The Zero Option

Published in cooperation with
the Peace Research Institute, Frankfurt, West Germany

The Zero Option

INF, West Germany, and Arms Control

Thomas Risse-Kappen

TRANSLATED BY LESLEY BOOTH

Westview Press
BOULDER & LONDON

Publications of the Peace Research Institute, Frankfurt, West Germany

This Westview softcover edition is printed on acid-free paper and bound in softcovers that carry the highest rating of the National Association of State Textbook Administrators, in consultation with the Association of American Publishers and the Book Manufacturers' Institute.

Copyright © 1988 by Westview Press, Inc.

Published in 1988 in the United States of America by Westview Press, Inc., 5500 Central Avenue, Boulder, Colorado 80301, and in the United Kingdom by Westview Press, Inc., 13 Brunswick Centre, London WC1N 1AF, England

Library of Congress Cataloging-in-Publication Data
Risse-Kappen, Thomas.
    The zero option.
    (Publications of the Peace Research Institute,
Frankfurt)
    1. Nuclear arms control. I. Title. II. Series.
JX1974.7.R537 1988   327.1'74   88-17398
ISBN 0-8133-7600-9

Printed and bound in the United States of America

The paper used in this publication meets the requirements of the American National Standard for Permanence of Paper for Printed Library Materials Z39.48-1984.

10   9   8   7   6   5   4   3   2   1

Contents

List of Abbreviations

ABM	Anti-Ballistic Missile Treaty
ACDA	U.S. Arms Control and Disarmament Agency
ACR	Arms Control Reporter
ALCM	Air-Launched Cruise Missile
ATACMS	Army Tactical Missile System
ATBM	Anti-Tactical Ballistic Missile
AW&ST	Aviation Week and Space Technology
CDE	Conference on Confidence- and Security-Building Measures and Disarmament in Europe
CDU/CSU	*Christlich-Demokratische Union Deutschlands/Christlich-Soziale Union Bayerns* (Christian Democratic Party)
CEP	Circular Error Probable
C^{3}I	Command, Control, Communication, and Intelligence
DPC	Defense Planning Committee (NATO)
EA	*Europa-Archiv*
FAZ	*Frankfurter Allgemeine Zeitung*
FBS	Forward Based Systems
FDP	*Freie Demokratische Partei* (Free Democratic Party)
FR	*Frankfurter Rundschau*
GLBM	Ground-Launched Ballistic Missile
GLCM	Ground-Launched Cruise Missile
HLG	High Level Group (NATO)
ICBM	Intercontinental Ballistic Missile
IDD	Integrated Decision Document
IHT	International Herald Tribune
INF	Intermediate Range Nuclear Forces
KStA	*Kölner Stadtanzeiger*
LRINF	Long-Range INF
LTDP	Long-Term Defense Plan
MBFR	Mutual Balanced Force Reductions
MIRV	Multiple Independently Targetable Reentry Vehicle
NPG	Nuclear Planning Group (NATO)
NST	Nuclear and Space Talks
PlPr	*Deutscher Bundestag: Stenographische Berichte* (Parliamentary Protocol)
SACEUR	Supreme Allied Commander Europe
SALT	Strategic Arms Limitation Talks
SCG	Special Consultative Group (NATO)
SDI	Strategic Defense Initiative
SLBM	Sea-Launched Ballistic Missile
SLCM	Sea-Launched Cruise Missile
SPD	*Sozialdemokratische Partei Deutschlands* (Social Democratic Party)

SRINF	Short-Range INF
START	Strategic Arms Reduction Talks
SZ	*Süddeutsche Zeitung*
SzS	*Stichworte zur Sicherheitspolitik* (security policy issues, ed. West German Press and Information Office)
TNF	Tactical/Theater Nuclear Forces
USPIT	U.S. Policy, Information, and Texts (issued by U.S. Embassy in Bonn)
WB	Wireless Bulletin from Washington (issued by U.S. Embassy in Bonn)
WEU	West European Union
WP/WTO	Warsaw Pact/Warsaw Treaty Organization

Preface

For almost 10 years now, I have studied the subject of intermediate-range nuclear forces (INF), most of that time as a member of the «arms race and arms control» research group at the Peace Research Institute Frankfurt (PRIF), West Germany, since 1981. This book is based, therefore, on a series of previous works, including a research report which was published in Spring 1985.

This study would not have been possible without the support of a number of people. It is partly founded on numerous interviews, most of them confidential, with officials of the West German government and the U.S. Administration. In particular I would like to thank Dr. Joseph Holik (Arms Control and Disarmament Advisor to the West German Government, Foreign Office, Bonn), Jürgen Ruhfus (West German Ambassador to the U.S., former Undersecretary of State, Foreign Office, Bonn), Dr. Friedrich Ruth (West German Ambassador to Italy, former Arms Control Advisor to the West German Government), Helmut Schmidt (former Chancellor of the Federal Republic), Dr. Walther Stützle (Stockholm Peace Research Institute, former head of planning staff, West German Defense Ministry), and Karsten Voigt (member of the *Bundestag*, SPD).

Discussions with my colleagues and friends at PRIF, particularly those in the «arms race and arms control» research group, have provided me with valuable comments and advice. Gert Krell and Harald Müller subjected the manuscript to a critical reading. I would like to thank them and Hans-Joachim Schmidt for the many discussions, suggestions and for their support.

I am particularly indebted to Leslie Booth who translated the manuscript into English. Leslie Evans and Brett Henry assisted me with editing the manuscript. Warm thanks go to them, too.

The study was part of a research project funded by the *Deutsche Forschungsgemeinschaft*, Bonn. The English version was edited during my stay at the Center for International and Strategic Affairs, University of California, Los Angeles, in spring 1988.

Los Angeles   Thomas Risse-Kappen

1

Introduction

The signing of the treaty between the United States and the Soviet Union on the worldwide disarmament of ground-launched intermediate-range nuclear missiles (INF)[1], on December 8, 1987, in Washington not only marks a milestone in the history of nuclear arms control; in signing the treaty, President Reagan and General Secretary Gorbachev have also concluded a chapter of East-West security relations which like few others before had been the subject of fierce debate in Europe for over 10 years. SALT negotiations, «forward based systems», «flexible response», SS-20, NATO's double-track decision, Pershing II, «walk-in-the-woods», «arms buildup», peace movements, British and French nuclear weapons and finally the «double-zero option» - these and other notions marked the up and down, the to and fro of the INF story.

Tracing their development is not only interesting in connection with the achievement of the zero-zero option - which came as a surprise to most of those involved and could hardly have been anticipated - but likewise focuses attention on the problems underlying East-West relations, security policy in the nuclear age, transatlantic relations, and public debate on war and peace.

The purpose of this study is to make sense of the muddle of domestic and foreign policy, of public demands and decision-making processes within the political systems involved, and to examine the interactions be-

---

1   The terminology used here is the official NATO language which became accepted in the early eighties:

INF   = Intermediate-range Nuclear Forces (150-5,500 km)
LRINF   = Long-range INF (1,000-5,500 km)
SRINF   = Short-range INF (150-1,000 km)
Note that the INF treaty differentiates between intermediate-range nuclear forces (1,000-5,500 km) and short-range nuclear missiles (500-1,000 km).

tween them. To do this, one has to distinguish between different levels of analysis and interaction patterns which overlap in empirical reality and become intertwined with one another through the constant flow of actions and interactions.

INF first cropped up as a subject of *American-Soviet relations*. True, intermediate-range missiles did not, for either the U.S. or the USSR, play a major role in the superpowers' security relationship, which is dominated by strategic nuclear weaponry. However, it was due to the very fact that the subject played a secondary role for both sides, that INF became an issue during the seventies, prompted by changes in the U.S.-Soviet security relationship. U.S.-Soviet relations represent the most important determinant for European security at the international level and as such form a decisive *independent variable* in this study. This is above all true for chapter 2, in which the evolution of NATO's double-track decision is analyzed.

The attempt to slow down the INF arms buildup, which failed initially in 1981-1983 and was not successful until 1986/87, was also the work of Washington and Moscow. In this respect the U.S.-Soviet relationship represents a *dependent variable* in this study, especially in chapters 3 and 4. In these chapters the INF negotiations since 1980 are discussed in detail.

The INF issue has, in addition, played a dominant role with respect to *East-West relations in Europe* since the seventies. Most European NATO members perceived the Soviet arms buildup, the SS-20 in particular, as a strategic threat which demonstrated a blatant disregard for West European security interests. At the same time, nobody wanted to be drawn into an unconstrained arms race, since an uncontrollable confrontation so close to the East-West border would have very strong repercussions. The Soviet leadership, on the other hand, may have seen the introduction of the «flexible response» doctrine by NATO as an attempt to confine (nuclear) war to Europe. Moreover, it is likely that the American «forward-based systems» (FBS) stationed in Europe, as well as the French and British nuclear arsenals, played a role in Moscow's threat perceptions. When relations between the two superpowers worsened dramatically after 1980, the Soviet Union tried to salvage European détente politics, so that the West European governments would have a moderating influence on Washington. Finally, the turnabout in Soviet INF policy under Gorbachev might indicate that the USSR has begun to reappraise its security policy towards Western Europe.

The role of INF in European East-West relations, is also examined in this study with regard to the relationship between West Germany and the Soviet Union. *German-Soviet relations* constitute an important *independent variable* and help to explain not only the West German government's INF policy but also indirectly NATO decisions. However, due to a lack of empirical data the Soviet decision-making process must remain largely in the dark. This means that any conclusions drawn regarding the motives for the Soviet actions have to be based on well-founded speculation.

Over and above this, INF has been a constant feature of the *relationship between the U.S. and Western Europe*. Indeed, many studies discuss the INF issue almost exclusively in this framework.[2] This study, on the other hand, attempts to show that neither NATO's double-track decision nor the West's contribution to the later INF negotiations can be satisfactorily explained if one concentrates solely on the interactions within the Alliance. That does not alter the fact that for well over ten years INF has had a decisive influence on the military relations between the U.S. and Western Europe. At issue was the old predicament of security dependence in an alliance of unequal partners - dependence which is increased by the existence of nuclear weapons.[3] Dennis Healey once described the problem by saying that a 5% probability of an American nuclear response would suffice to deter the Soviet Union from attacking Western Europe. The NATO allies, on the other hand, needed 95% certainty that the U.S. would use their nuclear weapons in the defense of Europe, in order to feel confident their security requirements would be met. Risk-sharing in the Alliance, maintaining the credibility of the U.S. nuclear guarantee, and military requirements for the implementation of flexible response are only some of the INF-related problems affecting NATO. In addition, the transatlantic debates on INF were always concerned with the future of détente policy and arms control. The American government saw the West European demands in the seventies as an attempt to hinder the conclusion of the SALT II treaty. Then in the eighties there

---

2   Cf. Hubertus Hoffmann, *Die Atompartner Bonn-Washington und die Modernisierung der taktischen Kernwaffen*, (Koblenz: Bernard & Graefe, 1986); Ernst-Christoph Meier, *Deutsch-amerikanische Sicherheitsbeziehungen und der NATO-Doppelbeschluss*, 2 vols, (Rheinfelden: Schäuble Verlag, 1986).

3   For more details see David N. Schwarz, *NATO's Nuclear Dilemmas* (Washington D.C.: Brookings, 1983).

seemed to be a reversal of roles. It was now the NATO allies who pressed for a continuation of U.S.-Soviet détente and arms-control. And in 1986/87 there appeared to be a further turnaround. It was now the American government which tried to persuade its allies to support the «zero-zero» option.

However, a closer look at transatlantic interactions with respect to INF reveals that it is an oversimplification to present American and West-European politics in this light. Nevertheless, it must be stressed that the Alliance's preoccupation with medium-range weapons stemmed from the desire to strengthen (extended) deterrence and continue Western arms control policy. The INF topic is therefore well suited to evaluate just how earnestly NATO actually implemented the double-track concept of the 1967 Harmel Report (deterrence + détente = security).

This study deals with the subject of INF as a NATO problem on two levels: it examines the decision-making processes within NATO but also the bilateral interactions between the U.S. and its allies, German-American relations in particular. As the major deployment country, West Germany played a dominant role in the issue from the start. The positions of other NATO countries are only given separate examination if they influenced the decision-making process of the Alliance.

The interrelation of actions in Alliance relations forms the decisive *dependent variable* in chapter 2 of the study which deals with the formulation of the NATO double-track decision. The INF decision was, after all, the result of West European and U.S. interactions against the background of arms control relations between the Soviet Union and the U.S. on the one hand, and European East-West relations on the other hand. However, in chapters 3 and 4 of the study, which examine INF negotiations, transatlantic relations form *independent variables*. Here the aim is to establish the degree to which American (and to some extent Soviet) arms control behavior on INF were influenced by Alliance decision-making processes.

The levels of interaction discussed so far concern international politics, i.e. the actions and interactions of state actors in their international environment. However, any study which aims to explain the evolution of the double-zero solution, is bound to conduct a systematic analysis of the *domestic environment* of security policy, i.e. the evolution of societal demands and their transformation into decisions within each respective political system. This is all the more true since INF was from the very start, and especially in Western Europe, a major subject of public controversy. Of course it came as no surprise that a NATO decision to deploy nuclear weapons in Western Europe capable of reaching Soviet territory, would prompt domestic controversy. The Social Democrats in Western Europe, for example, who in the seventies were the ruling parties or coalition partners in Great Britain, West Germany, and the Netherlands, reacted to NATO's INF policy with utmost scepticism. However, what requires explanation is the *extent* of the mass protests organized by peace movements in most of the deployment countries at the beginning of the eighties. In 1986/87 when it seemed likely that the zero option would be accepted, the fronts in the domestic debate shifted. It was now the West European conservatives who criticized the INF policy pursued by the U.S. and NATO.

It would be going too far to examine the debates in all the political systems involved. Moreover, a brief overview hardly suffices to provide an explanation of the policies pursued by individual governments. This study therefore concentrates solely on the West German domestic debates on INF (see 2.2, 2.5, 3.2, 4.4).[4] Firstly, West Germany was the principal INF deployment country. Secondly, it was West German domestic politics which was of particular significance for the formulation of NATO's double-track decision in 1979, for the zero option in 1981, and for the debates in the Alliance following the summit meeting in Reykjavik 1986.

As a significant determinant of NATO's INF policy, the public debates and political decision-making processes in West Germany form an *independent variable* in this study. At the same time, however, U.S.-Soviet relations, transatlantic affairs, and European East-West relations constantly influence the formulation of societal demands and their transformation to decisions within West Germany's political system. It is therefore a further aim of this study to use INF as an example to analyse the interaction patterns between the international system, the domestic environment and West Germany's political system.[5]

---

4   These paragraphs are based largely on my dissertation. Cf. Thomas Risse-Kappen, *Die Krise der Sicherheitspolitik. Neuorientierungen und Entscheidungsprozesse im politischen System der Bundesrepublik Deutschland, 1977-84* (Mainz, München: Grünewald-Kaiser, 1988).

5   This study is mainly devoted to the INF policy of the *West European* governments. *American* INF policy cannot therefore be dealt with in as much detail, as for example, the decision-making processes within West Germany.

The issue of intermediate-range nuclear weapons has polarized the West European public like no other topic in security policy during the past 10 years. It would be dishonest, therefore, for someone engaged in a political science study to claim that his is the position of the neutral observer. As this is not possible and never can be, since every science is bound by certain value orientations, it is all the more important to be frank about one's own premises. This study is committed to a program of vigorous arms control. It assumes that in the East-West conflict, cooperation with the opponent whilst maintaining one's own security interests is preferable to an unconstrained arms race and a politics of confrontation. This is why the INF policies pursued by the U.S., NATO, West Germany and the Soviet Union are assessed here according to the stability criteria of arms control and not primarily with regard to the improvement of their deterrence systems.[6] Concerning arms control, the following questions are addressed in this study:

- Did the actors involved endeavor, in their interactions with the international environment, to get their arms-control objectives satisfied, and what was the impact which the goal of «common security» had on their policies?
- To what degree were the actors' decisions influenced by the wish to slow down the dynamics of armament and to improve crisis stability?
- What conclusions can be drawn regarding the necessary preconditions for successful arms control?

---

6   Although this study is principally based on similar empirical material, it does, therefore, not come to the same conclusions as the studies mentioned in note 2 or the book by Lothar Ruehl, *Mittelstreckenwaffen in Europa* (Baden-Baden: Nomos, 1987).

2

Phase I: NATO's Double-Track Decision and the Federal Republic of Germany

2.1 Flexible Response and SALT: The Background up to Fall 1977

The debate surrounding the deployment of intermediate-range nuclear weapons in West Germany at the end of the seventies and the beginning of the eighties was not the first discussion of its kind. As early as December 1957, a NATO summit meeting decided to accept an American plan to base «Thor» and «Jupiter» missiles (range approx. 2,000 km) in Western Europe. Aside from complementing strategic deterrence until the U.S. had intercontinental ballistic missiles (ICBMs) of its own, these intermediate-range missiles served visibly to strengthen the American nuclear guarantee to Europe. The West German government of that time had in fact actively supported the deployment of U.S. *tactical* nuclear weapons and the Bundeswehr's possession of suitable launchers. But once medium-range missiles capable of targeting the Soviet Union from Western Europe were at issue, Bonn reacted more cautiously, partly for reasons of détente policy. Finally, no further consideration was given to the deployment of Thor and Jupiter missiles in West Germany. They were deployed in Turkey, in Italy, and Great Britain, but were withdrawn after the Cuban missile crisis. The fact that the Thor/Jupiter systems were one factor which led the Soviets to initiate the Cuban missile crisis in 1962 indicates what a delicate topic, even at that time, the basing of U.S. intermediate-range missiles in Western Europe was.

INF missiles were, however, based in West Germany in the *sixties*. Contrary to the attitude it took in the Thor/Jupiter case, the West German government now argued that it needed a weapon to counter the Soviet SS-4/SS-5 missiles. In December 1961, Franz Josef Strauss - then defense minister - introduced in a speech before the NATO council an argument which was to run through the debate in the seventies and eighties. Admittedly, U.S. strategic systems could still cover Soviet medium-range missiles. This would no longer be the case, however, once the USSR had achieved strategic parity in intercontinental ballistic missiles and, thus, could deter the U.S. from using its strategic arsenals for the defense of Western Europe by threatening to retaliate against the American homeland. At the same time, West Germany pressed for the development of a Pershing missile with a longer range than the 1 A version deployed at the end of the eighties (1,100 km rather than 720 km). Bonn also supported the plan of the then Supreme Allied Commander Europe (SACEUR) Norstad to build up a mobile force of intermediate-range missiles for Europe. The U.S. government of the day, on the other hand, was not convinced of the military value of new intermediate-range missiles for NATO. In the end, only 113 cruise missiles of the type «Mace B» (range 1,900 km) were deployed, and these were placed under the sole control of the U.S., who had rejected the West German government's request that the *Bundeswehr* be provided with launchers. The last Mace B, which cannot be compared to modern cruise missiles, was withdrawn from Europe in 1969.[1]

The history of NATO's double-track decision began to evolve at roughly the same time. It can be traced back to three factors: *military requirements*, *arms control*, and *Soviet INF modernization*. Initially, very little linked these factors. It was not until later that they became related to each other. This partly accounts for the contradictions of NATO's INF policy, including the debate over the zero option.

---

1   For the following see Catherine M. Kelleher, *Germany and the Politics of Nuclear Weapons* (New York: Columbia University Press, 1975); Ernst-Christoph Meier, *Deutsch-amerikanische Sicherheitsbeziehungen und der NATO-Doppelbeschluss*, vol.1 (Rheinfelden: Schäuble Verlag, 1986), pp.150-166, 202-239: David N. Schwartz, *NATO's Nuclear Dilemmas* (Washington D.C.: Brookings, 1983), pp.62-81.

a) Flexible Response

As regards *military policy*, the work of NATO's Nuclear Planning Group (NPG) should be mentioned. Funded in 1967, its main purpose was to grant NATO's non-nuclear weapon states a say in issues related to U.S. nuclear planning.[2] The NPG's main objective from the start was to define the flexible response doctrine more clearly and ensure its implementation as far as theater nuclear weapons are concerned. Once the «Provisional Political Guidelines» on nuclear first use had been passed in 1969, the group's concern was to examine in detail whether NATO's existing battlefield and medium-range nuclear forces met the requirements of flexible response. From the start, the conflicting interests of the U.S. and Western Europe in the Alliance were reflected in the Nuclear Planning Group. West Germany, for example, wanted the U.S. to commit itself to an early first use of nuclear weapons against the Soviet Union, for purposes of deterrence. For fear that they could be drawn too soon into a nuclear exchange with the Soviet Union, the United States rejected this strategy.

In November 1973, the NPG set up two study groups to examine the effects of new technologies on NATO's nuclear capabilities in Europe. They reached the conclusion that modernization of NATO's tactical nuclear weapons was unavoidable if the Alliance was to remain committed to the flexible response doctrine, to «deliberate escalation» (as nuclear first use is euphemistically termed), and the goal of escalation control in particular. Long-range INF, capable of striking military targets in Eastern Europe and the Western Soviet Union, were also under consideration at that time. It was almost an accepted fact within NATO that the Alliance's INF aircraft, especially the U.S. F-111 based in Great Britain, were scarcely capable of fulfilling their role in the framework of flexible response. Given improved Soviet air-defense capabilities, they were

---

2   For details see John M. Legge, *Theater Nuclear Weapons and the NATO Strategy of Flexible Response* (Santa Monica: RAND, 1983), pp.28-33; also Paul Buteux, *The Politics of Nuclear Consultation in NATO, 1965-1980* (Cambridge: Cambridge University Press, 1983); Helga Haftendorn, «Das doppelte Missverständnis. Zur Vorgeschichte des NATO-Doppelbeschlusses von 1979,» *Vierteljahreshefte für Zeitgeschichte*, no.2, 1985, pp.244-252. See also the «Schlesinger Report» of 1975: Dept. of Defense, *The Theater Nuclear Force Posture in Europe. A Report to the U.S. Congress* (Washington D.C.: GPO, 1975).

obliged to change the flight profile which in turn meant a reduction of their effective range. Thus, it was argued, they were no longer capable of accurately striking targets in the Western Soviet Union. This was the military background of what was later referred to as the «gap in NATO's escalation ladder».

These first considerations to modernize NATO's medium-range forces coincided with changes in the declared strategic nuclear doctrine of the *United States*. In 1974/75 the U.S. government introduced the «Schlesinger doctrine» which adapted declared strategy to actual strategic nuclear planning. More emphasis was placed on the ability to undertake flexible, selective and limited nuclear strikes against the opponent's military targets («limited nuclear options»). In April 1975, in a report to the U.S. Congress, Secretary of Defense Schlesinger set out the new doctrine's implications for NATO's nuclear strategy.[3] Schlesinger underlined again the original intentions of flexible response and placed the main emphasis in Europe on *conventional* defense, while tactical nuclear weapons would assume less importance. But the report also stated that the remaining nuclear weapons in Europe would have to be modernized with regard to their survivability, their operational capabilities, and command, control, communications and intelligence (C^3I).

At the same time, the first funds were approved in the U.S. for the development of the weapons systems for NATO's subsequent INF decision. In 1974 the United States signed a contract with Martin Marietta, for the development of a new warhead for Pershing I with reduced yield and a new guidance system. The weapons's accuracy was to be considerably improved by terminal-phase guidance. Moreover the missile was to be equipped with an earth-penetrating warhead, thus allowing attacks on hardened targets. The Department of Defense Annual Report for Fiscal Year 1975 announced the examination of the technical feasibility of a missile to succeed Pershing I with a longer range (i.e. Pershing II). However, Congress was not convinced of the need for the defense of Western Europe and cut off funds.[4]

---

3   Cf. ibid.

4   Cf. Gert Krell/Hans Joachim Schmidt, *Der Rüstungswettlauf in Europa* (Frankfurt am Main: Campus, 1982), pp.24-26; Hubertus Hoffmann, *Die Atompartner Washington-Bonn und die Modernisierung der taktischen Kernwaffen* (Koblenz: Bernard & Graefe, 1986), pp.142-146; Meier, *Sicherheitsbeziehungen*, note 1, vol.2, p.364.

On top of this, work had been carried out in the United States since the early seventies on the development of advanced, or second generation cruise missiles. This initially involved sea- and air-launched versions, but in 1976 the U.S. Tactical Air Command called for a ground-launched version. Development began one year later. However, the U.S. armed forces did not show overwhelming interest in the cruise missile option. The U.S. Army refused to assume responsiblity for the weapons, arguing that it was already in charge of Pershing II development. Finally, the Air Force was assigned the task. The forces' reluctance to assume responsiblity was partly due to their concern that development costs would further stretch their already tight budgets in the fight for scarce resources. The initiative for the development of the new cruise missile technologies came not so much from the armed forces, but from the *political leadership* in the Pentagon.[5]

But the greatest interest for the cruise missile option was shown by the West Europeans. Many defense ministries regarded them as the ideal weapon for extended deterrence. As unmanned missiles, they could fly at a fairly low altitude and thus evade radar and air-defense installations. What is more, the new generation of cruise missiles was to be equipped with an electronic navigation system, allowing constant correction of the flight path and leading to extremely high accuracy. The Europeans' desire for cruise missiles was vigorously supported by a small group of transatlantic experts who in the seventies had repeatedly argued the case for the modernization of nuclear weapons deployed in Western Europe. Most American members of this group were part of the anti-SALT coalition; on the West European side they belonged to the military elite, or were conservative military experts such as Uwe Nerlich of the government-sponsored Stiftung Wissenschaft und Politik. Worthy of mention in this connection is the «Euro-American Workshop» which was initiated by the former U.S. Defense Secretary Schlesinger and chaired by Albert Wohlstetter. Workshop participants were politicians and scientists from Western Europe and America. Thus, a cruise missile lobby developed on both sides of the Atlantic backed by American armaments companies. Its

---

5   Cf. Robert J. Art/Stephen E.Ockenden, «The Domestic Politics of Cruise Missile Development, 1970-1980,» in R. Betts (ed.), *Cruise Missiles* (Washington: Brookings, 1981), pp. 359-413.

members - professionals from various fields - tried to influence the national security elites including the top decision-makers.[6]

The decision-making process within NATO finally gained momentum in 1976/77 as a result of the Long-Term Defense Plan (LTDP) of the Defense Planning Committee (DPC).[7] However, the initial emphasis was on *conventional* forces. At the NATO summit meeting in May 1977, U.S. President Carter proposed a comprehensive plan aimed at strengthening NATO's conventional forces. The LTDP was set in motion. Nine study groups were created which were subordinate to the Defense Planning Committee. The tenth group was to investigate NATO's tactical nuclear capabilities and was placed under the control of the NPG. The latter group was assigned the work of the technology study groups and in October 1977 was renamed High Level Group (HLG). The group was responsible for preparing the military component of the double-track decision.

It is important to bear in mind that up to about mid-1977, NATO's *internal* decision-making process centered mainly around problems of military strategy and military operations. NATO's subsequent INF decision was therefore founded from the start on issues related to military strategy (although these issues did not prove to be the most crucial ones in bringing about the final decision). At stake was the implementation of the flexible response doctrine. Apparently, early on in the NATO decision-making process, no thought was given to including medium-range systems in arms control. The SS-20 played no role whatsoever. Not until later did NATO's Military Committee emphasize Soviet INF modernization. Anxious to avoid a public debate on the merits of flexible response

---

6   The first findings of this group's discussions on strategy appeared in *Beyond Nuclear Deterrence*, eds. Jörg J. Holst/Uwe Nerlich (New York: Crane, Russak, 1977). See on the role of this group Fred Kaplan, «Warring Over New Missiles for NATO,» *New York Times Magazine*, December 9, 1979, pp.48ff.

7   There now exist a fair number of works on the background to the NATO double-track decision, e.g., Haftendorn, «Missverständnis,» note 2; Hoffmann, *Atompartner*, note 4; Meier, *Sicherheitsbeziehungen*, note 1; Lothar Ruehl, *Mittelstreckenwaffen in Europa. Ihre Bedeutung in Strategie, Rüstungskontrolle und Bündnispolitik* (Baden-Baden: Nomos, 1987); Leon V. Sigal, *Nuclear Forces in Europe* (Washington D.C.: Brookings, 1984). Unless stated otherwise, the analysis which follows in this chapter summarizes the above.

as a military strategy, NATO presented the SS-20 to the public as the main justification for the double-track decision.

b) SALT and Extended Deterrence

The issue at stake for NATO - at least initially - was the routine modernization of weapons. For the decision-makers in the West German government, however, broader *security policy* considerations took priority from the beginning, the effect of the superpowers' bilateral negotiations on the security of Western Europe in particular. This forms the second determinant of the NATO double-track decision.

The U.S.-Soviet negotiations on the limitation of strategic arms (SALT) were for many West European governments connected with the problem of *extended deterrence*. How was the credibility of the U.S. nuclear guarantee for Western Europe to be maintained once strategic parity existed? Was America prepared, if worse came to worst, to risk New York for Frankfurt by escalating a military conflict in Europe to strategic nuclear war in order to avoid imminent conventional defeat in Europe? Or would the U.S. not take such a risk, since it would mean reckoning with Soviet retaliatory measures against their own territory? The set of problems related to decoupling posed the central issue for the decision-makers in Western Europe. Two lines of argument were taken. The first was based on a concern for *military strategy* in the narrow sense and stated that, once strategic parity existed between the superpowers, American ICBMs could no longer credibly deter an attack on Western Europe. Therefore, weapons systems were necessary which created a visible link between the nuclear battlefield weapons deployed in Europe and the American strategic forces, thereby coupling NATO defense to U.S. strategic deterrence. The second line of argument was founded on considerations of *deterrence policy* in general and emphasized that strategic parity would result in a greater accentuation of the already existing INF disparity in Europe. U.S. strategic weapons would no longer be available to deter the Soviets from using their intermediate-range nuclear forces. The notion of «eurostrategic parity» originated here. According to this line of argument, the Soviet SS-20 complicated the problem though the new missile had not been its actual cause. This aspect of the evolution of the double-track decision dates back to the start of the SALT process at the end of the sixties. Despite the principal support of

strategic arms control, three sets of problems dominated particularly the
West German position towards the SALT negotiations:
- First, the West German government repeatedly insisted that NATO be
  closely consulted by the U.S.; not only out of a desire to be kept informed on the American negotiating position, but also to be given the
  chance to influence U.S. arms-control policy to accommodate West
  German interests. In support of her demand, West Germany referred
  to the «Athens guidelines» of 1962, in which the U.S. had given an assurance that it would consult its allies on plans or provisions affecting
  those nuclear weapons assigned to NATO defense.[8]
- Second, the West German government was concerned, in common
  with other European allies, that the bilateralism of the superpowers
  should not have a detrimental effect on extended deterrence. Initially,
  the major issue at stake was how to deal with American nuclear
  weapons capable of reaching Soviet territory from third countries such
  as Europe, or from aircraft carriers, i.e., the forward-based systems
  (FBS). Later the emphasis shifted to the effects of the SALT process on
  the upgrading of nuclear weapons based in Europe.
- Third, there was the problem of the intermediate-range weapons fac-
  ing Western Europe: the SS-4 and SS-5, and later the SS-20. As mentioned above, Minister of Defense Franz Josef Strauss had already
  pointed out during the early sixties that the issue of the nuclear balance in Europe would become critical once the superpowers had
  achieved strategic parity.

West Germany's INF policy changed several times, however. In July,
1968 - i.e., before the SALT negotiations began - the West German Foreign Office informed the U.S. embassy in Bonn that in their opinion,
Soviet medium-range weapons should be included in the strategic arms
control process.[9] The second U.S. SALT proposal, which was presented

---

8   Cf. Heinrich Buch, « Die Rolle der Bundesrepublik bei SALT - Mitspieler
     oder Zuschauer?» in *Verwaltete Aussenpolitik*, eds. H. Haftendorn et al. (Köln:
     Wissenschaft & Politik, 1978), pp.115-134, 126.

9   See Jonathan Dean, *Watershed in Europe* (Lexington,Mass.: Lexington
     Books, 1987), p.118. For a more general analysis see Jane M.O. Sharp,
     «Understanding the INF debacle: Arms Control and Alliance Cohesion,»
     Arms Control, vol.5, no.3., 1984, pp.97-123, 109. On the topic following see
     Raymond Garthoff, *Détente and Confrontation* (Washington D.C.: Brookings,
     1985), pp.141/142.

to the Soviets in 1970, did include Soviet INF in the limitations, but not American FBS. The USSR termed it imbalanced and rejected it outright. In a counterproposal she suggested that the strategic systems SALT would limit, be defined as all weapons which could reach the territory of either superpower. This would have included American FBS but not Soviet INF.

The West German government seems to have concluded that cuts in Soviet intermediate-range forces could only be gained in return for corresponding cuts in American FBS. This would include, according to Soviet counting rules, the American F-4, F-111 and FB-111 intermediate-range aircraft (respective operating radiuses: 750 km; max. 1,800 km, and 2,700-2,900 km) as well as the A-6 and A-7 fighter aircraft based on carriers (respective operating radiuses: 1,500 and 1,200 km).[10] These systems were regarded by most West European governments as vital to extended deterrence. They therefore rejected their inclusion into SALT as well as that of the French and British nuclear forces. Already in the early seventies therefore, Bonn was faced with choosing between nuclear arms control for Europe, including negotiated constraints on Soviet INF, and leaving America's forward-based systems untouched for reasons of extended deterrence. This would have meant having to accept the already existing Soviet superiority in intermediate-range missiles. Bonn initially decided in favor of the latter option and against arms control. It no longer insisted on the inclusion of the SS-4 and SS-5 in the SALT process, assuming moreover that the USSR would withdraw these systems from operation anyhow. It was not until the mid-1970s that Chancellor Schmidt changed this policy.

The Americans took the European reservations into account and continued to reject the Soviet demand that FBS be included in the SALT process. General Secretary Brezhnev and Defense Minister Grechko presented the Soviet position on FBS once again at the Moscow summit meeting of summer 1973. Despite European fears that the U.S. might give in to Soviet persistence, the United States stuck by their decision. In the 1974 Vladivostok Accord the USSR backed down again. She also agreed to exclude FBS from SALT II, even though her military leadership obviously considered this an unjustified concession to the United

---

10 For details see Gert Krell, «Zählkriterien für die Mittelstreckenwaffen,» in *Kernwaffen im Ost-West-Vergleich*, eds. Krell/E. Forndran (Baden-Baden: Nomos, 1984), pp.175-226.

States. It was only when in 1977 Jimmy Carter made his new SALT proposal, which amounted to drastic cuts in Soviet land-based ICBMs with
no restrictions whatsoever on cruise missiles up to a range of 2,500 km
in which the United States had the numerical edge, that the Soviets responded by presenting their position on FBS once again. FBS now and
later acted as a kind of trump card which was always played when the
U.S., in the Soviets' opinion, demanded too much.[11]

The West European governments' concern over SALT I had been
that the United States might make concessions on FBS. With SALT II,
they now feared that the United States would agree to cuts which would
hinder the modernization of NATO's medium-range weapons. Cruise
missiles were their chief concern. The West German government was
worried that the U.S. might negotiate away the cruise missile option at
SALT II without securing corresponding cuts in Soviet INF. In early
1976 the Ford Administration made several proposals for dealing with
sea- and ground-launched cruise missiles. At the same time, the Soviet
new Backfire bomber, which the United States charged to have strategic
range, was to be subject to restrictions. In February 1976 the Americans
introduced a concept which largely predetermined the agreement which
could later be reached in SALT II. They proposed that the Backfire
problem be postponed, provided the USSR was prepared to guarantee
that it was not a strategic-range bomber. For sea- and ground-launched
cruise missiles, there was to be a ban on missile testing for a three-year
period. This applied to missiles with a range of over 2,500 km. Further,
the basing of systems with ranges over 600 km was to be banned. This
proposal was almost identical to the later SALT II protocol. The proposal to keep INF out of strategic arms control was not, therefore, an in-
vention of the Carter Administration. Rather it built upon proposals
made by the Ford/Kissinger government.

Most European governments were highly disturbed by these proposals. They feared that the contemplated three-year ban would gener-
ate so much of its own dynamics that in the end the cruise missile option

---

11   For a general account on this see Garthoff, *Détente*, note 9, pp.158, 186, 429,
     446/447, 464, 807/808. For the following ibid., pp.541-543. In a most recent
     volume on the Soviet SS-20 decision, Jonathan Haslam argues that the deci-
     sion to deploy the new INF missile was taken in light of the Vladivostok Ac-
     cord and its exclusion of the forward-based systems. See Jonathan Haslam:
     The SS-20 and the Arms Race (London: Macmillan, 1988).

would no longer be available to NATO. On top of this there were worries concerning the non-circumvention clause foreseen for SALT II and the non-transfer proviso demanded by the Soviet Union, which was aimed specifically at cruise missiles. In addition, the American concession on the Backfire bomber - exclusion from SALT cuts in return for an assurance that it did not have strategic range - meant that the Soviets would be free to deploy it as an INF bomber. The West German government therefore continually pressed upon the Americans that cuts in U.S. medium-range systems could only be accepted in return for corresponding cuts in the Soviet INF potential. (This condition was later, on German initiative, included in the arms control component of the double-track decision.) The West German government also voiced its opinion publicly since the beginning of 1977. Defense Minister Georg Leber repeatedly pointed to the consequences for European security were parity to be achieved at SALT.[12] In the end there were heated debates between the U.S. and the West Europeans over the non-circumvention clause during an NPG meeting in October 1977.

c) The SS-20

The debate surrounding SALT and NATO's INF modernization, became even more animated when in 1976 the USSR began deploying a new medium-range nuclear missile with three warheads, the SS-20. It was developed from the first two stages of an intercontinental missile, the SS-16, which had been taken out of production. At the end of 1977 the first missile bases were operational and new deployments increased steadily from then on. For each new SS-20, an old SS-4/5 missile was withdrawn from operation (cf. table 1). Whilst in NATO headquarters, the SS-20 was not presented as a justification for INF upgrading, the West German government in particular took this weapon very seriously. The SS-20 was seen as an instrument of political blackmail used by the Soviets against Western Europe, an opinion first expressed in August

---

12 Cf. e.g. Lebers speech to the *Internationale Wehrkundetagung* in Munich, February 2, 1977, *Bulletin* ed. by the Press and Information Office of the Federal Government (subsequently referred to as «Bulletin»), no.14, 1977, pp.128-130. For a more general account, see also James A. Thomson, «The LRTNF decision: evolution of US theatre nuclear policy 1975-9,» *International Affairs*, vol.40, 1984, no.4, pp.601-614.

1976 by Fred Iklé, then the director of the U.S. Arms Control and Disarmament Agency.

Table 1:   Evolution of Soviet SS-20 Deployments

Year	Number of Launchers
1977	10
1978	70
1979	140
1980	200
1981	270
1982	324
1983	369
1984	378
1986	441

Source: John Cartwright/Julian Critchley, *Cruise, Pershing, and SS-20. A North Atlantic Assembly Report* (London: Brassey's Defence Publ., 1985), p.22; IISS, *The Military Balance 1986-1987* (London: 1987), p.204.

What represented a strategic threat for Western Europe, was apparently for the Soviet Union, a «routine» modernization of their INF potential.[13] There had long been speculation in the West that the old SS-4 and SS-5 missiles with liquid propellant would either be withdrawn, or replaced by new systems. The Soviets appear to have decided in favor of modernization as far back as the mid-1960s. Several tests with new missiles failed and assigning strategic systems such as the SS-11 a regional role brought no advantages, since these missiles were included in the SALT agreement. Moreover, the USSR had failed in its attempt to get American

---

13   For the following see Haslam, *SS-20*, note 11; David Holloway, «The INF policy of the Soviet Union», in *The European Missile Crisis* (New York: St. Martin's Press, 1983), pp.92-114; Garthoff, *Détente*, note 9, pp.871-886; Stephen Meyer, *Soviet Theatre Forces. part 2: Capabilities and Implications*, Adelphi Paper 188, (London: IISS, 1984), pp.25-28.

FBS included in strategic arms control. And so the Soviets finally resorted to the SS-16. According to Jonathan Haslam, the SS-20 *deployment* decision was taken after the Vladivostok summit, when the Politbureau had to appease the Soviet military. The Strategic Rocket Forces appeared to be dissatisfied with Brezhnev's decision to once again exclude FBS from strategic limitations. The Soviets could justify their action by reference to the settlement agreed upon by President Nixon and General Secretary Brezhnev on the signing of SALT I in 1972, allowing both sides to modernize those weapons not affected by SALT. The USSR also pointed to the fact that they needed a force to counter the French, British and Chinese nuclear weapons, and the American FBS. They could argue that the SALT agreement meant intercontinental weapons were now needed for the role of strategic deterrence. This was similar to the argument taken by the West Europeans who called for the upgrading of the *West's* INF potential to compensate for the emergence of strategic parity between the U.S. and the Soviet Union.

The SS-20 allowed the USSR to modernize considerably a military option which was already available to them before. The targets covered by the SS-20 in Western Europe could equally well be attacked using ICBMs, SLBMs or nuclear-equipped bombers. However, the SS-20 gave the USSR three times the number of warheads available with the SS-4 and SS-5. In addition, the warheads could be directed at separate targets independently of one another (MIRV). The SS-20 was the first Soviet missile not to use liquid fuel. Its accuracy was considerably improved (approx. 300 m as opposed to the SS-4's 2,300 m) and this meant that the yield of the warhead could be substantially reduced. And finally, the SS-20 was mobile and was therefore less vulnerable than its predecessors. Unlike the SS-4 and SS-5, the SS-20 could in theory be employed «discriminately» against hardened military targets in Western Europe (counterforce). In practice, though, use of the SS-20 would have resulted in widespread devastation, given Western Europe's densely populated and highly industrialized areas. The SS-20 warhead had a yield of 150 kt TNT (ten times more than the Hiroshima bomb) and was simply not accurate enough to allow for selective counterforce strikes in a really damage-limiting way (The Pershing II is accurate to within 30 m).[14] It would

---

14 Missile accuracy is measured in terms of «Circular Error Probable» (CEP), or the diameter of a circle, centred on the target within which 50% of the weapons aimed at it are expected to fall. Claims that the USSR had in the

seem, therefore, that the development of a new intermediate-range missile was the result of a modernization decision by the political and military bureaucracy, and that the Soviet leadership under Brezhnev did not consider what effect the SS-20 might have on Western Europe in an era of détente politics.

2.2 Uno Actu: Helmut Schmidt and the Double-Track Decision

Was Helmut Schmidt the «father of the double-track decision»? Critics and advocates of the INF arms buildup alike have repeatedly emphasized he former chancellor's tremendous role in the decision-making process. Schmidt's own comments on the subject are contradictory.[15] However, it would be wrong to say that the West German chancellor of the day provided the impetus for NATO's INF modernization. The Alliance had already begun its preliminary studies, when he first voiced his opinion publicly.

And yet without the commitment of Helmut Schmidt and his closest advisors, the NATO double-track decision would probably not have come about in the form it did. In particular, it is unlikely that it would have combined modernization and arms control in *one resolution* («uno actu», as Helmut Schmidt expressed it in a margin note).

Schmidt's intensive involvement with problems of security policy began in the fifties when he was the SPD's most important defense expert after Fritz Erler. In 1961, his study *Verteidigung oder Vergeltung* («Defense or Retaliation») appeared, one of the first analyses on nuclear deter-

---

SS-20 «in-theater selective targeting capability» which it did not possess previously, are valid only if it is compared exclusively to the SS-4/5 and the conditions of nuclear war in Europe are ignored. For such an evaluation see Ruehl, *Mittelstreckenwaffen*, note 7, pp.115-138.

15   1982/83 - at the height of the domestic INF debate in West Germany - Schmidt tried to play down his own role in the making of the double-track decision. This was still the case in a talk to the author in June 1985. In his most recent comments on the subject, however, he assigns himself a more active role, at least as far as the zero option is concerned. See Helmut Schmidt, «The Zero Option Wouldn't Leave the West Uncovered,» *The International Herald Tribune* (IHT) and also, *Menschen und Mächte* (Berlin: Siedler, 1987) p.333.

rence issues to be published in German. It introduced the U.S. debate on NATO's new flexible response doctrine into the West German discussion. In 1969, his book *Strategie des Gleichgewichts* («The Strategy of Balance») appeared. The title reflected his own approach to security policy, balance of power being central to his concept of foreign and security policy. Schmidt regards military balance *as such* to be of secondary importance; he places the emphasis on the political relationship between the two alliances. Political, military, strategic and economic factors all come together. This concept of balance is aimed at maintaining political stability which is jeopardized when one side of the East-West relationship perceives itself to be the underling. The military factor is not in itself important; its significance derives from its potential influence on the political relationship: «Therefore the principle of parity is a requirement for a contractual partnership aimed at mutual security between East and West ...»[16]

This quotation clearly indicates Helmut Schmidt's firm support of NATO's 1967 Harmel Report which encompasses the two concepts of deterrence and détente. Schmidt supported this strategy back in 1961 and was one of the first Germans to refer to it: «Defense and deterrence strategies have rightly been described as two Siamese twins.»[17]

Arms control and deterrence had the same goal in Schmidt's view, namely stability, and he regarded the double-track decision to be based on this very concept. His comments in the seventies suggest that while favoring arms control to solve the INF problem, he was not prepared to allow the Soviets to compromise the feasibility of the Western military strategy. No other West German politician invested so much personal commitment in the issue of intermediate-range weapons as did Helmut Schmidt. He first drew attention to the problem as early as 1965:

«Should a joint nuclear system (the Multilateral Force/T.R.-K) not come about ..., it would nevertheless remain a serious task to create a nuclear counterbal-

---

16 Helmut Schmidt, «Beiträge zu einer Zwischenbilanz 1982», *Vorwärts-Extra*, April 15, 1982, p.IV. Also by Schmidt, *Strategie des Gleichgewichts* (Stuttgart: Seewald, 1969). See further *Verteidigung oder Vergeltung?* (Stuttgart: Seewald, 1961). For a general account see Thomas Risse-Kappen, *Die Krise der Sicherheitspolitik. Neuorientierungen und Entscheidungsprozesse im politischen System der Bundesrepublik Deutschland, 1977-1984* (Mainz-München: Grünewald-Kaiser, 1988).

17 Schmidt, *Verteidigung*, p. 159.

ance against the aforementioned Soviet intermediate-range nuclear missiles
which exclusively cover European targets.»[18]

As Chancellor, Schmidt was repeatedly accused of having abandoned the
twin concept of the Harmel Report. In addition, it was charged that
during his term in office, détente and arms control policy had given way
to deterrence. That does not hold true for the INF issue. Here, Schmidt
abandoned the policy of his predecessor and argued that medium-range
systems should be included in the SALT negotiations. In doing so he apparently accepted that the American FBS would be subject to arms control talks. According to Schmidt, he received an assurance in private
talks with U.S. President Ford during the latter's visit to West Germany
in July 1975, that the U.S. would insist on the inclusion of the Soviet intermediate-range weapons in SALT II.[19]

Were Ford really in agreement with this policy - which would have
complicated the negotiation of the SALT II treaty not inconsiderably -
American handling of the negotiations showed no sign of it. The SALT
proposals introduced in 1976, i.e., by the Ford Administration, nowhere
included the limitation of Soviet INF. Rather, they excluded them after
the USSR had given assurances that it would not equip the Backfire
bomber with strategic range (cf. 2.1).

Schmidt later turned to the Carter Administration which likewise refused to accommodate his terms. This rejection combined with Soviet
deployment of the SS-20, which only strengthened the existing disparity
in the INF area, prompted Schmidt to speak out in public. In May, 1977,
he declared before the NATO Council in London that SALT could lead
to a paralyzation of the Soviet and U.S. strategic nuclear systems. They
would then become weapons of last resort, serving to protect only those
who exercised control over them. Schmidt did not touch upon INF, but
stressed instead the implications for conventional parity in Europe. In an
interview with the British news magazine «The Economist» on October
6, he expressed his regret that the Thor and Jupiter missiles had been

---

18   Schmidt, «Introduction» to the 5th edition of *Verteidigung oder Vergeltung*
     (Stuttgart: Seewald, 1968), p.XVII. See also Schmidt's interview with six
     U.S. west coast journalists, July 22, 1982; interview with *New York Times* on
     September 16, 1984. Further personal interview with Schmidt by the au-
     thor.

19   See Helmut Schmidt, *Menschen*, note 15, p.210.

withdrawn at the beginning of the sixties rather than having been modernized.[20]

The Chancellor gained worldwide attention with his speech before the International Institute for Strategic Studies (IISS) in London on October 28, 1977. Jürgen Ruhfus, Schmidt's foreign policy advisor in the Chancellery, and Walther Stützle, director of the planning staff of the West German Defense Ministry, advised him. Schmidt's speech marked the first occasion that a West European head of government had spoken at length on the question of intermediate-range nuclear forces. Politically, it had a «pigeonholing effect»[21] and set the problem in the general context of East-West relations. Schmidt's argument ran as follows:

«(C)hanged strategic conditions confront us with new problems. SALT codifies the nuclear strategic balance between the Soviet Union and the United States. To put it another way: SALT neutralizes their strategic nuclear capabilities. In Europe this magnifies the significance of the disparities between East and West in nuclear tactical and conventional weapons. ... No one can deny that the principle of parity is a sensible one. However, its fulfillment must be the aim of all arms-limitation and arms-control negotiations and it must apply to all categories of weapons. Neither side can agree to diminish its security unilaterally. It is of vital interest to us all that the negotiations between the two super-powers on the limitation and reduction of nuclear strategic weapons should continue and lead to a lasting agreement. The nuclear powers have a special, an overwhelming responsibility in this field. On the other hand, we in Europe must be particularly careful to ensure that these negotiations do not neglect the components of NATO's deterrence strategy. We are all faced with the dilemma of having to meet the moral and political demand for arms limitation while at the same time maintaining a fully effective deterrent to war. ... But strategic arms limitations confined to the United States and the Soviet Union will inevitably impair the security of the West European members of the Alliance vis-à-vis Soviet military superiority in Europe if we do not succeed in removing the disparities of military power in Europe parallel to the SALT negotiations. So long as this is not the case we must maintain the balance of the full range of deterrence strategy. The Alliance must, therefore, be ready to make available the means to support its present

---

20 Interview quoted in Meier, *Sicherheitsbeziehungen*, note 1, vol.2, pp.392/393. On Schmidt's comments in May, 1977 cf. remarks to NATO Council, *Bulletin*, no.51, 1977, pp.467-470.

21 In discussion with the author, Walther Stützle called it literally a «political sorter».

strategy, which is still the right one, and to prevent any developments that could undermine the basis of this strategy.»[22]

Since neither the U.S. nor the Soviet Union were prepared to deal with the eurostrategic systems in SALT and to eliminate disparities, Schmidt feared that West European security interests would suffer as a result. His concern was to prevent the strategic arms control of the two superpowers from endangering *unilaterally* the operational feasibility of flexible response through constraints on NATO INF (SALT II protocol), whilst no *corresponding* restrictions were placed upon Soviet intermediate-range forces. As he saw it, the double-track decision should offer incentives for preventive arms control, yet leave no doubts whatsoever about the West's determination to modernize its INF should these efforts fail. This concept distinguished the Chancellor from the demands of the conservative strategic community.

Aside from arms-control motives, the Chancellor accepted the following defense-policy rationales in support of INF modernization:
- Of prime importance was the necessity to uphold extended deterrence in an era of strategic parity. Unlike military and strategic experts, however, Schmidt was less concerned with abstract calculations concerning nuclear scenarios, but rather with the *political* consequences of growing regional disparity.
- This interpretation is also backed by the dominant role which the SS-20 played in Schmidt's threat perception. If one were to accept the Soviet modernization of their medium-range weapons in the SALT II treaty, they might gain the impression that they could do as they wished in Europe. Although the Chancellor remained somewhat vague on this point, his main concern seems to have been that the Soviet superiority in INF could, *in a serious crisis*, represent an instrument of political blackmail against the West.[23]

With regard to the *basing mode*, Helmut Schmidt continued to favor, true to his convictions of the sixties, the deployment of new INF as sea-launched cruise missiles on surface ships that would patrol along the coast. These ships, he argued, would be distinguishable from U.S. stra-

---

22   Helmut Schmidt, «Alastair Buchan Memorial Lecture,» *Survival*, vol.20., no.1, 1978, pp.2-10, 3/4. On the background of the speech see Haftendorn, «Missverständnis», note 2, pp.259-261.

23   Cf. Schmidt, *Menschen*, note 15, p.92.

tegic submarines. This is further proof of the fact that «coupling» in the sense of visible deployment of American INF in Europe was not the main consideration for him.

In retrospect, Helmut Schmidt can be said to have made three misjudgments. Firstly, in publicly decrying the SALT policy of the Carter Administration, he unwittingly supported those people on both sides of the Atlantic who were not concerned with eliminating disparities through arms control, but with halting the SALT process itself. Schmidt provided *de facto* the SALT opponents in America with arguments which were exploited to the full in the U.S. domestic controversy surrounding SALT II. There was no doubting his support for strategic arms control, and one should not overestimate his influence on the domestic debate in America. Nevertheless, his actions hindered the policy of a government which like no other before it strove for serious arms control with the Soviets.

Secondly, Schmidt's arguments were exploited by those in Europe and NATO who were more interested in modernizing *Western* systems than limiting Soviet intermediate-range missiles. In the United States and NATO, the Chancellor's IISS speech was interpreted as a call for the buildup of Western INF and its implications for arms control were largely overlooked. Schmidt's comments in interviews only served to reinforce this view. His speech merely speeded up the decision-making process already underway within NATO (cf. 2.1). Schmidt formed a tactical alliance with the opponents of strategic arms control on both sides of the Atlantic, if only out of his understandable concern for arms control in Europe.

Thirdly, the Chancellor obviously underestimated the domestic problems involved in deploying nuclear weapons in Germany which could reach Soviet territory. Going by the experiences of the fifties, it was to be expected that the basing of new nuclear weapons would meet with public opposition. The debate triggered off by the neutron bomb in 1977/78 was merely a taste of things to come. In the pursuit of his policy, Schmidt subjected his party to considerable tensions. On the other hand, his own scope for action was considerably limited by the attitude of many Social Democrats. In the end, it was only by threatening to resign that he could secure the SPD's tolerance of his policy on the double-track decision, up until the change of government.

2.3 Prolog: The Neutron Bomb Between Bonn and Washington

The neutron bomb debate was of importance for the evolution of the double-track decision in several respects:
- Nuclear weapons were discussed publicly in West Germany for the first time since the early sixties, in particular in the SPD.
- The West German government's position anticipated major elements of their subsequent double-track policy regarding INF.
- President Carter's decision in April 1978 had far-reaching consequences for U.S. INF policy, for the assessment of Carter's politics by the West German government and for NATO's subsequent decision-making process.

Work had been carried out in the U.S. since the fifties on a nuclear weapon with increased radiation and reduced yield.[24] NATO's Nuclear Planning Group had discussed the neutron bomb since the early seventies, in connection with its evaluation of new technologies. This did not become public until June 1977 when reports appeared in American newspapers. President Carter then asked Congress to approve the application for funds to produce the neutron bomb. Egon Bahr, at the time the SPD's general secretary, was largely responsible for prompting discussion in West Germany with his article, «Is mankind going mad?». He described the neutron bomb, which killed people but caused very little structural damage, as a «symbol of the perversion of thought».[25] This assessment may have been factually unfounded but it voiced widespread public fears. Its main effect was to bring about a policy debate on nuclear weapons in the SPD.

The political pressure within the SPD to prevent the basing of the neutron bomb in West Germany is illustrated by the history of a resolu-

---

24   For an excellent survey of the American predecessors of the neutron bomb in the 1950s see Matthew Evangelista, *Innovation and the Arms Race. How the United States and the Soviet Union Develop New Military Technologies* (Ithaca, NY: Cornell Univ. Press, 1988), pp.86-154. Cf. for the following also Volker Matthée, *Die Neutronenwaffe zwischen Bündnis- und Innenpolitik* (Herford: Mittler & Sohn, 1985); Sherri L. Wasserman, *The Neutron Bomb Controversy* (New York: Praeger, 1983).

25   *Vorwärts*, July 21, 1977. On the domestic controversy over the neutron bomb see also Risse-Kappen, *Krise*, note 16.

tion on the issue passed during the SPD party congress in Hamburg in November 1977. The initial version presented by the party executive gave the West German government a fairly free hand whilst stressing the importance of arms control. When members on the left announced they would move for a motion against the neutron bomb, the party leadership became worried about losing its majority at the congress. Accordingly, the commission responsible for the resolutions reworded the draft in stronger terms. The key sentence of the version passed read: «The West German government is called upon to create, through its security and disarmament policy, conditions rendering deployment of the neutron bomb on West German soil unnecessary.»[26]

This considerably limited the West German government's scope of action. At the same time, the party indicated that it was unwilling to accept modernization decisions on INF without concomitant arms control measures. In the same resolution, the SPD expressed its great concern about the development of nuclear weapons which were included neither in SALT nor in MBFR. The party called for arms control negotiations on these systems.

The West German government now came under pressure from both the SPD and the U.S. government. The latter argued that *prior* to an American decision on production, the allies, above all West Germany, must agree to the deployment of the neutron bomb on their soil. The West German government came to the conclusion, obviously influenced by the simultaneous decision-making process within NATO, that the neutron bomb would improve deterrence; but Bonn failed to reach a decision regarding its deployment on West German territory. From the outset there was talk of introducing the weapon into arms control. The Bonn government favored its use as a bargaining chip for MBFR. The U.S. government, on the other hand, for whom arms control played only a secondary role in this context - namely that of allaying public fears in Western Europe - wished to set the neutron bomb off against the SS-20. This was a dubious move, since the former is a battlefield weapon and

---

26 SPD Parteitag Hamburg, November 15-19, 1977, *Dokumente Frieden*, published by SPD party executive, p.7. Draft version in, SPD-Parteitag Hamburg, *Anträge*, p.13.

the latter a long-range INF system. In the end, the West German government gave in to U.S. pressure.[27]

The whole issue became the subject of heavy infighting in Bonn, not only between the governing parties SPD and FDP, but also between the FDP-led Foreign Ministry and the SPD-led Defense Ministry. The former felt American demands should be complied with. There was disagreement on this point and on the general role arms control should play in the neutron bomb issue. On January 20, 1978, the Federal Security Council (*Bundessicherheitsrat*) in Bonn finally took the following policy decision:[28]

1. As a nonnuclear weapon state, the West German government does not participate in decisions on the production of nuclear weapons.
2. Should the U.S. decide to produce the neutron bomb, it should be included in arms control negotiations.
3. The West German government is prepared to accept the neutron bomb on its territory, unless the West is able to forgo deployment within two years of the U.S. production decision due to results of arms control.
4. The neutron bomb is not to be deployed on West German territory alone («non-singularity»).
5. West Germany may not come into a peculiar position as compared to the nuclear powers U.S., France, and Great Britain; it must consider its relationship with the USSR and Eastern Europe.

Bonn wanted the Alliance to take a *joint* decision on points 2-5. The West German government thus confirmed the commitment of 1954, when the Federal Republic joined NATO, not to take part in the production of nuclear weapons. The non-singularity demand which had been backed by Helmut Schmidt for many years, was to make it absolutely clear that the Federal Republic did not wish to assume a special nuclear role in Western Europe. West Germany already was filled with nuclear weapons on

---

27 For details see Hoffmann, *Atompartner*, note 4, pp.212-219, 269-287; Matthée, *Neutronenwaffe*, note 24, pp.145-149; Wasserman, *Neutron Bomb*, note 24, pp. 88-97.

28 For details see Lothar Ruehl, «Die Nicht-Entscheidung über die Neutronenwaffe», *Europa-Archiv*, no.5, 1979, pp.137-150, 147. Helmut Schmidt also listed the five points in his governmental declaration at the *Bundestag* of April 13, 1978, *Bulletin*, no.24, 1978, pp.321-326.

her soil; she was therefore vulnerable enough in this respect.[29] This also explains the government's insistance on a joint NATO resolution.

On the other hand, Bonn agreed to accept the neutron bomb on West German territory provided a number of conditions were met. These terms, which foresaw the inclusion of the neutron bomb in arms control and offered a zero option in the event of successful negotiations, were a concession to SPD criticism.

The West German government's terms on the neutron bomb issue largely anticipated its position on INF which began to evolve at roughly the same time. This refers to the concept of a *double-track decision* on modernization and arms control. Regarding *Ostpolitik* and détente policy and its allowances for the fears and concerns of West Germany's neighbors, it was identical with the position subsequently adopted on INF (non-participation in production decisions; no special nuclear role for West Germany; non-singularity). In addition, the West German government tried to satisfy *both* the demands of the SPD and the U.S. government. Here too, the parallels to INF are more than obvious.

In February and March 1978, general consensus was reached in NATO on the course of action to be taken. The U.S. would officially announce production of the neutron bomb; at the same time NATO would declare its intention to deploy the system within two years should no arms control results have been achieved. The neutron bomb was either to be traded off against the SS-20 or against reductions in Eastern tanks. Aside from West Germany, only Great Britain was to be a further deployment country. Thus the non-singularity requirement had just been met. The arms control offer was worded in such imprecise terms that it most resembled a fig leaf. Within NATO only vague ideas existed on where and how the neutron bomb should further arms control.

On March 14, 1978, the West German Federal Security Council passed the final resolution. Shortly afterwards NATO's Permanent Council was to make the decision. Carter's personal move to delay production of the neutron bomb came as a complete surprise to the West German government. It felt it had been treated very badly by the U.S. President, since it had consented to deploy the neutron bomb on its territory, despite massive protests at home and the fact that not all of its conditions had been satisfactorily fulfilled. Attempts to bring around the

---

29 Helmut Schmidt to the author.

American government failed. Bonn's statement of April 7, 1978, on Carter's decision was therefore worded with greatest diplomatic restraint. Notwithstanding this, the West German government remained true to its position of January and now made a more explicit link to the issue of intermediate-range weapons. The West would have to continue to use its technological capabilities in order to remove the existing disparities:

> «The West German government continues to believe that the neutron bomb has considerable potential as an instrument of arms control to eliminate disparities in the military balance, especially as far as intermediate-range weapons and tanks are concerned. We therefore consider the planned Alliance consultations on arms control, to be of particular importance; the West German government will continue to participate actively in these consultations.»[30]

This declaration illustrates a further connection between the debate on the neutron bomb and NATO's decision-making process on INF. Carter's handling of the matter eroded West German confidence in the United States' ability to pursue a consistent foreign policy. For Helmut Schmidt in particular, Carter's decision seems to have been a kind of crucial experience. He began to question the reliability of the American President and to doubt whether the U.S. was capable of taking European security interests seriously. This explains his constant references later to «predictability» and «calculability», which he designated basic foreign policy virtues in the nuclear age.[31] The repeated demands of the West German government to be comprehensively consulted by the U.S. should also be seen in this context.

Aside from the personal animosity between Schmidt and Carter, the German-U.S. differences of opinion on the neutron bomb stemmed from misunderstanding on two points. In NATO committees and in the defense ministeries concerned, consensus had developed over the years in favor of the weapon. But when the time came to take a decision, the lack of enthusiasm for the neutron bomb shared by political leaders on

---

30 Klaus Bölling, «Zur Entscheidung von Präsident Carter zur Neutronenwaffe,» *Bulletin*, no.32, 1978, p.293.

31 First mentioned in a speech before the UN Special Session on Disarmament, May 25, 1978, *Bulletin*, no.55, 1978, pp.529-535. See also Hartmut Soell, «Sich barfuss in die Tür der Weltpolitik klemmen,» *Frankfurter Allgemeine Zeitung* (FAZ), November 12, 1983, p.10.

both sides of the Atlantic became evident. Jimmy Carter, as an advocate of disarmament and an opponent of nuclear weapons, remained unconvinced of its advantages. Pushed to make a decision, he shifted the pressure to the Europeans, by making his acceptance conditional on their backing. He obviously overlooked the fact that in doing so he presented West Germany in particular with the dilemma of having to decide between the American security guarantee and its own status as a non-nuclear country.

On the other hand, Helmut Schmidt who had always rejected battlefield weapons, was not in favor of the neutron bomb either, if only for domestic motives. Pressured by the Americans, he believed he had no alternative but to consent to deployment. He seems to have made no allowances for the fact that Carter himself was no vigorous supporter of the neutron bomb. Once a compromise had, after much wrangling, been reached, Carter believed - rightly to an extent - that the allies' support was only half-hearted. He therefore decided not to produce the neutron bomb.[32] His decision made altercation within NATO inevitable.

2.4 Reassuring the Allies: The Position of the U.S. Government

As of the early eighties the opinion shared by many West German critics of the INF buildup was that Pershing II and cruise missiles were the ideal weapons for the «battlefield of the superpowers».[33] They could be employed, it was argued, either in a U.S. first-strike strategy against the Soviet Union («decapitation»), or in the limitation of nuclear war to Europe. It was also alleged that the United States was extremely interested in deploying these weapons in Western Europe. If this were so, then it ought to be evident in the evolution of the double-track decision. Did the American government impose the INF modernization on the Europeans? This was not the case at all.

---

32 See Jimmy Carter, *Keeping Faith* (Toronto: Bantam, 1982), pp.225-229; Cyrus Vance, *Hard Choices* (New York: Simon & Schuster, 1983), pp.94/95.

33 See e.g. Dieter S. Lutz, *Weltkrieg wider Willen?* (Reinbeck: Rowohlt, 1981); Alfred Mechtersheimer, *Rüstung und Frieden* (München: Langen-Müller & Herbig, 1982), pp.76-88.

Admittedly, there was keen interest among Pentagon staff in the mid-1970s in developing cruise missiles as a new technological option - an interest supported by the transatlantic «cruise missile lobby». The cruise missile was fervently declared the ideal weapon for a whole range of military options. This enthusiasm was not shared by the armed forces, however (cf. 2.1). When the Soviet Union tried, during SALT II negotiations, to achieve cuts in cruise missiles, she met with vehement opposition from the Pentagon. It was in this connection that the U.S. Defense Department considered the option of ground-launched long-range cruise missiles for the defense of Western Europe. It was argued they would enable SACEUR to cover military targets in the Western Soviet Union, thus relieving tactical air forces of their nuclear role.[34] NATO officials in Brussels gave their full backing to the Pentagon's plans (cf. 2.1).

On the other hand, the U.S. State Department, but also Carter's Defense Secretary Brown himself, opposed the wishes of the Pentagon bureaucracy and the West Europeans. Initially an attempt was made to appease European reservations regarding American SALT policy and the ever-louder calls for modernization of U.S. nuclear weapons in Europe. In June 1976, the number of Poseidon submarine-launched ballistic missiles (SLBMs) assigned to SACEUR was increased. SACEUR now had at its disposal 400 SLBM warheads with a range of 4,600 km. In 1977, the U.S. finally doubled the number of its F-111 bombers based in Great Britain from 80 to 164, in response to allied fears. Britain's Minister of Defense Mulley and his German counterpart Leber found these measures insufficient, however. In August, Harold Brown received a letter from Mulley in which the latter expressed his support for new NATO ground-launched intermediate-range missiles. His argument ran that the existing U.S. systems were not visibly available for extended deterrence. On top of that, the assignment of the Poseidon SLBMs to NATO could be canceled at any time on U.S. request.[35]

A week after Helmut Schmidt's IISS speech, U.S. Secretary of State Cyrus Vance declared before Congress that NATO was currently examining its nuclear weapons posture. In view of the existing SLBMs and forward-based systems (FBS), no additional ground- or sea-launched sys-

34 See Thomson, «Evolution,» note 12, pp.602/603; Art/Ockenden, «Domestic Politics,» note 5.
35 On the Mulley letter see Meier, *Sicherheitsbeziehungen*, note 1, vol.2, p.397.

tems were necessary for Europe. Defense Secretary Brown took a similarly cautious line of argument, partly against positions taken by lower-ranking officials of his own department. The American strategic potential, he argued, was fully capable of attacking all targets in the Soviet Union and of matching Soviet INF. Further, it was unrealistic to single out a regional equilibrium of the overall strategic balance.[36] The irony of the story is that these very arguments cropped up again after 1979, in the West German debate on INF. West European critics of the Pershings often failed to realize that their own considerations had initially been presented by the *Carter Administration* to reassure West Europeans demanding the upgrading of NATO's INF posture.

In summer 1977, the U.S. government decided that it should accommodate European concerns and provide the allies with comprehensive information on the cruise missile option. There was a heated debate between advocates of cruise missiles in the Pentagon and opponents in the State Department over who should be assigned this task. Finally, the State Department won the argument. Leslie Gelb, the director of the Bureau of Politico-Military Affairs, visited Brussels with a paper intended to give the NATO allies a balanced explanation of the situation. Verification problems were cited as one of the detrimental effects that cruise missiles would have on arms control. Further, the paper argued, it was questionable from a strategic viewpoint to call for cruise missiles for Europe. This could have a «decoupling» effect, because it would suggest a separate eurostrategic balance and thereby undermine the credibility of the U.S. nuclear guarantee. (West European opponents of INF deployment would later accuse the United States of the very opposite, namely of wanting to limit nuclear war to Europe.) Gelb's visit did nothing to allay European fears; rather it was seen as an unacceptable attempt at appeasement.[37]

David Aaron, the deputy of National Security Advisor Brzezinski, suffered the same fate when he visited Europe in late 1977. His mission was to inform the allies on the American view of the threat posed by Soviet intermediate-range weapons. NATO was again reassured that the U.S. strategic forces provided a sufficient counterbalance and that no addi-

---

36 See Garthoff, *Détente*, note 9, p.854; Krell/Schmidt, *Rüstungswettlauf*, note 4, p.19/20.

37 See Schwartz, *NATO's Dilemmas*, note 1, pp.211/212; Thomson, «Evolution,» note 12, pp. 604/605. For the following see Garthoff, *Détente*, note 9, p.857.

tional systems were necessary. Speaking before the NATO Council in December 1977, Harold Brown attempted to convince his European colleagues that SALT II would not put a stop to any of NATO's modernization options. Secretary of State Vance proposed the creation of a multilateral arms control forum so that the West Europeans could participate in the negotiations on INF. The West German government was among those to speak out against this and similar proposals made later, arguing that INF negotiations outside the SALT framework would encourage «decoupling».

A different policy was obviously pursued by proponents of cruise missiles in the Pentagon's office for International Security Affairs (ISA). In NATO's High Level Group, which was set up in October 1977 (cf. 2.1) and which convened under the chairmanship of David McGiffert, the Assistant Secretary of Defense for ISA, U.S. officials did not in any way oppose European demands. The British representative in particular, Michael Quinlan, expressed a firm call for INF modernization. He received strong support from both his West German colleague Wolfgang Altenburg (later Tandecki, Armed Forces General Staff, Defense Ministry) and the Norwegian representative Jörg Johan Holst. Michael Quinlan appears to have stressed above all the so-called «gap in NATO's escalation ladder», whilst the West German representative concentrated on the threat posed by the SS-20.[38] At the third meeting of the HLG in February 1978, McGiffert presented a paper containing several proposals for INF modernization. The option to build a large nuclear battlefield force was dismissed, since the West Europeans did not wish to fuel fears of a (nuclear) war limited to Europe. Equally rejected was the proposal to set up a comprehensive INF counterforce and countervalue capability against the Soviet Union. The concern here was that a separate eurostrategic balance might increase «decoupling» fears. A corresponding proposal to deploy 1,500 to 2,000 U.S. INF in Western Europe had been made by the U.S. Joint Chiefs of Staff in the course of the debate. On the other hand, there was backing for the proposal to modernize NATO's long-range INF. As early as March 1978, general consensus had been reached in the HLG that an evolutionary upward adjustment - as it was euphemistically termed - of NATO's intermediate-range posture was

---

38   According to Meier, *Sicherheitsbeziehungen*, note 1, vol.2, p.408.

necessary. The objective was to strengthen NATO's capability to cover targets in the Soviet Union.

In April 1978, officials in the White House and the State Department recognized that the representatives of the Pentagon had gone considerably further than the U.S. government was prepared to at that point. The National Security Council then sent its own representative to the HLG. The State Department feared above all that NATO's proposals might prevent the conclusion of the SALT II treaty.[39] As a counterargument to the military justification of the INF buildup, it was maintained that nuclear attacks against Soviet territory could lead to a strategic exchange between the superpowers, regardless of from where the U.S. missiles were started. Moreover, it was deemed possible that the Soviets lacked the necessary technical know-how to detect where U.S. INF came from so as to acknowledge the selectivity and the limitedness of the nuclear strike. In short, these U.S. officials feared the very opposite of what West German critics of the NATO decision later saw as American motivation for the deployment of the Pershing II and cruise missiles. Leading sections of the U.S. government argued that new INF in Western Europe might result in the United States being drawn into a nuclear exchange with the Soviet Union, rather than limiting (nuclear) war to Europe. These American critics of INF modernization were afraid of the very «coupling» which the West European advocates were asking for. Finally, it was argued that the task of implementing flexible response, i.e., selective and limited counterforce options, could just as easily be taken over by U.S. strategic forces; their command and control systems were equally capable of carrying out such flexible options.

By early 1978, there was no consensus in the U.S. Administration on how to deal with the issue. Then, in early summer, Washington abandoned its hitherto cautious position. From this time on, the U.S. showed resolve and leadership to bring about NATO's INF decision. This change of attitude was the result of the neutron bomb debacle. As of mid-1978, a consensus emerged in Washington that the U.S. must develop a coherent policy on medium-range weapons and assume the leadership in the Alliance's internal decision-making process, so as not to jeopardize Alliance cohesion. The opinion was that NATO could not afford a repeat of the brouhaha over the neutron bomb. Thus the overriding objective the

---

39   Cf. Schwartz, *NATO's Dilemmas*, note 1, pp.221/222; Garthoff, *Détente*, note 9, p.858.

U.S. government pursued with their INF policy came to be *Alliance cohesion*. At the NATO summit in Washington at the end of May 1978, President Carter called for an evaluation of the modernization of intermediate-range systems in view of the Soviet arms buildup. At the same time, he linked modernization to arms control, thus adopting a position put forward by the West Germans, among others. The communiqué issued by the NATO Council also reflects this position, albeit in very vague terms.[40]

During summer 1978, various sections of the U.S. Administration conducted, on the President's instructions, a comprehensive study on INF and arms control: the «Presidential Review Memorandum 38» (PRM 38). PRM 38 supported the HLG consensus on long-range INF for political and military reasons; NATO would have to stand firmly behind the modernization of its INF potential if the SS-20 were to be restricted through arms control. The U.S. therefore pleaded for an integrated solution consisting of a modernization decision and an offer to negotiate. This approach was accepted, partly thanks to efforts by the West German government, which endorsed it during a bilateral West German-U.S. meeting on July 31, 1978. In connection with PRM 38, the Americans assured the Europeans on several occasions that flexible response would remain NATO strategy and that the U.S. nuclear guarantee would still be valid. Should the Europeans find this inadequate, then they would have to be prepared to share the risk and make their territory available for American medium-range weapons. At the NPG Council of Ministers Meeting in October 1978, an initial decision was taken in favor of INF systems capable of reaching targets in the USSR.[41]

In 1978/79, up to the passing of the NATO double-track decision, U.S. government representatives worked all out in the Alliance for a joint decision, exerting pressure on the West Europeans to reach consensus. American determination was motivated by concern for Alliance cohesion. The decision-makers in Washington remained unconvinced of

---

40 See the communiqué of the North Atlantic Council Meeting, May 30-31, 1978, *Bulletin*, no.60, 1978, pp.569-572. See also President Carter's speech to the NATO Council, May 31, 1978, *Current Policy*, ed. Bureau of Public Affairs, U.S. Dept. of State, no.22, June 1978.

41 Cf. the communiqué, *Bulletin*, no.121, 1978, p.1126. See on the subject Ruehl, *Mittelstreckenwaffen*, note 7, p.183. Also interviews by the author. On PRM 38 see Schwartz, *NATO's Dilemmas*, note 1, pp.224/225.

the military value of new intermediate-range weapons in Europe. However, they backed HLG consensus in order to appease America's allies and to ensure European support for SALT II, support which was considered necessary in the U.S. domestic debate over the treaty. The following quote by U.S. Security Advisor Brzezinski expresses, according to Garthoff, the prevalent opinion in the Carter government:

«I was personally never persuaded that we needed TNF for military reasons. I was persuaded reluctanctly that we needed it to obtain European support for SALT.... We felt we were responding to the European desire in shaping the TNF, but we were also very conscious of the fact that Europeans were ambivalent.»[42]

An examination of the evolution of NATO's double-track decision reveals very little evidence that the arms buildup was imposed upon the Europeans by the U.S. Rather, the opposite was true. West European responsiblity for NATO's decision cannot be denied.

2.5 Modernization and/or Arms Control? The West German Domestic Debate in 1978/79

The debate over the neutron bomb showed clearly that the planned deployment of new medium-range weapons capable of reaching targets in the Soviet Union, would not pass without domestic debate. As early as fall 1977, SPD spokesmen had adopted a critical stance to the modernization of medium-range weapons, in particular to cruise missiles. The aforementioned party conference resolution in Hamburg in November 1977 contained a call, formulated by Walther Stützle, for arms control negotiations to cover those weapons which were included neither in SALT nor MBFR. In addition, the resolution stipulated that before qualitatively new weapons systems were introduced, assurances must be given that they would not constitute an obstacle to arms control.[43]

The decision-making process within the West German government and NATO was observed by the SPD security elite with great concern. For example, in a speech before the *Bundestag* on April 13, 1978, Alfons Pawelczyk, the party's spokesman on arms control, aired his criticism of the arguments put foward by the West German government and Chan-

---

42 Quoted in Garthoff, *Détente*, note 9, p.859 (note). See ibid., pp. 858/859.
43 Cf. the Hamburg party resolution, note 26, p.7.

cellor Schmidt. Although there was no denying the Soviet Union's increasing edge in intermediate-range weapons, nobody could prove that the Warsaw Pact derived any new military option as a result. Pawelczyk warned against the argument that the strategic forces would be neutralized as a result of U.S.-Soviet parity. U.S. nuclear weapons were sufficient to cover the Soviet INF potential. Those disagreeing with this argument were sowing mistrust in the U.S. guarantee to the Alliance and therefore acting in an irresponsible manner likely to jeopardize national security.

Despite this criticism, the West German government defined a contrary position in fall 1978. During summer, a policy decision had been taken in Bonn to strive for a double-track decision integrating modernization and arms control. The West German government continuously backed such an approach to INF and finally helped to bring about its acceptance by the United States and NATO, aided by the support of other West European governments. In its official policy statement of fall 1978, the West German government presented arms control as merely complementing the modernization decision. Arms control was meant to help eliminate disparities in INF but was not intended to replace NATO INF modernization.[45]

Another component of the double-track decision can also be attributed to the Dutch and the West German governments, especially to Helmut Schmidt. For him, the INF decision was linked to a reduction of nuclear battlefield weapons whose role he had always viewed with skepticism. Shifting the emphasis within NATO's nuclear capabilities to systems with longer ranges accommodated the old West European desire to assign nuclear weapons a «deterrence» role and to limit their military function as far as possible. This explains the connection between the modernization decision and the announcement contained in the 1979 communiqué, that 1,000 nuclear battlefield warheads were to be withdrawn.

The West German government rejected a massive increase in launchers for longer-range INF, so as not to arouse the suspicion that they wished to create a separate eurostrategic balance. NATO's overall

---

44   See Deutscher Bundestag: *Stenographische Protokolle* («PlPr»), 8/83, pp.6511-6517, in particular 6513-6515.

45   Cf. Ruehl, *Mittelstreckenwaffen*, note 7, pp.180-187.

number of nuclear warheads was not to be increased. Over and above this, Bonn strove for a joint Alliance decision and was vehemently opposed from the start to the basing of intermediate-range systems in West Germany alone. Finally, the West German government made it clear that it was not prepared under any circumstances to accept longer-range INF systems as part of a «double-key» arrangement with the U.S. (*Bundeswehr* control of the launchers; U.S. control of the warheads). The new medium-range weapons were to be deployed under the sole control of the United States, so that the USSR should have no reason whatsoever to think that West Germany had a «finger on the trigger» of systems capable of reaching Soviet territory.

At the same time, the West German government lent its support to a modernization option which was intended to visibly distinguish between U.S. INF based in Europe and the strategic potential of the United States. Additional submarine-launched missiles under NATO Supreme Command and submarine-launched cruise missiles were both dismissed as being inadequate. However, no decision was taken on particular weapons systems until early 1979. The decision-making process was still in a stage at which different options were examined. In intensive talks between ministries and in the Federal Security Council, INF modernization was discussed at length. It remains unclear, however, to what extent arms control influenced the choice of particular weapons systems.

The fact that the West German decision-makers consented to the modernization of NATO's INF potential must be seen in connection with Soviet intransigence. The issue was playing an increasing role in *German-Soviet relations*, especially during General Secretary Brezhnev's visit to West Germany in May 1978. Chancellor Schmidt stressed to the Soviet leadership the growing disparity in intermediate-range weapons and called upon the Soviet Union to agree to cuts in the SS-20. Otherwise it would have to face a countermove by the West. Brezhnev remained noncommital. However, the meeting was the first occasion that West Germany and the Soviet Union had discussed the military balance in tactical nuclear forces. The Soviet leadership created the impression that it did not intend using the SS-20 to drastically increase the number of its medium-range missiles. But no concrete assurances were given. The joint declaration of May 6, 1978 stated:

«Both sides consider it important that nobody seeks military superiority. They consider that approximate equivalence and parity are sufficient for the main-

tenance of security. In their opinion, appropriate disarmament and arms limitation measures in the nuclear and conventional areas which are in keeping
with this principle, would be of great importance.»[46]

The West German government considered Soviet readiness for arms
control and its acceptance of the principle of parity a foreign policy success. Above all, the SPD hoped that Soviet restraint might eliminate the
necessity of a NATO decision on modernization. It soon emerged, however, that the Soviets were not prepared to make substantial concessions
which went beyond verbal declarations. Their acceptance of the parity
principle was of very little value to the West German government since
the USSR had claimed during Brezhnev's visit that parity already existed
on INF, a position which it reaffirmed on numerous occasions.

At the summit meeting of the four Western heads of government in
Guadeloupe in January 1979 (cf. 2.6), Chancellor Schmidt presented
Bonn's position. The West German government announced its support
for SALT II and was prepared to accept the deployment of new INF on
West German soil under the following conditions:[47]

1. The U.S. assume their nuclear leadership role in NATO by means of a
    binding political decision.
2. The deployment decision is to result from a joint NATO resolution. West
    Germany will not let itself be pushed into a leadership role.
3. NATO's deployment decision should coincide with an American offer to the
    Soviet Union to negotiate on intermediate-range weapons in the framework
    of SALT III.
4. Ground-launched LRINF in West Germany must be under the sole control
    of the U.S.
5. INF must not be based exclusively on West German territory («non-singu-
    larity»).

The above terms indicated a certain hesitation on the part of the West
German government, though it had given the impression in the Alliance
that it would fully back INF modernization. This hesitation stemmed
from domestic motives. Bonn was urging arms control moves in the face
of increasing opposition to its INF policy, especially from the ranks of
the SPD. The major domestic controversies over NATO's policy prior to

---

46 *Bulletin*, no.44, 1978, pp.429/430. See also Ruehl, *Mittelstreckenwaffen*, note 7,
    pp.228/229; Schmidt, *Menschen*, note 15, pp.90-94.
47 See Schmidt's speech to the SPD parliamentary group, February 6, 1979;
    Schmidt, *Menschen*, note 15, pp. 230-232.

the INF decision in December 1979 involved the SPD leadership and the party's arms control experts on the one hand, and the West German Government on the other. Following the debate on the neutron bomb, the party's advocates of *unilateral disarmament* quickly disassociated themselves from security policy issues and concentrated their attention, up to 1980, almost exclusively on the civilian use of nuclear energy.

The *FDP* - with the exception of a minority around its special Committee on Foreign and Inter-German Policy and its chairman William Borm - devoted hardly any time to debate on INF. While security policy spokespersons of the *CDU/CSU* called first exclusively for an INF modernization decision, the double-track approach did not receive official party support until fall 1979.[48] Therefore, prior to 1980, the domestic opposition to the double-track decision was almost entirely confined to the arms control elite of the SPD.

SPD criticism grew considerably stronger in the wake of the Guadeloupe summit meeting. It appears that, prior to the conference, SPD politicians had prevented the Chancellor from presenting President Carter with a written statement committing West Germany to the deployment of intermediate-range missiles on its territory. After Guadeloupe, the leader of the SPD Parliamentary Group, Herbert Wehner, out of his concern for the future of détente policy, launched a sharp personal attack on the national security and arms control policy of the West German government. On the INF issue Wehner wrote:

> «It is not in keeping with West Germany's situation to allege that additional weapons are necessary and by this argument to increase the likelihood that West Germany become a deployment country for such additional systems, instead of bringing the weight of the Alliance to bear for arms limitation and disarmament.»[49]

In response to this criticism, which brought about a heated domestic debate, the West German government defined its position publicly in February 1979. This took the form of a reply to a parliamentary questionnaire from the SPD/FDP and CDU/CSU *Bundestag* factions. The Soviet INF buildup was described as a strategic threat to NATO which could only be compensated for by resorting to American strategic sys-

---

48 For details see Risse-Kappen, *Krise*, note 16.

49 Herbert Wehner, «Deutsche Politik auf dem Prüfstand,» *Die Neue Gesellschaft*, no.2, 1979, p.93.

tems. Though the West German government supported the SALT II treaty, it nevertheless stressed that the cruise missile option would still be available to NATO once the Protocol had run out. The following sentences sum up West Germany's INF policy at the time:

> «The West German government assumes that this [the elimination of the INF disparities] can be achieved by combined efforts in defense policy and arms control. The integrated nature of NATO's military strategy requires an arms control concept in conformity with it. The Alliance must reply in kind to the Warsaw Pact arms buildup and prepare itself for the developments which will come to fruition in the eighties. What is important is that Alliance solidarity, the continuum of capabilities in NATO's defense posture, and the cohesion of the European-American partnership remain visible both through defense and arms control policies.»[50]

The opposite standpoint was voiced by SPD politicians Horst Ehmke and Alfons Pawelczyk in the *Bundestag* on March 8, 1979. The arguments they used foreshadowed most of those which were to shape the peace debate after 1980 (cf. 3.2):[51]

- There had always been Soviet superiority in intermediate-range weapons. This superiority can continue to be met by the American strategic forces.
- European «decoupling» fears cannot be overcome by military and technical means. Those who do not believe that the U.S. would use its ICBMs in response to a nuclear attack on Western Europe should ask themselves whether U.S. INF systems in Western Europe would really alter the situation.
- The technological dimension of the nuclear arms race with its trend toward greater accuracy, reliability, and improved guidance, increases nuclear warfighting capabilities. If this trend continues, a situation could arise in which one side is able to eliminate the forces of the other with a nuclear first strike.
- The deployment of ground-launched INF in West Germany capable of reaching Soviet territory, jeopardizes détente; therefore the basing of new INF systems at sea should be considered.
- Since neither the range nor the payload (conventional or nuclear) of cruise missiles can be verified, they pose additional problems for arms control.

The SPD asked that clear priority be given to negotiations over a deployment decision.

---

50 «Antwort der Bundesregierung auf die Grossen Anfragen von SPD/FDP und CDU/CSU», February 16, 1979, *Bundestagsdrucksache* (Drs.) 8/2587, p.21. See ibid. pp.20, 22.

51 See *PlPr* 8/141, pp.11119-11127 (Pawelczyk) and 11178-11188 (Ehmke).

The party's skepticism towards a Western deployment decision in no way meant that it was prepared to accept the Soviet INF arms buildup. Both in public statements and in talks, it repeatedly reminded the USSR that the West would react if the Soviets did not exercise restraint. SPD politicians tried on several occasions to take Soviet declarations expressing willingness to negotiate literally and exploit them to the full. In particular, they referred to Brezhnev's statement of November 2, 1977, in which he suggested that production of all kinds of nuclear weapons be stopped. It was this and similar proposals which had led the SPD to discuss the possibility of a moratorium. During various visits to Moscow, SPD politicians called upon the Soviet Union to impose a moratorium on the deployment of the SS-20.[52] The proposal was rejected. It is unlikely, though, that the SPD would have tolerated the NATO double-track decision and that the decision would have found sufficient domestic support in West Germany, had the Soviet Union announced a timely moratorium on the SS-20 arms buildup.

The SPD arms control elite did not regard either the military-strategic (implementation of flexible response) or the alliance justification («coupling») of the NATO decision as watertight. They did however accept, in the light of Soviet policy, the «bargaining chip» argument - i.e., that the USSR could only be moved to accept negotiations on the SS-20 if faced with the threat of new Western INF systems. During the entire inner-party debate up to the change of government in 1982, this justification was the main argument used to commit the SPD majority to support the Bonn government's INF policy.

Due to the domestic situation and because it seemed increasingly apparent that the U.S. was pursuing modernization and dragging its feet over arms control, the West German government went all out at the beginning of 1979 to convince NATO to make an INF arms control offer to the Soviets. Together with the Dutch government, it argued that NATO needed an elaborated arms control concept for dealing with INF in the framework of SALT III, prior to a modernization decision. To this

---

52 See e.g. Alfons Pawelczyk's interview with the radio station *Sender Freies Berlin,* September 23, 1978 (Bundespresse- und Informationsamt [BPA], Nachrichtenabteilung, *Rundfunkauswahl Deutschland*); «Pawelczyk in Alleingesprächen mit Falin und Sagladin,» *FAZ*, March 17, 1979. On Brezhnev see his speech on the 60th anniversary of the October Revolution, November 2, 1977.

aim the West German government's Arms Control Advisor, Ambassador Friedrich Ruth, suggested that a special advisory group be created in NATO (Special Group, later Special Consultative Group) to deal with INF arms control issues. This would allow NATO members to be involved in the formulation of the U.S. negotiating position, thus preventing renewed bilateralism between the two superpowers at the cost of the Europeans.

At the same time, the West German Foreign and Defense Ministries were commissioned to work out an arms control policy for INF. And so the stance which the West German government had been committed to since 1978 was not elaborated until a year later. This is probably the main reason the government failed to evaluate thoroughly how the INF modernization decision would affect political and military stability in Europe. After all, there was already fairly extensive consensus in NATO's HLG at the beginning of 1979 regarding the choice of weapons systems (cf. 2.6).

The drawing up of a position on arms control policy led to controversy between the Defense Ministry and the Foreign Office which in part mirrored the party-political fronts between SPD and FDP.[53] It was agreed that there should be bilateral negotations between the U.S. and the USSR on INF within the framework of SALT III. However, the Defense Ministry favored a *global ceiling* on strategic and intermediate-range weapons within SALT III with a subceiling for INF, thereby preserving Alliance unity and enabling compromise on problematic issues (e.g. FBS), whilst the Foreign Ministry wished to add INF as a separate issue to the existing SALT II framework. It wanted to ensure that specific negotiations on INF take place and that the Soviet Union be forced to make concrete concessions regarding its medium-range posture. Finally, the West German government adopted the first approach.

As for the negotiating objective on INF, there was still agreement within the German government in spring 1979 that total renunciation of deployment was out of the question, even in return for substantial Soviet concessions. Indeed, it was assumed it would be necessary to retain a minimum force of about 200 systems in order to guarantee the imple-

---

53   The West German Defense Minister at the time, Hans Apel, was a Social Democrat, while Foreign Minister Hans-Dietrich Genscher was chairman of the Free Democratic Party (FDP).

mentation of NATO's flexible response strategy. Arms control was to *complement* modernization, but not replace it.[54]

The SPD however, argued from the start that a «zero option» should be possible. This and other INF issues were discussed by a working group of the party's executive board. The group was chaired by Alfons Pawelczyk and members included Hans Apel, Horst Ehmke, Walter Stützle, Karsten Voigt, and some advisors from the outside. The working group had a decisive influence on the consultation process between SPD and the Bonn government. It prepared the motion for the party congress in Berlin at the end of 1979, which was to largely shape the SPD position on INF. The party leadership accepted the double-track decision at a meeting in the Chancellery on May 19, 1979. Its decision appears to have been influenced by the «bargaining chip» argument, the wish to maintain support for the government in general, and the conviction that Chancellor Schmidt, himself SPD, would bring about an arms control success.[55]

SPD acceptance of the double-track decision was further encouraged by the continued intransigence of the Soviet Union. In June 1979, during a short visit Schmidt made to Moscow following the signing of the SALT II treaty, the Chancellor once again approached the Soviet leadership regarding the SS-20. And once again the Soviet Union showed a lack of willingness to take West European security interests seriously. Not only that, the Soviets insisted that forward-based systems must be dealt with in SALT III. In particular, they argued that U.S. attempts to circumvent SALT II restrictions by introducing new FBS - a reference to NATO's INF modernization - would have to be dealt with. Schmidt's position was weakened by the fact that President Carter had apparently not specifically addressed the SS-20 issue during his talks with the Soviet leadership at the Vienna summit meeting, but had merely made a general appeal for INF to be discussed in the framework of SALT III.[56]

Whilst Soviet intransigence had been a decisive factor in SPD toleration of the double-track decision at their party congress in Berlin in early December 1979, the *basing mode* remained a matter of contention to the very last moment. Both the SPD working group and Helmut

---

54   See Ruehl, *Mittelstreckenwaffen*, note 7, pp.180/181, 204/205.

55   See Soell, «Barfuss,» note 31.

56   Cf. Schmidt's account in *Menschen*, note 15, pp.100/101.

Schmidt himself proposed the sea-launched option on several occasions. In July 1979, the German government called upon NATO to give serious consideration to sea-launched cruise missiles (SLCMs) aboard surface ships which would patrol along the European Atlantic coast. The proposal was promptly rejected by other allied governments and then dropped by the West German government too, not least of all since it did not factor in the five essentials formulated at the Guadeloupe summit.

The SALT II controversy in the U.S. Congress also formed part of the debate within the SPD. The arms control component of the double-track decision and the entire discussion prior to the NATO resolution were based on a continuation of the SALT process. It was feared that, in the absence of a strategic arms control regime, an uncontrollable arms race in INF might occur. During a visit to the United States in early October 1979, Defense Minister Apel therefore drew attention to the link between SALT II ratification and NATO's double-track decision. There was a debate in the SPD on making explicitly such a linkage which was to have consequences both for the party congress in Berlin but also later on. The West German government did not endorse a linkage between the INF decision and SALT II ratification for fear it might have a detrimental effect on the ratification process in the U.S. Senate and even lead to the complete paralyzation of NATO. In a joint meeting of the Foreign and the Defense Committees of the *Bundestag* on October 17, 1979, which dealt with the double-track decision in detail, agreement was reached on this point among all parties.

The decisive domestic debate which immediately preceded the passing of the NATO decision, however, was concerned with the possibility of a *zero option*.[57] The SPD finally, if reluctantly, tolerated the double-track decision provided Western deployment would be cancelled in the event of acceptable Soviet concessions.

Schmidt was prompted by the debate in the SPD to hint for the first time, in November 1979, that under ideal circumstances it might not be necessary to deploy the Pershing II and cruise missiles. In a speech to the SPD parliamentary group he announced that an ideal solution would

---

57 This aspect is ignored in almost all the studies quoted in note 7, which usually refer to the NATO consensus that arms control should *complement* modernization and not *substitute* for it.

mean no NATO INF deployments and «that the Soviet Union would get rid of much of what it has produced.»[58]

However, the zero option favored by the SPD security politicians was at no time identical with the subsequent U.S. negotiating position of November 1981. The key section of the party conference resolution reached in Berlin, which owed its wording to Alfons Pawelczyk and Karsten Voigt, ran as follows:

«For these reasons the West German government should only consent to the deployment of intermediate-range weapons in Europe whose development is to be the sole responsibility of the United States... under the revocable condition that they not be introduced should arms control negotiations lead to satisfactory results. The aim of negotiations is to eliminate the necessity of additional intermediate-range weapons in Western Europe through a reduction of Soviet INF and a mutually agreed limitation of those missiles by East and West in Europe.»[59]

The SPD did *not* call for the total elimination of the SS-20. Moreover, the above wording left open the inclusion of forward-based systems and third-country forces. The party also insisted that arms control be given political priority while at the same time determining defense policy options in case negotiations should fail. «Automatism» in deployment was explicitly ruled out; instead, the SPD supported consideration of a possible moratorium during the term of negotiations. The SPD can, therefore, at most be said to have tolerated the double-track decision; its position was not one of unconditional acceptance. The party's interpretation of the double-track decision represented the broadest possible reading and foreshadowed the SPD's clear mistrust of NATO's INF policy.

In assessing the extent to which the SPD debate influenced the West German government's decision-making process, it should be stressed that the SPD did not invent the double-track decision. However, the skepticism of leading Social Democrats did help Bonn, together with the backing of other West European governments, to get the integrated decision accepted by NATO. It was clear to all concerned that the party

---

58 Speech to the SPD *Bundestag* faction, *Informationen der sozialdemokratischen Bundestagsfraktion*, no.1140, November 15, 1979. See also Schmidt's speech at the SPD party congress in Berlin, December 3-7, 1979, *Protokoll*, pp.157-201, 193/194.

59 «Beschlüsse zur Aussen-, Deutschland-, Friedens- und Sicherheitspolitik», SPD-Parteitag Berlin, December 3-7, 1979, *Protokoll*, pp.10-22, 21.

would not have tolerated the NATO resolution without a serious arms control offer. Just how serious Helmut Schmidt himself judged the situation to be is evident in the fact that he threatened the party council with his resignation on the eve of the party congress in December 1979. The SPD (and the Dutch Social Democrats) did however invent the zero option as early as summer 1979. Had there been no debate prior to NATO's decision, it is difficult to imagine that this proposal would have been adopted in somewhat altered form as the Western INF negotiating position two years later.

2.6 Decision: The Evolution of NATO's Double-Track Concept[60]

After the NPG in October 1979 had approved the modernization of U.S. medium-range missiles in Europe, the U.S. presented the High Level Group (HLG) with a paper containing the following options:
- ground-launched cruise missiles (GLCMs);
- Pershing II with extended range;
- development of a new, mobile intermediate-range missile;
- modernization of the FB-111A intermediate-range bomber;
- sea-launched cruise missiles (SLCMs).

A combination of Pershing II and ground-launched cruise missiles soon emerged as the favored option. The military backed the Pershing II which was considered a suitable weapon for ensuring the implementation of flexible response (selectivity in order to assure damage limitation; high penetrability; reliability). Not only was Pershing II rated higher in military utility than the ground-launched cruise missile, NATO also feared that in the late eighties the Soviet Union might be able to detect and shoot down the cruise missile version which was planned for deployment.

---

60 For an account on this see, apart from the works in note 7, John Cartwright/Julian Critchley, *Cruise, Pershing and SS-20. A North Atlantic Assembly Report* (London: Brassey's Defence Publications, 1985); Raymond L. Garthoff, «The NATO Decisions on Theater Nuclear Forces,» *Political Science Quarterly*, vol.98, no.2, 1983, pp.197-214; Schwartz, *NATO's Dilemmas*, note 1; Thomson, «Evolution,» note 12.

The summit meeting of the USA, Great Britain, France, and West Germany, January 5-6, 1979, on the island of Guadeloupe involved the respective heads of government in the decision-making process. According to Helmut Schmidt's account, a *general policy decision* was taken in favor of combining INF modernization and arms control. The British Prime Minister Callaghan would have proposed a double-track decision. Schmidt, whom the other summit participants described as extremely hesitant, presented the West German position (cf. 2.5).[61]

A further decision, which had considerable impact on the subsequent INF arms control negotiations, was taken at the summit meeting. It was to be expected that, during negotiations on medium-range systems, the Soviets would bring up the topic of British and French nuclear weapons - whose inclusion in SALT the U.S. had repeatedly rejected. France consented to NATO's INF decision on condition that its nuclear weapons not be included in negotiations on intermediate-range weapons.[62] From this time on, neither the U.S. nor NATO gave any further consideration to the inclusion of French and British nuclear weapons in INF talks.

Following the Guadeloupe summit, the most immediate task was to work out the precise details of the double-track decision. A look at the timetable of events reveals that the planned combination of modernization and arms control was only partly adhered to. When the Special Group (SG) was brought into the process on April 6, 1979, at Bonn's suggestion, consensus had already been reached in the HLG on the basing of 200-600 warheads on Pershing II and cruise missiles. This consensus was confirmed by the Nuclear Planning Group which convened at the end of April. The Special Group for arms control decided to adopt HLG considerations as a starting point for its own work. Thus the modernization decision assumed priority and arms control considerations took a back seat. Agreement was also reached relatively quickly in the SG that arms control should assume a complementary function to INF

---

61 Cf. Schmidt, *Menschen*, note 15, pp.231/232; also Carter, *Keeping Faith*, note 32, pp.234/235. However, I was not able to confirm by other sources Schmidt's account of the Guadeloupe events, in particular his insistence that British Prime Minister Callaghan proposed the double-track approach.

62 See «Ein veraltetes nukleares Rückgrat - aber französisch,» *Süddeutsche Zeitung* (SZ), February 16, 1979. See also press conference of President Valery Giscard d'Estaing, February 15, 1979, *Europa-Archiv*, vol.34, 1979, pp.177-186, 181/182.

modernization, but not substitute for it. Prior to the first SG meeting, the American, British and West German representatives had obviously come to an agreement that a zero option in the form under consideration by Belgium and the Netherlands was unacceptable.[63] Regardless of arms control results, the deployment of a certain number of systems was considered to be unavoidable. Thus Helmut Schmidt's position of 1977/78 to give priority to an arms control solution for the INF problem got brushed aside.

In the course of summer 1979, the SG worked out a series of criteria for INF arms control. These were later included in the «Integrated Decision Document» (IDD):[64]

- Once it had been decided that USA and USSR should conduct bilateral negotiations on INF systems, it was further specified that they take place within the «framework of SALT III». This, however, remained open to interpretation. Did it, for example, envisage one set of talks to include strategic and intermediate-range systems? It would seem more likely that separate negotiations were foreseen which would be combined later.
- On West German initiative, the principle was adopted that any future limitation of U.S. medium-range weapons be accompanied by appropriate cuts in Soviet systems. *De jure* parity should furthermore apply for mutual reductions of medium-range systems. On the one hand, this was in accordance with the Jackson Amendment to the SALT I treaty of 1972. On the other hand, the wording *de jure* provided certain leeway for trade-offs.
- INF were to be negotiated step-by-step, dealing initially exclusively with ground-launched LRINF. This was an indication that the West was not prepared to trade off the Soviet SS-4, SS-5, and SS-20 against Western medium-range aircraft. In addition, ground-launched systems were considered easier to negotiate, in view of the difficulty of devising mutually acceptable counting rules for aircraft - an argument which is not to be dismissed.[65]
- It was finally agreed that, in keeping with European demands, the SG should continue to exist during negotiations as the Special Consultative Group (SCG). This ensured West European involvement in the bilateral arms control process of the superpowers for the first time.

---

63 According to Meier, *Sicherheitsbeziehungen*, note 1, vol.2, p.432.
64 The IDD was not published. See however the communiqué of the special meeting of NATO's Foreign and Defense Ministers, December 12, 1979, in *American Foreign Policy. Basic Documents. 1977-1980*, ed. Dept. of State (Washington D.C.: GPO, 1983), pp.494-496.
65 For details see Krell, «Zählkriterien,» note 10.

Parallel to the NATO decision-making process on criteria for arms control, the HLG continued its work on the modernization option. The sea-based version was finally abandoned, in part because ground-launched systems were thought to have a greater deterrent effect, since they could be visibly and unmistakably identified with the defense of Western Europe. Moreover, ground-launched systems, in particular Pershing II, would allow a higher degree of flexibility and selectivity and thus be more suited to the implementation of flexible response. A final reason was that no West European country was prepared to make harbors available for the ships sea-basing required.

In summer 1979, a consensus was also reached on the number of 572 systems, i.e., 108 Pershing II missiles, which would replace the corresponding number of U.S. Army Pershing IA missiles stationed in West Germany, and 454 cruise missiles (in units of 4 launchers with 4 GLCMs each). The military objective was to have sufficient systems available which could survive a Soviet preemptive attack, penetrate Soviet air defenses, and satisfy NATO's targeting requirements. The West German non-singularity principle also meant that missile deployment must be spread among several countries in Western Europe. Deploying more than 600 systems, on the other hand, might have revived Soviet fears of a first strike and created the impression that the West sought a separate eurostrategic balance. This was unacceptable to the West Europeans for the very «coupling» concerns for which they had raised the INF issue in the first place. Their aim was to achieve «calculated inferiority». Finally, NATO wanted to retain room for bargaining above the minimum requirement of 200 systems.

HLG and SG had completed their work in September 1979. At the beginning of October the draft for the Integrated Decision Document was forwarded to NATO's decision-making bodies.

The Soviet leadership now accused NATO and the U.S. of using the planned decision to circumvent the provisions of the SALT II treaty. In addition, the FBS issue became a topic again. Brezhnev's speech of October 6, 1979, is also to be seen in this context. The General Secretary hinted that the Soviet Union might be prepared to reduce intermediate-range weapons, should NATO forgo the basing of new INF. Brezhnev further announced the unilateral withdrawal of 20,000 soldiers and

1,000 tanks from East Germany.[66] The Soviet offer came too late to in-fluence the NATO decision, but it did have one specific impact. In re-sponse to the Soviet initiative and following a Dutch suggestion which received immediate backing from the West German government (cf. 2.5) NATO included the unilateral withdrawal of 1,000 nuclear battlefield warheads from Western Europe in the double-track decision. Aside from the aforementioned concession, the Soviet campaign which culminated in an extremely aggressive press conference given by Foreign Minister Andrej Gromyko in Bonn, hindered rather than promoted the pursuit of Soviet aims.

The West German discussion on the zero option does not seem to have reached NATO (cf. 2.5) until shortly before the decisive meeting of the Nuclear Planning Group in November 1979. At Helmut Schmidt's insistence, the IDD mentioned zero Western INF in exchange for drastic Soviet concessions as a conceivable, albeit highly unlikely, outcome of negotiations. The final sentence of the NATO communiqué («NATO's TNF requirements will be examined in the light of concrete results reached through negotiations.») has also been interpreted in Bonn since then as indicating the vague possibility of a zero option. There was no agreement on this point within NATO, however. The majority consen-sus in 1979 seemed rather to rule out a zero option. Further, the word-ing *«concrete* results» severely limited Social Democrat hopes of a mora-torium from the outset.

Once all the preparatory steps had been taken, the NPG Council of Ministers convened to set its seal of approval on the double-track resolu-tion, November 13-14, 1979. The final decision was taken at a special meeting of NATO's Foreign and Defense Ministers on December 12, 1979, in Brussels. The communiqué of the meeting summarized the In-tegrated Decision Document. It first pointed to the growing Soviet nu-clear arms buildup, in particular to the SS-20, whilst the corresponding Western potential had remained unchanged. The communiqué conclu-ded that these trends could «cast doubt on the credibility of the Alliance's deterrent strategy by highlighting the gap in the spectrum of NATO's available nuclear response to aggression.»[67]

---

66   See Brezhnev speech, October 6, 1979, *Survival*, vol.22, no.1, 1980, pp.28-30.

67   NATO communiqué, note 64, p.495.

NATO's overall interests would best be met by the simultaneous pursuit of two strategies which complemented one another, namely modernization and arms control. The communiqué also maintained that, in deploying 108 Pershing II to replace the U.S. Pershing IA and 464 ground-launched cruise missiles, the number of U.S. nuclear weapons in Western Europe would not increase. There would be a shift in emphasis on longer-range systems though. Finally, the communiqué listed the aforementioned arms control criteria, and the Integrated Decision Document further stipulated that third-party systems were not to be counted in U.S.-Soviet negotiations.[68]

The NATO double-track decision foresaw the following distribution of the 572 INF systems which were to be deployed from the end of 1983 on:
- 108 Pershing II and 96 cruise missiles (GLCMs) in West Germany;
- 160 GLCMs in Great Britain;
- 112 GLCMs in Italy;
- 48 GLCMs in Belgium and the Netherlands respectively.

2.7 Conclusions: The Double-Track Decision - Who Wanted What and Why?

Itself the product of technological options, threat perceptions, domestic requirements, considerations of arms control, Alliance policy, and military strategy, the NATO double-track resolution illustrates how such factors may combine to produce a decision whose grounds are highly contradictory. First of all, there were the technological innovations which enabled cruise missiles to fly over enemy territory undetected by radar and reconnaissance systems and to strike military targets with extreme precision. In addition to that, missile accuracy had been improved using terminal guidance which meant that yields could be substantially lowered, thereby reducing collateral damage. This was the *technological* background of the NATO decision.

These newly available technologies were ideally suited to the trends in *military strategy* towards emphasis on counterforce rather than countervalue options. In fact, counterforce options have featured in the nuclear strategic planning of both sides since nuclear weapons first existed.

---

68 According to Ruehl, *Mittelstreckenwaffen*, note 7, pp. 207/208.

However, NATO reappraised such limited options in connection with the introduction of flexible response in 1967. Agreement was quickly reached in the Nuclear Planning Group that nuclear weapons were needed for selective, controlled escalation, should NATO be faced with conventional defeat in Europe. In view of the existing strategic parity between the superpowers, it was argued, it would not be credible to escalate immediately to strategic nuclear war. Such considerations were related to Soviet armament insofar as the problem only existed as a result of the Soviet strategic buildup and of the fact that NATO's LRINF aircraft were no longer considered capable of penetrating Soviet air defenses.

It is quite doubtful, however, whether this rationale for Pershing II and cruise missiles on grounds of military strategy was really justifiable. It remains extremely dubious whether it would be possible to use nuclear weapons in the densely populated and highly industrialized Central Europe in a controlled and selective manner if one considers the likely origins of military conflicts and the resulting escalation processes.[69] And even if one accepts the logic of flexible response, this by no means makes it imperative to deploy *ground*-launched INF. NATO's internal discussion on air- and sea-launched alternatives made that clear. True, the highly accurate Pershing II with its short flight time was an almost «ideal» counterforce weapon to threaten time-urgent hardened targets. Making it the cornerstone of flexible response, however, would mean interpreting NATO's doctrine in a way sure to create massive problems for the West Europeans themselves. The emphasis would then be on escalation control which was always at variance with the «coupling» interests of the NATO allies. Indeed, INF modernization was to be kept quantitatively limited for this very reason.

The main justification the West Europeans had for land-basing was that it would have a «coupling» effect. Whether Pershing II would «couple» rather than «decouple» Western Europe and the U.S. strategic arsenal is difficult to determine. On the one hand, the USSR had always

---

69 See, for example, William M. Arkin/Richard F. Fieldhouse, *Nuclear Battle-fields* (Cambridge, Mass.: Ballinger, 1985). For a critique of flexible response see Krell/Schmidt, *Rüstungswettlauf*, note 4, pp.79-82. For a summarizing critique of the military justification of NATO's INF decision see Dieter Senghaas, *Die Zukunft Europas* (Frankfurt am Main: Suhrkamp, 1986) pp.217-266; Sigal, *Nuclear Forces*, note 7.

said that, in the event of an attack against their territory involving American nuclear weapons, it would respond with retaliatory strikes against the U.S. homeland. In this sense, Pershing II could be said to have a «coupling» effect - via Moscow, one might say. On the other hand, one could just as easily argue that a missile which had been visibly launched against the Soviet Union from Western Europe ought to signal to the USSR the American desire to limit nuclear war.[70] In that sense, Pershing II would serve to «decouple» the U.S. from Europe. Which argument is the more convincing remains a matter of deterrence metaphysics.

It may be dubious to justify land-basing with considerations of military strategy. Nevertheless, such considerations were dominant *within NATO headquarters*.

Yet it is highly questionable whether these requirements alone would have led the Alliance to take such a decision. The Thor/Jupiter issue of 1957 had illustrated clearly that the land-basing of nuclear weapons capable of targeting the Soviet Union remained a very delicate subject. On top of this, the Pershing II decision did not have the «advantage» of the fifties' cold war environment, but had to taken in a period of relatively relaxed East-West relations. Finally, the domestic situation in the principal deployment countries - Great Britain, the Netherlands, and West Germany - must be taken into account. All things considered, it seems highly unlikely that the NATO INF decision would have come about as some kind of routine modernization on grounds of technological developments and requirements of military strategy alone.

It was the *political decision-makers in Western Europe* and above all in West Germany, who turned the INF problem into an Alliance issue and thus opened the «window of opportunity» for the double-track decision. Helmut Schmidt, in particular, was eager to eliminate the disparity in intermediate-range weapons in Europe which could no longer be compensated for by U.S. strategic superiority. This problem was aggravated by the SS-20 buildup. Decision-makers such as Schmidt saw SS-20 deployment as proof of Soviet unwillingness to either take West European se-

---

70   Stephan Tiedtke in particular repeatedly stressed that the USSR might perceive the situation so. See his essay, «Sowjetische Militärstrategie und die Sicherheitspolitische Stabilität in Europa,« *Militärpolitik Dokumentation*, no.53-55 (Frankfurt am Main: 1986), pp.27-40.

curity interests into account or to place them on a similar footing to U.S. interests.

One can easily doubt whether the SS-20 was really the instrument of political blackmail that Schmidt took it to be.[71] The missile can hardly be said to have provided the USSR with a new military option; it could only be termed an effective counterforce weapon if one left aside the civilian damage to a densely populated Western Europe. On the other hand, the SS-20 certainly represented a considerable upgrading of the SS-4 and SS-5, and its deployment brought the USSR a substantial increase in the number of warheads available for targeting Western Europe. It certainly seems more plausible to explain the Western INF buildup as a political reaction to the SS-20 rather than on grounds of military strategy alone. The USSR under Brezhnev was not prepared to consider West European security interests and to follow up political détente in Europe with military détente.

What is more, to assume defensive motives for NATO's INF decision is in accordance with the double-track concept. To modernize and to negotiate simultaneously only made sense if the objective were truly to remove the disparity in intermediate-range weapons. Moreover, the offer to negotiate was necessary to build sufficient *domestic* support for the deployment decision.

Whilst the top political leaders in *Western Europe* were largely responsible for the NATO decision, it was the *U.S.* who finally met their demands and in 1978/79 pushed through an Alliance resolution. Leaving aside Pentagon officials, the Carter Administration was unconvinced of the political or military necessity of the INF arms buildup. Its concern was that refusal to accommodate European demands might jeopardize NATO cohesion. The swapping of roles in 1979 - the U.S. pushing for armament, the West Europeans insistent on arms control - came about due to mutual misunderstanding of one another's motives.[72]

In sum, the main actors supported the NATO decision for greatly differing reasons:

---

71   See Senghaas, *Zukunft*, note 69, pp.217-266.

72   According to Haftendorn, «Missverständnis,» note 2, p.286. On the whole it is misleading to interpret the evolution of the double-track decision as pure transatlantic misunderstanding. It was more a case of *real* differences in security policies and perceptions between the U.S. and Western Europe.

- *military strategy*: implementing flexible response to ensure escalation control;
- *Alliance policy*: strengthening of the U.S. nuclear guarantee for Western Europe given the «codification» of strategic parity in SALT II;
- *defensive motives*: reacting against the threat posed by the SS-20;
- *arms control*: including intermediate-range weapons in the East-West arms control process;
- *détente policy*: complementing political détente in the military area;
- *domestic policy*: justifying a modernization decision by the simultaneous offer to negotiate.

These goals were only in part compatible with one another. The military-strategic goal of ensuring escalation control was only compatible with «coupling», as long as there were no comprehensive eurostrategic counterforce posture involving the risk of nuclear war limited to Europe. This was why the West German government spoke up in NATO against the reduction in any significant way of the *risk* of escalation to strategic nuclear war - an objective which ran contrary to the goal of perfect escalation *control*. No less problematic was the relationship between the goals of «coupling» and of providing a counterweight to the SS-20. The latter would logically have required NATO to match Soviet INF in numbers. Yet West European governments considered calculated inferiority, both in conventional and nuclear weapons in Europe, a prerequisite for «coupling».

There were even stronger contradictions between military-political objectives and motives of arms control policy. The uneasy relationship between the declared eurostrategic inferiority in the modernization component and the criterion of *de jure* parity in the arms control track has already been mentioned. More importantly, the modernization component of the double-track decision violated important stability criteria for arms control. The military-strategic objective called for an effective counterforce weapon. The Pershing II met this requirement but also posed substantial problems for crisis stability in Europe due to its extremely short warning time. A counterforce weapon of this nature, suitable for selective strikes against time-urgent military targets in the Western Soviet Union (command and communication facilities, missile bases etc.) was bound to feed Soviet threat perceptions. From the Soviet viewpoint the U.S. was trying to secure escalation dominance and at the same time «decouple» itself from the strategic nuclear risk. Pershing II thus increased the danger of preemptive instability in crises. *This* line of argument did not play a decisive role either in NATO's decision-making process or in West Germany. Public criticism prior to the NATO double-track decision was likewise directed almost exclusively at cruise missiles. Pershing II was seen merely as a modernization of Pershing IA. Not until 1982/83 did Chancellor Schmidt and Defense Minister Apel recognize the stability problems regarding Pershing II. Both later conceded in public that its deployment in West Germany alone had been a mistake. Their reappraisal of the situation was greatly influenced by Soviet threat perceptions.[73]

Finally, the interpretation of the double-track decision shared by Helmut Schmidt and the SPD, that arms control results could *replace* the modernization of NATO's medium-range weapons, was incompatible with the Alliance policy and military strategic rationales of the INF decision. Both the implementation of flexible response and «coupling» made Western basing a necessity regardless of Soviet behavior. A zero option was inconsistent with this. The conflict of aims first emerged in 1979 in the internal NATO debate. At issue was whether arms control could, or even should, replace modernization. This had serious consequences for the subsequent negotiations. Without this conflict of aims there would be no explanation for the debate over the zero option in 1986/87.

It is part and parcel of politics in general that some degree of incompatibility exists between individual goals - in security policy this is unavoidable. The problem can be dealt with by setting priorities and understanding the interrelations between them. A policy only becomes problematic and inconsistent when one attempts to create the impression that all objectives can be achieved at the same time and equally well. This was the main problem of NATO's INF policy; there was no internal agreement on priorities. Was the emphasis on arms control or on modernization? Was NATO prepared to forgo in part the implementation of flexible response and «coupling» in return for an arms control success, as the zero option would suggest? Or was deployment to take place come what may, with arms control only being allowed to influence the *extent* of deployment? On these two decisive issues, no policy consensus existed prior to the NATO decision. Thus the conflict of goals remained and was

---

73 See Helmut Schmidt, speech at the SPD party congress, Cologne, November 19, 1983, *Protokoll*, pp.98-118, 107; Hans Apel, interview with *Der Spiegel*, October 31, 1983, p.31.

merely put off until negotiations, or rather until their outcome. It is even possible that some of those involved hoped the Soviets would continue to be intransigent.

Given this setting, a first attempt can be made to assess INF policy up to 1979 in terms of arms control. It must first be stressed that the concept of a double-track decision represented progress when compared to the arms control practice up to that time. The Alliance was prepared to negotiate a modernization decision *prior* to the deployment of the new weapons in question. West Germany, for example, was bound to support serious arms control if only for domestic motives. The threat to deploy new medium-range missiles must also be seen against the background of the Soviet arms buildup of the seventies. Had the USSR made a substantial concession (a moratorium in summer 1979 would probably have been sufficient), then it would have been impossible to secure domestic acceptance of the double-track decision in West Germany and in other West European countries.

Yet, NATO's INF policy was by no means so consistent that the double-track decision could be termed an offer of preventive arms control. This would have required a clearer statement that arms control was to take precedence. NATO could, for example, in 1979 have declared its willingness to forgo INF modernization in return for corresponding Soviet concessions. While the double-track decision combined *uno actu* a modernization decision and an offer to negotiate, the Integrated Decision Document was not integrated in the sense that the two tracks of the document were subject to, or based on the same criteria.

Indeed, the double-track decision allowed several interpretations. Which of these would finally assert itself could not be foreseen on December 12, 1979. Whether the NATO decision could be used to further arms control policy depended on American-Soviet relations, public demands on both sides of the Atlantic, and not least of all on whether the principal deployment country, West Germany, would use its scope of action in the furtherance of arms control.

3

Phase II: Negotiations and Deployment 1980-1983

3.1 Damage Limitation: Afghanistan, Reagan, and West Germany

In the early eighties, there were important changes in the international environment which were crucial for the success or failure of an INF policy geared towards preventive arms control:
- The Soviet intervention in Afghanistan put the lid on the détente policy pursued by the two superpowers in the seventies. It remains unclear whether the Soviet leadership was influenced in its decision to intervene by the NATO double-track decision. At any rate, Western Europe came under pressure to follow the U.S. lead and adjust to the policy of sanctions pursued by the Carter Administration.
- Ratification of the SALT II treaty by the U.S. Senate, which already seemed endangered in the course of 1979, was withdrawn from consideration due to the Afghanistan intervention. The negotiating approach of the double-track decision, i.e., treating INF «in the framework of SALT III», was therefore no longer applicable shortly after the NATO resolution was passed.
- Even during Carter's term there was a change in U.S. foreign and security policy. In addition to that, Ronald Reagan's election as the new U.S. President in November 1980 brought an administration to office whose foreign policy credo was the rejection of the détente and arms control policies of the seventies. The foreign and security policy goals of the new U.S. government (reassertion of American superiority; global containment of Soviet power; arms control only after the U.S. had gained strength) were clearly at variance, during Reagan's first

term, with NATO's two-pillar concept as incorporated in the Harmel Report.

Given these changes, the West German government pursued a policy of «damage limitation» in the East-West relationship. Détente policy, which had the backing of an overwhelming majority among the West German public, was pursued with the aim of retaining as much as possible of what had been achieved and continuing West German *Ostpolitik* on a low key, despite the worsened relations between the superpowers.[1] Joining the boycott of the Olympic Games was a typical example of accommo-dating American demands by a symbolic protest whilst continuing with her own détente policy in other areas. Western Europe and the U.S. seemed to exchange roles. Having warned against exclusive bilateralism between the U.S. and the Soviet Union - NATO's double-track decision was a consequence of this concern -, the allies now aimed to soften the confrontational course which Moscow and Washington were on. In both instances the aim was preservation of European security interests. Whilst in the seventies the fear had been that American-Soviet arms control could jeopardize NATO's *deterrence* policy, in the early eighties the con-cern was for the second track of the Harmel concept: détente and arms control.

A policy of damage limitation was also pursued in connection with SALT II and INF. Following the failure to ratify SALT II, the West Ger-man government argued that both sides should pledge to abide by its provisions so that at least the spirit of the SALT regime might be main-tained. Given the threat to the second component of the double-track decision, a further task in 1980 was to ensure that INF negotiations be-gin even though the course foreseen in the SALT II Protocol was no longer available. In its first statements on the Afghanistan crisis, the West German government emphasized that nuclear arms control must continue and that the offer to negotiate on INF must be upheld.[2] West

---

1   See Helmut Schmidt's governmental declarations of January 17, 1980, *Bulletin*, no.8, 1980, pp.61-65, and of February 28, 1980, *Bulletin*, no.22, 1980, pp.177-183. Cf. also Helga Haftendorn, *Security and Détente. The For-eign Policy of the Federal Republic of Germany 1955-1982* (New York: Praeger, 1985), pp.145-148, 254-260; Philip Windsor, *Germany and the Western Al-liance: Lessons from the 1980 Crisis*, Adelphi Paper 170 (London: IISS, 1981).

2   Cf. the governmental declaration of January 17, 1980, note 1; Chancellor Schmidt, interview with *Der Spiegel*, no.6, February 4, 1980.

Germany and France consulted very closely on foreign policy matters at this time, and again a year later when Reagan entered office.

The first objective was to encourage Soviet willingness to negotiate. In April 1980, the West German Chancellor announced that he would accept a standing Soviet invitation to visit Moscow. In an attempt to soften Soviet intransigence, Helmut Schmidt refloated the idea of a moratorium. At the time, the SPD was in the middle of its election campaign against the Christian Democrat candidate for the chancellery, Franz Joseph Strauss, - a campaign stressing the SPD's peace policy. Speaking at an election rally in Essen on April 12, 1980, Schmidt explained that, while the West, for technical reasons alone, would not be able to deploy the new INF systems in the coming 2-4 years, the Soviet Union was basing a new SS-20 every week:

> «The first step toward solving this problem might be for both sides to forgo the deployment of new, additional ... intermediate-range systems for a given number of years, so that negotiations and mutual limitations ... could take place in this period of time.»[3]

Schmidt opposed the line of argument, backed also by the West German government up to that date, that this would seal Soviet superiority. The West was not exposing itself to additional risk, he argued, since Soviet superiority would continue to increase daily *without* a moratorium. In his speech, Schmidt took up the debate within the SPD, as well as considerations which he had already presented to the parliamentary group in the Bundestag on November 13, 1979. However, on that occasion, he had made a similar plea to that of Foreign Minister Genscher, i.e., for a *unilateral* Soviet moratorium.[4]

Schmidt's initiative not only met with a cool reception from the Soviet Union but also from the American government and the West German Foreign Minister. Dissatisfied with the poor support from their West European alliance partners in the Afghanistan crisis, the United States saw the moratorium proposal as further evidence of Bonn's unreliability in foreign policy matters. Genscher and the Foreign Ministry argued that a bilateral moratorium was incompatible with the double-

---

3   Speech at an election rally in Essen, April 12, 1980, *SPD-Mitteilung für die Presse*, 228/80, p.8.

4   See speech to the SPD parliamentary group, November 13, 1979, *Informationen der sozialdemokratischen Bundestagsfraktion*, no.1140, 1979.

track decision. To support this argument, they referred to the final sentence of the 1979 document (*«concrete* negotiation results»») and further pointed out that such a moratorium would have been incompatible with the integrated nature of the INF decision. The Foreign Ministry also acted in accordance with the West German government's policy; since 1977 it had consistently rejected moratorium proposals made by the SPD. However, had the proposal for a temporary moratorium starting *prior* to negotiations been accepted, the only consequence for NATO would have been having to formally acknowledge a given state of affairs which could not be altered before 1983 on account of technical realities anyway. For the USSR it would have meant, in hindsight, having to forgo deployment of more than 150 SS-20 missiles with over 450 warheads (cf. table 1, p.18).

The controversy within the West German government was laid to rest by the Chancellor himself who stressed that it had never been his intention to call NATO's double-track decision into question. At the same time he referred to the West German government's earlier call for a unilateral Soviet moratorium. What is remarkable, is that Helmut Schmidt's proposal received only luke-warm backing from the SPD. The party executive committee passed a resolution in support of the moratorium but avoided arguing on the issue with the FDP, possibly for motives of coalition politics - 1980 being an election year - but also for fear that they might be accused of unreliability in security policy.

Finally, the U.S. government intervened. After Schmidt had presented his moratorium proposal in modified form to the SPD party congress in Essen on June 9, 1980, he received an explicit letter from Carter warning him against any deviation from the double-track decision. The controversy led to a heated argument between Schmidt and Carter on the occasion of the economic summit meeting in late June 1980.[5]

During his visit to Moscow June 30-July 1, 1980, the West German Chancellor succeeded in persuading the Soviet Union to enter INF talks and to withdraw their earlier refusal to negotiate after NATO had passed

---

5   See Jimmy Carter, *Keeping Faith* (Toronto: Bantam, 1982), pp.535-538. Carter describes his discussion with Schmidt in Vienna as the most invigorating talk he ever had with a foreign statesman (p.538). See also the somewhat different account by Helmut Schmidt, *Menschen und Mächte* (Berlin: Siedler, 1987), pp.226-263.

the 1979 decision. Schmidt made it absolutely clear to the Soviets that the West German government was committed to both parts of the NATO decision and that deployment in West Germany would go ahead, should there be no concrete negotiating results by the end of 1983. The Soviet leadership said it was willing to enter into preliminary INF negotiations outside the SALT framework. It still refused to enter into SALT III talks before the SALT II treaty was ratified. It was the Soviet Union, then, who *first* spoke up for separating the two levels of negotiations and for removing INF from the SALT context. The West German government accepted this because its main concern was that negotiations get underway. The following hints on the Soviet negotiating position emerged in Moscow:[6]

- As claimed in 1978/79, eurostrategic parity was said to exist already. The Soviets stuck by this position even after negotiations were well underway and only abandoned it later tacitly.
- There were to be bilateral U.S.-Soviet negotiations on intermediate-range weapons *in Europe*. The USSR, therefore, gave INF talks a regional focus by excluding its INF based in Soviet Asia.
- As was to be expected, the Soviet Union renewed a call from the SALT process that American «forward-based systems» (FBS) be included in negotiations.
- Significantly, the Soviet leadership did not specifically insist on the inclusion of British and French nuclear weapons in INF negotiations. In reply to questions from the Chancellor, Foreign Minister Gromyko explained that these systems belonged to the strategic area and would have to be taken into consideration there.[7]

And so in 1980, the West German government achieved a major foreign policy success with its double-track policy which led ultimately to the start of U.S.-Soviet preliminary talks in October/November 1980. In summer 1980, the main problem of negotiations was seen to be the FBS problem. The issue immediately became a subject of controversy within

---

6   Cf. Lothar Ruehl, *Mittelstreckenwaffen in Europa* (Baden-Baden: Nomos, 1987), pp.242-247. On Schmidt's Moscow visit in general see *Bulletin*, no.79, 1980, pp.661-665.

7   The protocol extract including Gromyko's declaration is quoted in Jürgen Todenhöfer's speech in the *Bundestag* on October 10, 1983, *PlPr* 10/29, pp.1952/1953; also in Schmidt, *Menschen*, note 5, p.118.

the Bonn government. On his return from Moscow, Chancellor Schmidt had said he found the Soviet request reasonable. However, corresponding Soviet INF aircraft would also have to be taken into account. He dismissed the argument that this would complicate negotiations.[8] The Foreign Ministry countered that the double-track decision stipulated a step-by-step approach. The controversy continued up to 1981. When the USSR repeated her insistence on the inclusion of FBS during a visit to Moscow by Foreign Minister Genscher in April, the latter spoke out in an after-dinner speech against complicating the problem and thus hindering the achievement of negotiating results. Defense Minister Apel (SPD), on the other hand, said in a July 1981 interview that he could appreciate the Soviet position.[9] The controversy between the Foreign and the Defense Ministries, which dated back to the preparation of NATO's double-track decision, continued through the entire term of the Social-Liberal coalition. The Defense Ministry, headed by a Social Democrat, generally supported an arms control policy geared to compromise even if this was likely to create negotiating problems as in the case of FBS and Soviet INF aircraft.

In U.S.-Soviet preliminary talks in October 1980, the United States introduced a position which had largely been developed by the Special Consultative Group (SCG). The group had reached consensus on the following negotiation principles:[10]
- «step-by-step» approach (aircraft to be dealt with at a later stage);
- global limitation of LRINF missiles with a regional subceiling for Europe;
- warheads on lauchers as a counting unit.

These first talks brought no concrete results but did clarify the negotiating positions of both sides. The Soviet Union proposed, in keeping with the position presented during Helmut Schmidt's visit to Moscow, to

---

8   Cf. Chancellor Schmidt, interview with *Der Spiegel*, no.28, July 7, 1980, particularly pp.28/29.

9   For the account, see Genscher's after-dinner speech during his visit in Moscow, April 2-4, 1981, *Bulletin*, no.34, 1981, pp.295/296; Hans Apel, interview with *Der Spiegel*, July 13, 1981.

10 See in particular John Cartwright/Julian Critchley, *Cruise, Pershing and SS-20. A North Atlantic Assembly Report* (London: Brassey's Defence Publ., 1985), pp.24-27; Ruehl, *Mittelstreckenwaffen*, note 6, pp.246/247.

«freeze» INF systems at existing levels on both sides. It claimed once again that rough parity already existed in European-based intermediate-range forces, including American FBS. This balance would be seriously disturbed by the deployment of new U.S. INF. In February 1981, the Soviet General Secretary offered a mutually agreed moratorium for the duration of the talks. Two days later, on February 25, the West German government rejected the proposal for the reasons already mentioned.[11] NATO followed suit.

In the meantime, INF negotiations were in jeopardy again following President Reagan's entry into office. The new U.S. Administration was initially not prepared to enter into arms control talks, and subsequent concessions during Reagan's first term were the result of vigorous bureaucratic infighting.[12] If at the beginning of 1980 the West German government's energies were directed towards compelling the *Soviets* to negotiate, a year later it worked with the same energy for the resumption of talks by the *U.S.* At the same time, the emergence and growth of the peace movements led to a drop in domestic support for the double-track decision (cf. 3.2). Thus the West German government came under pressure from two sides. With clear reference to both the domestic controversy and American policy, Helmut Schmidt stated on January 30, 1981:

> «I have to point out that the double-track decision of 1979 is to date the only existing American commitment in the Alliance to arms control negotiations which ... deal with weapons in an area directly relevant to Europe and also to West Germany. The United States of America must continue to uphold this obligation.»[13]

Schmidt categorically dismissed any criticism of the principle of parity. He suggested that the INF talks in Geneva be continued, even if the SALT process were initially interrupted. However, he stressed the con-

---

11 Cf. the declaration in BPA (ed.), *Stichworte zur Sicherheitspolitik* (SzS), no.3, 1981, p.7.

12 For a detailed account of the bureaucratic infighting see Strobe Talbott, *Deadly Gambits* (New York: A. Knopf, 1984). Whilst he is the best-informed source on the U.S. decision-making process, Talbott's description of the part played by NATO allies is sometimes inaccurate.

13 Speech in the *Bundestag* on January 30, 1981, quoted from *SzS*, no.2, 1981, p.5.

nection between INF and strategic arms control. The West German government therefore accepted the temporary delinking of INF and SALT, in order to limit damage to arms control.

The West European insistence that the U.S. government give a binding assurance that negotiations would be resumed was finally successful. On February 26, 1981, Reagan declared his support for the double-track decision to British Prime Minister Thatcher. A similarly worded joint declaration was issued by Secretary of State Haig and Foreign Minister Genscher on March 9, 1981. During a meeting of NATO's Council of Ministers in May, the United States finally set the end of the year as the time to begin INF negotiations. During Schmidt's visit to Washington on May 22, 1981, the U.S. President, at the Chancellor's request, fixed a more specific date. Negotiations were now to begin between mid-November and mid-December. In the joint communiqué, the links to strategic arms control were also laid down, thus dispelling West German fears for the time being.[14] The Americans had been pinned down to a definite date though their negotiating position at this time was by no means clear.

At this point, mention should be made of the channels open to the West European governments through which they could influence the U.S. position. The first level was, of course, bilateral talks between the heads of government and their foreign and defense ministers, as well as the multilateral exchanges within NATO. Here political decisions were taken and directives given to the respective government agencies.

At the operative level the *Special Consultative Group* (SCG) was the decisive forum in which NATO members could present their position. The SCG convened under U.S. chairmanship, either Richard Burt, head of the Bureau of Politico-Military Affairs in the State Departement (later U.S. Ambassador in Bonn), or Lawrence Eagleburger, at the time Assistant Secretary of State for European Affairs. Moreover, the *High Level Group* also continued to convene, generally chaired by Richard Perle, Assistant Secretary of Defense for International Security Policy. Perle was Burt's counterpart in the Pentagon. The bureaucratic infighting between

---

14 See Reagan's declaration in February and its background in Talbott, *Deadly Gambits*, note 12, p.45; the Haig/Genscher declaration in *Bulletin*, no.41, 1981, pp.354-356. On Schmidt's visit to Washington see the joint declaration ibid., no.49, 1981, pp.421/422; Talbott, *Deadly Gambits*, note 12, p.50.

the Pentagon and the State Department, personified in «the two Richards», was thus also reflected in NATO.

West German participants in SCG meetings described consultations as being very extensive.[15] Every negotiation proposal the Americans made, every detail of the negotiations was discussed at length. This was especially true of the «Quint» subgroup composed of the five deployment countries: Belgium, Great Britain, Italy, the Netherlands, and West Germany. Due to this close consultation process it is often difficult to discern the origin of a negotiating proposal.

Aside from NATO fora, the bilateral cooperation between officials in the respective ministeries must also be mentioned, one example being the contact between the West German Arms Control Advisor and Richard Burt. The position which Burt introduced to the American decision-making process seems frequently to have stemmed from talks with Ambassador Ruth as well as consultations in the SCG. Finally, the close personal relationship between Chancellor Schmidt and the American chief negotiator at the first INF talks in Geneva, Paul Nitze, should also be mentioned, as this had a direct influence on the latter's handling of negotiations.

The disadvantage of this complicated consultation process was that it often took a long time to work out a negotiating position - generally between four and six months. The reason becomes clear when one looks at the various stages that a proposal had to pass through before becoming official U.S. bargaining position:

1. Formulation of a proposal, e.g., within the U.S. State Department;
2. Acceptance of the position by the U.S. government;
3. Introduction to the SCG and to the bilateral channels with West European governments;
4. Evaluation of the proposal in the European capitals;
5. Opinion-forming in the SCG;
6. Decision by the U.S. government and bi- or multilateral consultation of the allies;
7. Introduction of the American negotiating position in Geneva.

---

15 Interviews with the author. Talbott's account (*Deadly Gambits*, note 12) contrasts to this description. A reason for this could be that positions which Eagleburger and Burt introduced into the U.S. decision-making process, were in part the result of SCG consultations.

This summary shows clearly that the West European governments had an unusually large number of channels at the *institutional* level with which to influence the American INF policy. Never before in the nuclear arms control process between the superpowers had NATO allies had so many ways through which to make their position clear. On the other hand, one should not overlook the fact that, despite this, it is not possible to talk of an *integrated decision-making process*. The reason for this was that negotiations in Geneva were led, at the express wish of the West Europeans in the seventies, solely by the U.S. Despite the fact that the SCG could discuss individual options, *decisions* were made exclusively in Washington. The Alliance fora and the numerous bilateral contacts served to ensure West European *involvement*, but this involvement did not include *decision-making*, as crucial turning points in the Geneva negotiations would later show.

3.2 Negotiations Begin, Support Dwindles: Effects of the Peace Debate in West Germany

It is not possible here to examine in detail the peace debate in Western Europe since 1980. Rather, emphasis will be again on the West German debate and on the effects the discussion had on the government's INF policy.[16]

First, it must be stressed that the heated debate after 1980 was *partly* the result of the decision-makers' disregard for democratic and public discussion prior to NATO's INF decision of 1979. To avoid a discussion on NATO strategy and the credibility of the U.S. nuclear guarantee, attention was focused in public almost exclusively on the SS-20. The fact was overlooked that the decision to deploy nuclear missiles in West Germany capable of reaching Soviet territory was not a «routine» modernization decision but one with far-reaching consequences which required extensive public consideration.

---

16   For more details see Thomas Risse-Kappen, *Die Krise der Sicherheitspolitik. Neuorientierungen und Entscheidungsprozesse im politischen System der Bundesrepublik Deutschland 1977-84* (Mainz-München: Grünewald-Kaiser, 1988). For the Netherlands see Philip P. Everts (ed.), *Controversies at Home. Domestic Factors in the Foreign Policy of the Netherlands* (Dordrecht: Martinus Nijhoff, 1985).

The imminent deployment of new intermediate-range missiles became the *major issue* of the peace movements, and, given the experiences of the fifties, it was to be expected that *any* deployment of nuclear weapons would meet with opposition. However, it is not enough to claim that NATO's double-track decision as such triggered the opposition of the new peace movements.[17] Those who regard the double-track decision itself as the decisive catalyst for the formation of the new peace movements have no plausible explanation for this mass opposition not taking off until roughly a year *after* its passing.

The development of the new peace movements into a mass movement, however, can be explained if one calls to mind the stages of its mobilization and actions. The first phase, which could be termed *sensitization*, coincided with the debate on the neutron bomb in 1977/78. As of this time, the peace movements began to center their activities on arms control issues. The transition to the phase of *manifest articulation of protest* took place in the course of 1980. It was not the double-track decision which triggered this phase; rather, *mass* protests against the imminent deployment only began in connection with the crisis of détente policy and the drastic deterioration of U.S.-Soviet relations in the aftermath of the Afghanistan intervention in early 1980. The foreign policy pursued by the Reagan Administration, together with its arms buildup and the use of nuclear-militarist rhetoric during Reagan's first years in office, encouraged a further spread of the new peace movements. Important factions of the West German public took Reagan's speeches seriously and, thus, became afraid that war between the superpowers was imminent.

In this phase, petitions in particular were used in order to get the discussion moving. The «*Krefelder Appell*» (Krefeld Appeal) deserves special mention here. It led to the first coalition between groups associated with the Moscow-oriented (West) German Communist Party (DKP) and the ecological movement, above all the Green Party. The «*Krefelder Appell*» which its initiators claim was signed by several million people, was aimed

---

17   There are no comprehensive studies to date on the new peace movements in West Germany. See, however, Reiner Steinweg (ed.), *Die neue Friedensbewegung, Friedensanalysen 16* (Frankfurt am Main: Suhrkamp, 1982); Josef Janning inter alia (eds.), *Friedensbewegungen. Entwicklung und Folgen in der Bundesrepublik Deutschland, Europa und den USA* (Köln: Wissenschaft & Politik, 1987).

solely at preventing the deployment of new Western INF. It did not originally mention the SS-20 at all.

In 1981 the *demonstration phase* of the new peace movements began, involving large numbers of protesters rallying in public. During the Protestant Church Congress in Hamburg in 1981, the first large-scale demonstration took place under the motto, «Be afraid, nuclear death threatens us all - resist!». In Hamburg, peace organisations banded together to form an alliance which then organized subsequent large-scale demonstrations. Later this same alliance became nationwide with the name Coordination Committee (*Koordinierungsausschuss der Friedensbewegung*). Some 300,000 people gathered for the demonstration in Bonn on October 10, 1981. The protest coinciding with the NATO summit meeting in Bonn on June 10, 1982 attracted 400,000 demonstrators. Since 1981, there have also been a large number of activities organized by local peace groups. Above all, the «Peace Weeks» which began in November 1980 and were staged nationwide by Christian oganizations gained national importance. The tradional «Easter Marches», an institution dating back to the *Kampf dem Atomtod* («Fight Against Atomic Death!») movement of the late fifties, were also revived.

While the above activities continued through to 1983, as of mid-1982 a phase of *intensified protest* began. In summer 1982, demonstrators staged a week-long symbolic blockade of the Gross-Engstingen nuclear storage site, after months of preparation. Similar actions of civil disobedience took place nationwide on the anniversary of the double-track decision, December 12, 1982. They were repeated throughout 1983 at various military facilities, for the most part peacefully.

What did these and similar activities of the peace movements achieve? Most importantly, the new peace movements triggered a basic change in the security policy culture of West Germany. For the first time since the fifties, security policy issues were discussed in public and were no longer dominated by a few experts. The influence of the peace movements - strengthened by the media - outlived the deployment debate and continued after 1983. At the societal level, the peace debate had the greatest influence on the churches.[18] Within the protestant church in

---

18 For details see Thomas Risse-Kappen, «'Final Respite' or 'Unconditional No'? The Church and the Question of Peace in the Federal Republic of Germany», *Bulletin of Peace Proposals*, vol.15, no.3, 1984, pp.205-212.

particular there were heated discussions on the ethical problems connected with nuclear deterrence.

The peace movements could rely their protests on the latent unease with the deployment of nuclear weapons in the West German general public, feelings which had not changed very much since the debate on nuclear armament of the fifties. Public opinion revealed the following trends:

- The more nuclear weapons were presented as a means of warfighting, the more likely they were to be rejected. Defense of the Federal Republic involving nuclear weapons on West German soil was rejected in 1977/78 by 61%, in 1983 by 72%, and in 1986 by 62% of the respondents.[19] In 1983, roughly two-thirds of the population were against the deployment of intermediate-range weapons, the data did not change since then (cf. table 2).
- However, the more nuclear weapons were referred to in the context of war prevention, parity and arms control, the more likely they were to be tolerated. Whilst the number of *deployment* opponents increased steadily up to 1983, at the same time there were constant majorities in favor of NATO's *double-track decision*, provided it was presented with both its components (cf. table 3). This finding may seem paradoxical at first glance; but it can be explained by the fact that most people were ready to believe that the USSR would only consent to compromises if threatened with basing. Further surveys confirmed that the INF decision only received public acceptance when its arms control component was emphasized.

---

19 Data according to SINUS, *Sicherheitspolitik, Bündnispolitik, Friedensbewegung* (München-Bonn: October 1983) p.36; Sebastian Knauer, *Lieben wir die USA?* (Hamburg: Stern-Buch, 1987), p.98. See also data in Petra Heinlein/Hans Rattinger, *Sicherheitspolitik und öffentliche Meinung* (Berlin: Wissenschaftlicher Autoren-Verlag, 1986).

Table 2: Attitudes Towards INF Deployment 1983/84

	8/1983	8-9/1983	11/1983	11-12/1983	5-6/1984
Opposed:	66%	66%	62%	57%	66%
Favorable:	31%	16%	37%	28%	29%
Undec./N.A.:	3%	18%	1%	15%	5%

Source: *Various similar surveys, according to Karl-Heinz Reuband, «Die Friedensbewegung nach Stationierungsbeginn: Soziale Unterstützung in der Bevölkerung als Handlungspotential», Sicherheit und Frieden, vol.3, no.3, 1983, pp.147-156, 151.*

Table 3: Attitudes to the NATO Double-Track Decision

«For some time now, there has been the so-called NATO double-track decision. NATO members have agreed to base intermediate-range missiles in Central Europe to counterbalance corresponding Soviet missiles, but also to start negotiations with the Soviet Union on arms reduction. All in all, do you agree with this double-track decision or do you disagree?»

	5/1981	8/1981	10/1981	12/1981	1/1982	6/1982	12/1982	8/1983
Agree:	53%	49%	50%	48%	52%	54%	51%	49%
Disagree:	20%	26%	22%	22%	22%	24%	25%	23%
Undecided:	27%	25%	28%	30%	26%	22%	24%	28%

Source: *IfD Allensbach data according to Gebhard Schweigler: Grundlagen der aussenpolitischen Orientierung der Bundesrepublik Deutschland (Baden-Baden; Nomos, 1985), p.194.*

Regarding *content*, the new peace movements popularized arguments which had already been brought forward prior to the NATO double-track decision by the arms control elite of the SPD against the modernization of Western medium-range missiles. However, the rejection of

U.S. defense policy far exceeded what SPD politicians and peace researchers had themselves voiced prior to 1979. The peace movements argued that the new intermediate-range weapons served to limit war to Europe; thus, the United States could relieve itself of the nuclear risk. This argument culminated in the thesis of the «battlefield of the superpowers», according to which the U.S. and the USSR wanted to limit nuclear war to Europe and be in a position to win. Another argument claimed the Pershing II and cruise missiles were part of a U.S. first-strike strategy against the Soviet Union aimed at eliminating its most important command and control centers with a «decapitation» strike. Declarations from members of the Reagan Administration did nothing but pour oil into the fire begun by allegation.

The claims that U.S. policy was aimed at the limitation of nuclear war to Europe or part of a first-strike strategy against the Soviet Union are only plausible when seen as a political-psychological reaction both to the change in American foreign policy after 1980 and to the militarist rhetoric of Reagan's first term in office. They had very little to do with NATO's double-track decision and its evolution (cf. 2.4). As already shown, the double-track decision was largely the result of West European initiatives. Admittedly, Pershing II and cruise missiles were ideally suited to the trend in U.S. nuclear strategy towards more flexible and more selective counterforce options in the sense of the «countervailing strategy». However, declaring INF modernization the linchpin of U.S. nuclear armament was a gross exaggeration of its real significance. In addition, the very people in the Pentagon who were genuinely interested in strategic superiority (e.g. Fred Iklé and Richard Perle) were by no means convinced of the *military* necessity of these weapons.[20]

By making U.S. policy the main target of criticism, the new peace movements were in part responsible for the West European, and particularly the West German, involvement in the nuclear arms race being passed over in the course of the debate. The West Germans were assigned the role of the victim of the superpowers, and their active participation in the arms race was forgotten. This resulted in West Germany's scope of action being equally ignored. Such a perception was bound to encourage resignation in the long term. How were even millions of demonstrators to prevent deployment when it stemmed from the global

---

20   Cf. Talbott, *Deadly Gambits*, note 12, pp.43/44.

confrontations of the two superpowers? The sense of being a victim, combined with apocalyptic visions of the future may explain why the peace movements so quickly lost the ability to mobilize large numbers of people once they had failed in their main aim of preventing deployment in late 1983.

Aside from the new peace movements, the *SPD* remained, at least until the change of government in 1982, the most important domestic factor for West German INF policy. The party's arms control wing kept up its criticism of the West German government. In December 1980, for example, Karsten Voigt, the foreign policy spokesman, pointed to the discrepancy between the NATO decision and recent SPD resolutions. He once again questioned the double-track decision which had been deprived of its underlying arms control concept - namely SALT II ratification.[21] While the SPD *majority* continued to tolerate NATO policy, the party's disarmament wing, led by Erhard Eppler and Oskar Lafontaine, which had newly emerged at the same time as the peace movements, rejected it on principle. In 1981, the SPD debate focused on the sea-basing option but also turned again to the moratorium proposal. Schmidt obviously perceived the debate to be so dangerous that in May 1981 he again threatened to resign, thereby linking acceptance of the double-track decision to confidence in the party's ability to support the government in general.

At the SPD party congress in Munich in April 1982, the inner-party «coalition» formed in Berlin in 1979 between the «Helmut Schmidt wing» and the arms control majority stood firm against the disarmers. The latter could gather as many delegates as in Berlin, when, in a vote on an INF moratorium, 40% of the delegates backed the disarmers' position. The party majority argued it was important to maintain confidence in the government and also presented the same bargaining chip concept as in Berlin. Now, however, they further charged that the *United States* could only be persuaded to enter into serious negotiations if the West German government continued to support the double-track decision. There were very few attempts to justify deployment with arguments related to defense policy. The most important deviation from the platform

---

21 See Karsten Voigt, «Warnung vor der Sackgasse. Ein Jahr nach dem Berliner SPD Parteitag und dem NATO-Nachrüstungsbeschluss,» *Sozialdemokratischer Pressedienst*, no.239, December 12, 1980. For a general account see Risse-Kappen, *Krise*, note 16.

adopted in Berlin was the call to include French and British nuclear weapons in the arms control process of the superpowers. However, this was worded in such general terms that even Helmut Schmidt could agree to it without jeopardizing the NATO consensus of early 1979.[22]

Although NATO's INF policy differed from the official SPD position on several points, the party majority continued to back it for the following reasons:
- general support for the social-liberal government;
- trust in Helmut Schmidt's ability to bring about a compromise between the superpowers;
- «damage limitation» given the confrontational atmosphere between the superpowers.

Two of these motives became irrelevant with the change of government in fall 1982 and the SPD's new position as an opposition party. The Social Democrats' rejection of INF deployment in 1983 thus almost became inevitable and could probably only have been prevented by an arms control agreement in Geneva. The party conference in Cologne in November 1983 sealed the SPD's rejection of INF missile deployment with an overwhelming majority, and established a new inner-party alliance between the arms control and disarmament wings. Thus the SPD put an end to a debate which had always been critical of the double-track decision. After all, the party had only *tolerated* the INF policy pursued by NATO and the West German government under certain preconditions and according to their own interpretation (cf. 2.5).

The double-track decision was also the cause of heated debate in the *Free Democratic Party*. Foreign Minister Genscher presented the party with a similar ultimatum to the one Helmut Schmidt delivered to the SPD. However, a third of the delegates who attended the FDP party congress in Cologne at the end of May 1981 voted against the double-track policy. This vote was significant as it clearly showed that the double-track decision no longer had 100% backing in the FDP. Moreover, a motion for the sea-basing of intermediate-range weapons was supported by 40% of the delegates. Thus the size of the inner-party minority at the time was similar to that of the SPD. It seems questionable whether the FDP would have accepted deployment in fall 1983 had there been no

---

22 See *Beschlüsse zur Aussen-, Friedens- und Sicherheitspolitik*, SPD-Parteitag München, April 19-23, 1982.

change of government and the subsequent withdrawal of the Social-Liberal wing from the party. For, in spite of the change in the coalition, numbers of deployment opponents at the party conference in Karlsruhe in 1983 were no less than they had been in 1981 in Cologne.[23]

Whilst there were heated arguments over INF deployment in both the SPD and the FDP, the CDU/CSU maintained almost 100% support for NATO's double-track decision. While the party had finally come around in the course of the peace debate to a stronger emphasis on arms control policy, it merely followed the NATO position with regard to INF. The more the double-track decision was criticized and debated in the SPD, the more the CDU/CSU tried to present itself as domestic guarantor of West German security policy and to emphasize its full support of the double-track decision. However, the CDU also had to adapt to the altered domestic climate. The following statement was made by the CDU federal committee in Berlin on May 10, 1982: «The CDU continues to support the NATO double-track decision, which is a timetable for disarmament. The firmer the support for both components of this decision, the better the chances for controlled disarmament on both sides.»[24]

Whilst the public debate and the new peace movements clearly affected *all* parties, they cannot be said to have specifically influenced Western INF policy. When in the course of 1981 the new peace movements formed mass movements, NATO and the West German government had long since reached their decisions. Not only that, the negotiating options were also established in part. And, as was already mentioned, the peace movments were unable to achieve their most important aim, namely the prevention of Pershing II and cruise missile deployment.

On the other hand, governments in Western Europe, particularly in London, the Hague, Brussels and Bonn now had to contend with public demands which called into question the very role of nuclear weapons in deterrence. Had no serious efforts been made in terms of arms control, there would have been a grave crisis of legitimacy regarding Western se-

---

23 On the FDP debate see *Politik für Frieden und Sicherheit. Die Debatte auf dem F.D.P.-Bundesparteitag*, edited by the Friedrich-Naumann-Stiftung (Bonn, 1981); *Friedens- und Sicherheitspolitik für die 80er Jahre*, resolution of the 34th FDP Bundesparteitag, Karlsruhe, November 18-19, 1983.

24 «Berliner Erklärung», May 5, 1982, *CDU-Dokumentation*, no.16, May 13, 1982, p.3.

curity policy as a whole. In that respect, public pressure in Western Europe encouraged U.S. readiness to negotiate. It seems doubtful whether negotiations would have taken place in Geneva at all if not for the West European and later the American peace movements. One factor accounting for the interest in serious talks shown by some actors in the U.S. decision-making process, such as chief negotiator Nitze, was the fear that, otherwise, the debate in Europe would bring about NATO's collapse. The most significant influence of the new peace movements on the Geneva talks was, however, that the Western negotiating proposal of 1981 - the *global, mutual zero option* - responded to public demands. Without the pressure of the deployment opponents in Europe, it seems unlikely that NATO would have come around to this position.

3.3   A German-American Baby: The Zero Proposal

It was not until early summer 1981 that the Reagan Administration, after six months of pressuring by the West Europeans, agreed to accept the basic principles of the Integrated Decision Document and declared its willingness to negotiate on intermediate-range weapons. A further six months was to pass before the Americans reached agreement on a negotiating position. Throughout 1981, there were discussions in the Alliance about negotiating positions consistent with the criteria of the double-track decision. While every conceivable combination of numbers was discussed, a final negotiating position was not decided on. One of the ideas floated within the West German government was to set a low upper limit for intermediate-range missiles on both sides, below the figure of 572 warheads foreseen in the double-track decision. This proposal, allowing the West to deploy a certain number of Pershing II and cruise missiles, was incorporated into the subsequent American offer of September 1983 (cf. 3.4).

More decisive for the American negotiating position of 1981 were thoughts along the lines of a zero option. This proposal was introduced by the West German government to the internal Alliance decision-making process and supported by the Netherlands from the beginning. The Schmidt-Genscher government was mainly responsible for getting the zero option accepted by NATO and especially by the United States, where it was backed by those who used it to block the INF talks. In 1981, its implications for the future could not be foreseen.

The notion of forgoing deployment of Pershing II and cruise missiles altogether in return for acceptable Soviet concessions can be traced back to the debate of the West German and Dutch Social Democrats prior to the double-track decision in 1979. Thus, the arms control elite of the SPD is at least partly responsible for the idea of a zero option. It was first discussed at length in a working group which was created in order to prepare the security policy resolution passed at the Berlin party congress in December 1979 (cf. 2.5). It was in Berlin that the SPD committed itself to a zero option as its negotiating aim on INF. However, it should be remembered that the party did not at any time demand that the Soviet Union forgo *all* its SS-20 missiles. In April 1980, for example, Alfons Pawelczyk defined the Berlin resolution in more precise terms, saying that deployment of new U.S. systems could be abandoned provided the USSR make drastic cuts in its own medium-range weapons and, moreover, allow the U.S. a certain degree of superiority in nuclear strategic warheads.[25] When in 1981 it was certain that INF negotiations were to begin separately from strategic arms control, the SPD resolutions continued to make vague references to «deep cuts» in the Soviet arsenals as a precondition for Western zero INF. However, a series of comments indicated that the party would not include Soviet INF based in Asia in a zero option and was prepared to grant the Soviet Union some sort of compensation for French and British nuclear forces on whatever negotiating level (strategic or INF). In fall 1981, prior to the beginning of the negotiations, Egon Bahr in particular considered that an acceptable solution would be for the West to abandon deployment in return for the SS-20 being reduced to the number of third-party systems.[26] He thus suggested exactly what was to become the Soviet bargaining position later on (cf. 3.4).

The FDP had also committed itself to a zero option at its party conference in Freiburg in June 1980. The election program passed in Freiburg for the parliamentary elections of that year stated: «The FDP will do everything in its power to ensure that the negotiation offer made to

---

25 Cf. Alfons Pawelczyk's speech at the security policy information meeting of the SPD parliamentary group in Cologne, April 19-20, 1980, *Sicherheit für die 80er Jahre* (Bonn, 1980), pp.87-98, 94.

26 Cf. Egon Bahr, *Was wird aus den Deutschen?* (Reinbeck: Rowohlt, 1982), pp.180/181. The discussion underlying the book took place during Fall 1981.

the Warsaw Pact and coupled to NATO's modernization decision re-
ceives vigorous support. Our aim must be total renunciation of the production and basing of medium-range nuclear weapons on both sides.»[27]

Unlike the SPD, the Free Democrats called for the *total* elimination of
Soviet INF in return for Western non-deployment. It was therefore not
without reason that the FDP leadership and in particular Foreign Minister Genscher, later repeatedly insisted that in Freiburg the Liberals had
«invented» the subsequent global zero option put forward by NATO and
the U.S..

Chancellor Schmidt favored a *European* zero option, i.e., Western renunciation of deployment provided the USSR withdraw all SS-20 missiles from areas within striking range of Western Europe. By the end of
1979, Schmidt had already said on various occasions that under ideal
conditions, which he considered unlikely, he could conceive of a negotiated result which would eliminate the necessity of deploying Pershing II
and cruise missiles. Though he did not have a specific proposal in mind
at that time, he did support the European zero option in 1981. This is
evident in an interview published on November 29, 1981, prior to the
start of negotiations in Geneva:

> «If for example the Soviets have 250 SS-20 missiles with triple warheads and a
> number of them were to be moved from European Russia to the area behind
> the Urals, then what is important is how far behind the Urals ... if they are
> deployed far behind the Urals then they would not be able to reach Europe.
> This is where the real problems start.»[28]

In the West German government, on the other hand, the position of the
Foreign Ministry gained acceptance in the course of 1981. The Arms
Control Department proposed that the United States and the Soviet
Union renounce all ground-launched LRINF missiles. This *global zero op-
tion*, which later became the U.S. negotiating position, was supported
from the outset by Foreign Minister Genscher. Internal debates concen-

27 *Wahlprogramm der Freien Demokratischen Partei für die Bundestagswahlen am
    5.10.1980*, Freiburg, June 7, 1980, p.12.

28 Interview with the radio station *Deutschlandfunk*, November 29, 1981, quo-
    ted from SzS, no.12, 1981, pp.23-29, 25. In his book, *Menschen und Mächte*,
    Schmidt says that the zero option was his invention (note 5, p.142; see also
    ibid., p.333). However, during my conversation with him in June 1985, he
    emphasized that he had been committed to a *European zero option*. I received
    confirmation of *this* account in the course of several other interviews.

trated mainly on the conflict of goals between the military requirements
for INF modernization and a zero option. Military experts objected that
if the aim of NATO strategy, i.e., deliberate, controlled escalation, was to
be maintained, some intermediate-range weapons would have to be deployed regardless of Soviet cuts. Only Pershing II would allow the precise targeting of time-urgent military installations in the Western part of
the Soviet Union. In the end, however, a decision was taken in favor of a
zero option, above all for domestic motives. It was argued by Foreign
Ministry officials that a global zero option would involve so many concessions by the Soviets that in this unlikely case the West could give priority to arms control. The government backed a *global* zero option on
the grounds that an unequal ceiling was considered unacceptable in
terms of Alliance policy; it might have created the impression that separate eurostrategic parity was being sought. Once again «decoupling»
fears played a role. Throughout the whole summer and fall of 1981, the
West German government tried to influence the decision-making process of the U.S. government in favor of a global zero option. At the end
of October, the West German Security Council decided, on Helmut
Schmidt's recommendation, to strive for a zero option as the *prime negotiating goal* on INF.

Paradoxically, the West German government thereby endorsed the
position of those top Pentagon officials in the U.S. who were vigorously
opposed to arms control. The proposal for a zero option finally gained
acceptance in the Alliance thanks to a strange coalition between advocates of arms control, such as Helmut Schmidt, and vehement opponents, such as Richard Perle. In late summer and fall 1981 in Washington, there was intensive bureaucratic infighting involving four different
factions.[29]

The key role in the Pentagon was played by *Richard Perle* who was
not convinced of the military necessity of Pershing II and cruise missiles.
For him, arms control did not mean the negotiation of compromises;
rather, he understood the U.S.-Soviet talks as the continuation of the
global power competition between the superpowers by different means.
He was not interested whether a position was negotiable or not. Consequently, he supported the zero option from the outset simply because he
did not believe it would be carried through. Were the Soviet Union to

---

29   For a detailed account see Talbott, *Deadly Gambits*, note 12, pp.56-70.

agree to it, against all expectations, all the better. The politics of strength would have won the day.

Ironically, Perle was the inventor of a version of the zero option which was put forward by Soviet General Secretary Gorbachev five-and-a-half years later in the form of the «double zero proposal». Perle argued that the zero option should not only include *longer-range* INF, but should from the outset also incorporate *shorter-range* systems (500-1,000 km). This would affect the range spectrum which the USSR was just modernizing by the introduction of the SS-12 mod (900 km; known for a time as the SS-22) and the SS-23 (500 km). Perle's aim was to prevent the Soviet Union from being in a position to threaten the same targets in Western Europe with their new short-range missiles, should they decide to scrap the SS-20. Finally, Perle argued that the United States should not present the zero option in Geneva as a starting position, but «without ifs and buts».

Perle's main opponent in the State Department was *Richard Burt*. He supported the global zero option as a *starting position*, but wanted at the same time to signal flexibility to the Soviets so as to avoid any public suspicion that the U.S. was not serious about arms control. He doubted that a negotiation success could be achieved prior to deployment in 1983. INF arms control was for him above all a matter of «Alliance management». However, he was prepared to take European suggestions into account because he put Alliance cohesion first. U.S. Secretary of State Haig finally adopted Burt's position, though the former NATO Supreme Allied Commander rejected in principle the total renunciation of deployment by the West.

Paul Nitze, the U.S. chief negotiator, and a few people in the Arms Control and Disarmament Agency (ACDA) were the only Administration officials who had a genuine interest in an arms control success. Nitze supported Burt's position believing this would give him more scope for the handling of the negotiations. He was not so much concerned about a particular starting position in Geneva, but his main objective was that the U.S. demonstrate flexibility to the Soviets.

The *U.S. military* stood somewhere between these two positions. The Joint Chiefs of Staff (JCS), unlike the NATO military, had no particular interest in the new intermediate-range weapons. In light of the rejection of their proposal in the seventies that 1,500-2,000 missiles be based in Europe, 108 Pershing II missiles did not represent a significant military option for them. For this reason the Joint Chiefs could live with a zero option. Their more immediate concern was to avoid getting INF aircraft or shorter-range missiles included in negotiations.

At a meeting of the National Security Council on November 12, 1981, President Reagan decided in favor of a *global zero option on longer-range INF*. This decision went against the State Department which had wanted to include the notion of «equal ceilings» in the negotiating offer in order to signal flexibility to the Soviets. On the other hand, Reagan did not take up Perle's proposal of a zero option for shorter-range INF, though it was favored by the Pentagon. The West European governments united to oppose the «extended» zero option which they felt would complicate negotiations. Their position was supported by the State Department, the ACDA and by the Joint Chiefs. Reagan finally decided merely to seek «concurrent constraints on short-range INF (SRINF)».

There were few principal opponents to a zero option in the conservative Reagan Administration, whose main problem was choosing between two different versions. The main opponents were to be found in Western Europe. At the top of the list was NATO's *military command*.[30] Taking the line that NATO's double-track decision was justified in terms of deterrence, they argued that a minimum number of Western missiles would have to be deployed, because the military option opened by Pershing II could not be discounted. In West Germany, it was above all the CDU/CSU who up to fall 1981 rejected a zero option as eyewash which distracted attention from the necessity of deployment. Sharp criticism of the zero option came above all from right-wing defense members of the CDU/CSU (later known as *Stahlhelmflügel*, i.e. the «steel helmet wing»). On June 3, 1981, Manfred Wörner spoke before the *Bundestag* of the «total illusion of a so-called zero option». The turnabout of the CDU/CSU did not take place till *after* President Reagan had declared the global zero option to be U.S. negotiating position. CDU chairman Helmut Kohl announced the turnabout on December 3, 1981.[31] This meant that at the end of 1981 there was at least a declaratory all-party consensus on the zero option.

What explanation is there for the fact that at the end of 1981 a Western negotiating position was adopted in Geneva which neither advocates

---

30 For details see Cartwright/Critchley, *Cruise*, note 10, pp.26/27.

31 See Manfred Wörner's speech to the *Bundestag* on June 3, 1981, *PlPr* 9/41, p.2253; Helmut Kohl's speech to the *Bundestag* on December 3, 1981, *PlPr* 9/70, p.4062.

nor opponents of serious arms control believed to be within reach? Having helped to achieve NATO and U.S. acceptance of the zero option, those West Europeans seriously interested in arms control faced two problems. They had to contend with an American administration whose election success rested on its criticism of the arms control practiced to date by the West. Little preparedness for compromises was to be expected from the U.S. in Geneva. Despite their squabbles over other matters, there was consensus in the U.S. government that deployment was almost unavoidable. The zero option served to appease the West European public; the overriding motive of the U.S. was to maintain NATO cohesion, not arms control.

The second problem was that, due to the changes in American politics, the governments in Great Britain, the Federal Republic of Germany, and the Netherlands faced growing domestic pressure. Security policy consensus began to fall off. Therefore, one can conclude that the zero option would never have been adopted as the Western negotiating position if not for domestic demands, the criticism of the social democratic parties, and the mass demonstrations by the new peace movements.

Moreover, this concept was a compromise between arms control advocates and opponents on both sides of the Atlantic. In 1981, both sides agreed on one point only, that the zero option was probably non-negotiable. It ignored the basic asymmetries on INF in expecting the Soviet Union to equate her entire SS-20 force with the American INF systems to be deployed in Western Europe alone. In addition, de-linking the INF negotiations from the overall context of strategic arms control made the negotiation of trade-offs more difficult. And, given what emerged as the Soviet negotiating position at that time, it was thought extremely unlikely that the USSR would accept equal global ceilings. Not without reason did NATO's original double-track decision only contain a call for *de jure* equality thus allowing some compromise.

Those people in NATO and in the U.S. who, for various reasons, considered Western deployment of medium-range missiles to be unavoidable, supported the global zero option *because* they considered it to be non-negotiable. The intransigent arms control opponents in the Pentagon used it in order to block the INF negotiations in Geneva until deployment began. NATO's military could tolerate the zero option because it was deemed highly improbable that the Soviets would accept it.

Conversely, people such as Paul Nitze and Helmut Schmidt supported the zero option *even though* they did not consider it to be negotiable. Proponents of arms control on both sides of the Atlantic saw the American offer as a starting position to be enlarged upon. They hoped that the negotiation process would gradually develop its own dynamics. After all, Western deployment was not due to begin for another two years. At the same time, this group argued from the start that the zero option should not be seen as a «take-it-or-leave-it» position. Chancellor Schmidt, for example, had already spoken up for greater flexibility on both sides in an interview a day before the talks commenced in Geneva. If both superpowers remained firmly rooted to their starting positions there were no chance for compromise. He also asked that, while missiles alone should be dealt with in the first negotiating phase, at the same time an agreement in principle should be reached for further talks on INF aircraft, i.e., including U.S. forward based systems (FBS).[32] General opinion in the SCG was likewise that the United States should be more flexible in its negotiating approach as stated in the notion of equal ceilings «at the lowest possible level».

Out of domestic and Alliance motives, the West had committed itself to a negotiating position which those people interested in a compromise wished to alter as soon as possible, whilst arms control opponents wished to use it in order to prevent this very compromise. Almost nobody could guess in November 1981 that President Reagan and General Secretary Gorbachev would sign a treaty six years later which was nearly identical to this Western proposal. Just five days after Reagan's speech the *then* Soviet leadership gave the zero option a curt *«njet»*.

3.4 A Missed Opportunity: Negotiations 1981-1983

On November 23, 1981, Soviet General Secretary Brezhnev visited Bonn and gave his official rejection of the global zero option. Various compromises were sounded out during his talks. The Soviet leadership further clarified its position for Geneva. Brezhnev presented the fol-

---

32 Interview with *Deutschlandfunk*, note 28.

lowing negotiating proposal which was introduced to the Geneva talks in
February 1982:[33]
- Reduction of American and Soviet intermediate-range missiles and
  aircraft deployed in Europe to an initial 600 and later 300 systems;
- Permission to modernize systems already in deployment but with a
  ban on deployment of *new* weapons (a reference to Pershing II and
  cruise missiles);
- Moratorium during negotiations and, in this case, withdrawal of part
  of the Soviet Union's INF in anticipation of an agreement.

The Soviet position was designed to prevent Western deployment while
allowing the USSR to keep all the SS-20 missiles (about 250) installed up
to the end of 1981. However, in this case they would have had to forgo
almost all of their INF aircraft. It remained unclear initially whether the
USSR would actually insist on the inclusion of British and French nuclear weapons. The West German government placed its trust in the assurance made to the Chancellor in summer 1980. The issue was finally
settled with the presentation of a Soviet draft treaty on May 25, 1982.
From this time on, the Soviets insisted on counting British and French
nuclear forces as part of Western INF, a position which had been rejected outright by the West since the Guadeloupe summit in early 1979.
(The SCG, for example, never discussed inclusion of third-party systems.) Thus, the USSR contributed to the stalemate in INF negotiations.
It is possible that this condition was made in response to the global zero
proposal which seems to have taken the Soviets by surprise.

On December 11, 1981, the U.S. presented its zero proposal in
Geneva. At the beginning of February 1982 it was set out in precise
terms in the form of a draft treaty:
- Worldwide elimination of all ground-launched LRINF (1,000-5,000
  km) i.e., the scrapping of all Soviet SS-4, SS-5, and SS-20 missiles in
  return for non-deployment of 572 Pershing II and ground-launched
  cruise missiles;
- Concurrent constraints on ground-launched SRINF (500-1,000 km)
  with the Soviet SS-23 and SS-12 mod missiles to be limited to the
  number deployed in early 1982;

33 See Special Consultative Group, *Progress Report to Ministers* (NATO Press
    Service, December 8, 1983); Ruehl, *Mittelstreckenwaffen*, note 6, pp.250-271.

- Nuclear-capable INF aircraft to be dealt with in follow-on negotiations.

Thus at the start of INF negotiations the positions of both sides were miles apart. The main issues on which there were differences concerned which systems ought to be included, where and how:[34]

- *Global or regional approach to limitations*: Western insistence that the SS-20 missiles based in Asia should be subject to limitations was understandable since these are mobile missiles and could be moved quickly to Europe. A further factor was that U.S. allies in Asia insisted on receiving the same treatment as West European countries. On the other hand, Soviet insistence that the missiles deployed in the European zone be treated separately was just as reasonable, since they felt most threatened by the U.S. INF systems deployed in Western Europe.
- *Treatment of aircraft*: As expected, the USSR made a renewed call for the inclusion of American FBS in INF negotiations, having failed to get these systems included in SALT. Naturally this would have meant that the Soviet medium-range Backfire (Tu-26), Badger (Tu-16), and Blinder (Tu-22) bombers would also have to be taken into account. The U.S. and NATO argued, justly to an extent, that including aircraft in the first round of talks would lead to unnecessary complications regarding counting rules. It would have involved settling the problems raised by dual-capable aircraft and the difficulty of discerning ranges of different types of aircraft with different flight profiles. NATO rejected outright the Soviet demand that aircraft and missiles be counted under the same ceiling.
- *Third-country systems*: NATO had made it clear from the start that the inclusion of French and British nuclear weapons, in whatever form, was out of the question. With the exception of 18 French SSBS-3 missiles and the Mirage IV bomber, the systems concerned had strategic range. Moreover, it was unthinkable that these weapons be dealt with directly in *bilateral* U.S.-Soviet negotiations. This would also have called the U.S. superpower status into question. The Soviet Union would have been granted as many nuclear weapons as the U.S., Great Britain and France *together*. However, the Soviet demand was reasonable considering that the British and French forces could reach Soviet territory from Europe. Further, Great Britain is a full member of NATO. While the potentials of the two countries are insignificant given the strategic «overarmament» of the superpowers, both the French and the British have modernization programs underway which will multiply their warhead arsenals.

---

34 See in particular Gert Krell, «Zählkriterien für die Mittelstreckenwaffen,» in *Kernwaffen im Ost-West Vergleich*, ed. Krell/E. Forndran (Baden-Baden: Nomos, 1984) pp.175-226.

- Further differences in the negotiating positions touched the inclusion of short-range INF (SRINF) and the question of whether the systems to be limited should be scrapped or merely removed from their deployment zone.

Finally, at the beginning of the negotiations, the two sides differed completely in their assessments of the INF balance of forces (see tables 4 and 5).

Table 4:   The INF Balance of Forces - U.S. Assessment

NATO			USSR
		Missiles	
	0	SS-20	250
		SS-4/5	350
		SS-12/22	100
		SS-N-5	30
		Aircraft	
F-111	164	Backfire	45
F-4	265	Badger/Blinder	350
A-6/-7	68	Fencer, Flogger, Fitter	2,700
FB-111 in U.S.	63		
in sum:	560		3,825

Source: John Cartwright/Julian Critchley: Cruise, Pershing and SS-20. A North Atlantic Assembly Report (London: Brassey's Defence Publications, 1985), p.29. (The data were made available by Richard Burt in late 1981.)

The figures served to underscore the respective negotiating positions. The Soviet aim was to claim eurostrategic parity which the planned Western modernization would seriously upset. This purported balance was a result of the Soviets, firstly, *including* French and British nuclear weapons, secondly, *excluding* some of their own aircraft, while *including* American systems (F-4, A-6/7), and, thirdly, basing their figures on launchers rather than warheads as counting units. Otherwise the SS-20 with its triple warheads, would have made a significant difference and swung the balance in favor of the USSR.

Table 5:   **The INF Balance of Forces - Soviet Assessment**

U.S. and NATO			USSR
		Missiles	
French INF	18	SS-20	243
French SLBM	80	SS-4/-5	253
British Polaris	64	SS-N-5	18
		Aircraft	
U.S. FB-111	65	Backfire	
F-111	172	Badger	461
F-4	246	Blinder	
A-6/-7	240		
French Mirage IV	46		
British Vulcan	55		
in sum	986		975

Source: as table 4. *(The figures were published by the Soviet Union in December 1981.)*

However, the American comparison was also influenced in part by propaganda aims. Admittedly, Soviet superiority in ground-launched missiles could not be denied, however hard one tried. For aircraft, however, the relationship would have been more balanced had fair comparisons been made and the aircraft with a combat radius under 1,000 km been excluded. In any event, they did not feature in the American negotiating proposal. However, the U.S. and NATO were eager to display Soviet superiority in the most drastic possible terms.

Given the *incompatible* negotiating positions, talks quickly ground to a halt. The opinion in Bonn was that both sides must give. In light of the domestic debate, the West German government realized that significant progress would have to be made in Geneva at the latest one year before the scheduled start of Western deployment. Therefore, in spring 1982 it was indicated to Chief Negotiator Nitze that the U.S. position in Geneva raised doubts over the Western willingness to achieve a compromise. This was where the «walk-in-the-woods» had its origin - the great missed opportunity of the first round of INF negotiations.[35] Here also, the close personal relationship between Paul Nitze and Chancellor Helmut Schmidt has to be taken into account.

The Nitze-Kvitsinsky compromise which was worked out in July 1982 during a walk in the woods around lake Geneva ran as follows:
- 225 LRINF launchers and aircraft in Europe with a subceiling of 75 missile launchers. The USSR to be allowed only ballistic missiles (i.e., 225 SS-20 warheads), the U.S. only cruise missile deployment (i.e., 300);
- Limitation of the U.S. F-111 and FB-111 and Soviet Backfire, Badger and Blinder aircraft to 150 on each side;
- Reduction of Soviet LRINF based in Asia to 90 launchers;
- «Freezing» of short-range INF at existing levels;
- Agreement on adequate verification to be worked out within three months.

The principal opponents of arms control in Washington (and presumably those in Moscow, too) were responsible for the failure of the compromise. It would have been an arms control solution of the INF problem acceptable to both sides, *if* they had been prepared to abandon some deterrence objectives of their respective INF policies. The «walk-in-the-woods» proposal was in accordance with all the basic stability criteria of arms control. It would have put an end to the INF arms race and at the same time would have substantially improved crisis stability in Central Europe. The major concession for the West would have been forgoing Pershing II deployment. All other elements of the compromise, especially the inclusion of a regional subceiling for Europe, had already been discussed by the SCG in 1980. Furthermore, using launchers as the main counting unit, which resulted in a complicated formula for the reductions, prevented the impression that the West had accepted separate eu-

---

35 For the most extensive account of the «walk-in-the-woods» in July 1982 and the subsequent internal wrangling in the U.S., see Talbott, *Deadly Gambits*, pp.116-151. For details of the compromise see also SCG, *Progress Report*, note 33, p.17.

rostrategic parity. The inclusion of aircraft in the first phase of reductions was made up for by the fact that they would be counted separately.

It was the *raison d'être* of Nitze's initiative that West Europeans, in particular the West Germans, support the compromise. Chancellor Schmidt would certainly have tried to influence both the U.S. and the Soviet Union and would have used West Germany's international standing to bring about acceptance of the «walk-in-the-woods» compromise had he been informed about it during his term of office.[36] Such efforts might at least have been successful in Washington. For, the decision to reject the compromise, which came about on Richard Perle's insistence, was the result of a very narrow majority and was only reached after lengthy internal discussions on September 13, 1982. Soviet rejection became known in Geneva on September 29.

It was because they feared that Schmidt's activities might secure support for the compromise that arms control opponents in the U.S. Administration made sure the West Europeans were not consulted prior to a decision being taken in Washington. In fact, despite efforts by the U.S. government to keep the matter secret, at the beginning of September 1982, scraps of information regarding movement in INF talks did trickle through to some lower-level officials of the West German government. Details were not made known, however. At any rate, none of the decision-makers were informed, first and foremost the Chancellor. In not consulting the allies, the U.S. government broke with its commitment contained in the double-track decision and failed to abide by normal SCG procedures.

Considering the explosive nature of the subject and the personal commitment of the West German Chancellor, a number of points remain unclear. One has to take into account that the Social-Liberal coalition was beginning to dissolve in summer 1982; in September, government business had largely come to a halt. Had the American government perhaps been informed that the FDP was about to change the coalition? Was the belief in Washington that it was therefore not necessary to further consider Schmidt and the SPD (U.S. government circles did not disguise the fact that they would prefer a CDU/CSU-headed gov-

---

36 Author's interview with Helmut Schmidt. He later voiced his support of the «walk-in-the-woods» compromise on numerous occasions in public and sharply criticized the lack of consultation by the Americans. See Schmidt, *Menschen*, note 5, pp.333-335.

ernment anyway)? What was the background of Foreign Minister Genscher's comment in the *Bundestag* on September 16 that the zero option
was not a position of «all or nothing»?[37] Why did Ambassador Nitze not
inform Helmut Schmidt when the decision-making process in Washington was underway, although he usually kept him up-to-date on such matters? Be that as it may, on October 14, 1982, shortly after Helmut Kohl's
entry into office, Bonn was informed by the Director of the U.S. Arms
Control and Disarmament Agency, Eugene Rostow, of the details of the
«walk-in-the woods» proposal. However, the new West German government was so occupied with domestic issues at this time that the political decision-makers devoted a minimum of attention to the INF issue.
The sensitive nature of the compromise was initially not recognized. The
assessment of the compromise in Bonn concentrated on the possible renunciation of Pershing II. In the end the U.S. position was internally endorsed, i.e., the informal channels between the negotiators in Geneva
were to be kept open, but Pershing II - the renunciation of which constituted the essential concession by the West - was to be brought back into
the package. The view in the German government was that the Alliance
should not have to forgo unilaterally and in perpetuity the right to deploy medium-range ballistic missiles in Europe. Thus the aim to implement NATO's flexible response doctrine was given priority over an arms
control compromise. There was also criticism within the government
over the arrangement for the SS-20 missiles based in Asia, since these
weapons were mobile and could be moved quickly to Europe.[38] At any
rate the CDU/CSU-headed government did not see any reason originally
to reintroduce the «walk-in-the-woods» proposal in NATO deliberations
and then work for U.S. acceptance.

Aside from this reluctance, the change of government little altered
Bonn's INF policy. For years the CDU/CSU had lent their support to
Genscher's foreign and security policy against the SPD, and since the
end of 1979 their support of the double-track decision had been unbro-
ken. After first warning against the global zero option, they backed it
once NATO had accepted it. The reason for this attitude was a shift of
power within the party in favor of the party's foreign policy experts
(including Alois Mertes and Volker Rühle), who accepted *Ostpolitik* in

---

37   See *PlPr* 9/114, p.7058.

38   See Ruehl, *Mittelstreckenwaffen*, note 6, pp.301/302.

principle and supported arms control as complementing deterrence. Here again, the peace debate had a considerable influence to enforce the inner-party position of moderate Christian Democrats. On the whole, however, the Kohl/Genscher government was less dependent domestically on an arms control success in Geneva than the Social-Liberal coalition. Whilst Helmut Schmidt had to contend above all with criticism from the SPD left, Helmut Kohl's double-track policy came under attack from the right wing and the security policy elite of the CDU/CSU, whose chief concern was to maintain a credible deterrent. The arms control critics *within* the Christian-Liberal government were mostly to be found among top-level officials in the Defense Ministry. The West German government experienced some sort of role-swapping. While during Schmidt's term the Defense Ministry had supported a policy more directed towards an arms control compromise than the Foreign Ministry, it was now the Foreign Ministry under Hans-Dietrich Genscher which adopted the more moderate position, setting itself against the right-wing of the CDU/CSU parliamentary group.

Meanwhile, there had been a return to normalcy in Geneva following the «walk-in-the-woods» interlude. Neither side had found a way around the impasse. It was the Soviets who first gave a little.[39] They indicated that they were prepared to accept a subceiling for aircraft and missiles in Europe and to reduce the SS-20 in the European zone to the number of British and French nuclear missiles (162 at the time) with zero U.S. INF. The Soviet proposal was officially announced on December 21, 1982, by General Secretary Andropov and was followed by a corresponding draft treaty in Geneva on February 2, 1983. The USSR reserved the right to increase the number of their SS-20 missiles based in Europe should the number of French and British systems increase. As was to be expected, the proposal was promptly rejected by the U.S.

The new Soviet offer did result, however, in increasing criticism from NATO of America's rigid insistence on a global zero option. Kohl's government, for example, put the case both in the SCG and vis-à-vis the U.S. for an «interim solution». Alternatives to the zero option involving every conceivable combination of numbers had already been discussed in the SCG and in Bonn in 1981/82. In considering possible interim solutions a major objective was to avoid singularity of West Germany and

---

39   For details see SCG, *Progress Report*, note 33, pp.20-24.

not to set the common ceiling too low, as Western deployment of less than 200 INF was not considered to make military sense. Within the West German government, there was a preference for an offer comprising a global ceiling with a subceiling for Europe and not compensating for all Soviet systems based in the Far East by deployments in Western Europe. It took almost a year to persuade the United States to accept the concept. At the beginning of 1983, the German Chancellery apparently even reconsidered renouncing Pershing II in return for corresponding concessions by the Soviets.[40]

The announcement by President Reagan on March 29, 1983, of a first interim solution did not signal that the logic of the global zero option had been abandoned. It introduced the principle of equal ceilings without specifying the numbers, though between 50 and 450 warheads worldwide was considered appropriate. The proposal had obviously not been discussed thoroughly in the SCG. Just four days before Reagan's announcement, SCG delegation leaders met informally in Brussels to discuss the new American proposal. Though public statements supported the proposal, the West Europeans would have preferred the introduction of a much more flexible approach as early as March, partly for domestic reasons. It would have allowed them to make a serious counteroffer to the Andropov move.

The talks in Geneva remained at stalemate despite minor concessions on both sides. At the beginning of May, the U.S. presented its proposal for a «zero plus» option in the form of a draft treaty. At the same time, General Secretary Andropov set out his proposal in more specific terms; warheads were now accepted as a counting unit for INF. At the end of August, the USSR finally agreed to the Western condition that the missiles to be reduced would have to be scrapped.

Within NATO and in the U.S. the struggle for a more flexible U.S. negotiating position continued. The West German government was able to win SCG consensus for their favored interim solution. Richard Burt then introduced it to the American decision-making process.[41] The ne-

---

40 See «The Euromissile Problem Isn't Over,» *Washington Post*, March 10, 1983. The content of the Washington Post article was confirmed by interviews in Bonn.

41 According to Talbott, *Deadly Gambits*, note 12, pp.155/156, 171-180, the proposal was worked out by Burt. However, it had already been discussed by the West German government in 1981. It was introduced in 1982 at the lat-

gotiation timetable meant that the final opportunity for presenting this first deviation from the global zero option in Geneva was September, if agreement were to be reached before the start of Western deployment. Declarations made by the West German Chancellor and the Foreign Minister in July 1983 were intended to speed up American acceptance of the proposal. Both repeatedly spoke of the «walk-in-the-woods» formula as a possible compromise requiring the USSR to drop its insistence that third-party systems be included. The West's side of the bargain - renunciation of Pershing II - was no longer mentioned publicly, although it continued to be discussed by some government departments. The West German government's official position was that Pershing II be included from the start in possible reductions of the 572 Western systems, proportionally to its share in the weapons mix (approximately 20%).[42] This brought protests from the CDU/CSU. Without consulting the Chancellor, the parliamentary group leader, Alfred Dregger, and the spokesman for disarmament policy, Jürgen Todenhöfer, publicly warned against giving up the Pershing II outside of a global zero option. They argued that it was the only weapon which could counter the SS-20.[43] Though such statements made it more difficult for the West German government to achieve American acceptance of its position, they had almost no impact on Bonn's INF policy. After intensive SCG consultations and letters from President Reagan to the heads of West European governments, the U.S. finally introduced the new interim solution to the Geneva talks on September 22:[44]

- The U.S. no longer insisted on compensation for *all* Soviet INF missiles worldwide by deployments in Western Europe. This meant, *de*

est by the SCG, from where Burt probably took it to the American decision-making process.

42　See the declaration by government spokesman Boenisch on July 18, 1983, *Bulletin*, no.79, 1983, pp.733/734; Kohl's interview with the *Washington Post* as quoted by government spokesman Boenisch on July 22, 1983, SzS, no.8, 1983, p.46; Kohl's interview with the television network *ARD* on July 22, 1983, ibid., pp.14/15; Genscher's interview with *Radio Luxemburg* on July 31, 1983, ibid., pp.15-18.

43　See Jürgen Todenhöfer, «Verzicht auf Pershing II?», *Deutschland-Union-Dienst*, no.134, July 18, 1983, p.4; Alfred Dregger, interview with *Der Spiegel*, no.33, August 15, 1983.

44　For details see SCG, *Progress Report*, note 33, pp.29-33.

facto, the introduction of a regional subceiling. However, the Americans reserved the right in principle to match Soviet missiles worldwide.
- Reductions of NATO's scheduled deployments would include the Pershing II from the beginning, and overall reductions would take place proportionally according to the share of Pershing II and GLCMs in the weapons mix.
- Specific types of aircraft should be included in a first treaty.

Thus two months before Western deployment - almost to the day - and some three-and-a-half years after NATO's double-track decision, the U.S. had introduced a position to the talks which not only preserved the basic aims of Western INF policy (implementation of flexible response, «coupling», reduction of Soviet INF) but also offered the Soviet Union flexibility on the issues most important to her, i.e., limitation of FBS and a regional subceiling for Europe. However, it was too late at the end of September to bring about an agreement before the start of Western deployment.

At the end of October, the Soviet Union also softened on its negotiating position, although she did not change its basics. She was now prepared to limit the number of her SS-20 missiles in Europe to 140, compensating for the British and French nuclear forces, to completely dismantle her remaining SS-4 missiles, and to freeze the number of SS-20 based in Asia. This final offer represented the only substantial concession, in that the USSR had until then refused to limit the Asian systems. At the end of 1983, these systems amounted to a considerable 135 of a total 378 SS-20 missiles (cf. table 1, p.18). In spite of this compromise on the Asian systems, the negotiating positions on INF deployed in Europe remained incompatible.

Shortly before the beginning of Western deployment, intensive consultations were renewed in the Alliance. The purpose was to add a specific number to the American offer of September. Finally, on November 15, the U.S. proposed a global ceiling of 420 warheads in Geneva which would have left the USSR freedom to determine the extent of Western deployment according to the number of her own INF remaining in Europe.

At about the same time, NATO's Nuclear Planning Group decided on October 28 in Montebello to reduce unilaterally the number of U.S. nuclear warheads based in Western Europe - particularly those on battlefield weapons - by a further 1,400.[45] This was the result of discussions by the High Level Group (HLG) which had prepared a study on NATO's nuclear arsenals. The study concluded that the planned deployment of Pershing II and cruise missiles would shift the emphasis in NATO's nuclear posture from battlefield weapons to medium-range systems. The HLG further maintained that the nuclear battlefield arsenal was too large and outdated to meet the requirements of flexible response. In particular the West German government and Defense Minister Wörner argued that the atomic mines on West German territory should be completely withdrawn. However, the Montebello decision laid down not only a reduction in but also *modernization* of the remaining arsenal, at least in principle. This applied above all to nuclear-capable artillery, air-launched systems, and short-range missiles such as «Lance».

The hectic activities in fall 1983 could not prevent the failure of the first round of INF negotiations. On November 22, the Christian-Liberal majority of the German *Bundestag* voted in favor of renewing its support for the deployment of ground-launched INF. The deployment of Pershing II began one day later despite massive protests by the peace movements. At the same time, the USSR broke off the INF negotiations in Geneva and also walked out of the strategic arms talks.

3.5 Conclusions: Mutual Stalemate

The start of Western INF deployment signalled the failure of the attempt to use the double-track decision as an instrument of preventive arms control and to include weapon systems in a treaty *prior* to basing. It is sometimes argued that failure was due to the double-track decision itself. Given the fact that since the end of the sixties NATO had practically left the way open for the USSR in the area of intermediate-range weapons, the Alliance had first to make clear to the USSR its determination to deploy and convince her that the arms control offer was not a means of escape: «(The) double-track decision compelled NATO allies to prove their steadfastness. This excluded the possibility of using the time up to the end of 1983 for constructive negotiations.»[46]

---

45 See Cartwright/Critchley, *Cruise*, note 10, pp.46-51.

46 Ruehl, *Mittelstreckenwaffen*, note 6, p.329.

Since Pershing II and the cruise missiles could not be deployed before the end of 1983 for technical reasons, the West's only alternative would have been not to negotiate *at all* prior to the start of deployment. In addition, it remains incomprehensible why steadfastness should automatically result in intransigence. Helmut Schmidt, for example, tried on several occasions to make clear to the Soviets that he would support deployment should there not be an acceptable arms control agreement. At the same time he argued repeatedly during his time as Chancellor that the West should adopt a more flexible approach to negotiations. It was not so much the concept of a double-track decision, in the sense of preventive arms limitation, which failed at the end of 1983. Rather, *neither* side was interested in an agreement - at least not on the available terms. First of all, the political relations between the U.S. and the Soviet Union worsened dramatically following Soviet intervention in Afghanistan. The turnaround in U.S. foreign policy had already set in under Carter. When Ronald Reagan became President in 1981, the U.S. experienced the most conservative government since the fifties. His election campaign was based on the outright rejection of the U.S. arms control and détente policy of the seventies.

Under these circumstances, arms control success in Geneva was unlikely from the outset. The Reagan Administration was concerned during its first term to regain American strength through armament and was not interested in arms limitation. It was only with great reluctance that it consented to the procedure laid down in NATO's double-track decision and to negotiations. In light of this, Paul Nitze was like a man shouting for help who hears only his own echo. The majority of the U.S. government did not see arms control as the search for an agreement based on mutually acceptable compromises, but the continuation of the East-West confrontation by other means. U.S. INF policy in the framework of the Alliance was a «combination of therapy and trickery.»[47] The global zero option was thought to fulfill this function almost perfectly. It was easy to understand and therefore an ideal means with which to score points in the fight for the trust of the Western public. Many of its supporters gave it their backing because they assumed that the Soviet Union would never agree to it. How could they guess that General Secretary Gorbachev would take up the proposal several years later?

---

47   Talbott, *Deadly Gambits*, note 12, p.62, on Richard Burt's strategy.

The Soviet Union under Brezhnev and later Andropov was by no means more willing to compromise than the United States. It pursued arms control on INF as a large-scale public relations campaign aimed at the West Europeans. Soviet policy since the seventies created the impression that the USSR was not prepared to take West European security interests seriously. Whether it hoped that this tactic could prevent deployment in Western Europe, or whether it even reckoned on the success of the peace movements has to be a matter of speculation. The fact remains that from the outset the USSR used the issue of the French and British nuclear forces to block negotiations in Geneva. In doing so, she must have been aware that quite apart from the intransigence of the Reagan Administration, the U.S. was not capable of compromising on the problem of third-country forces due to NATO decisions. Andropov's proposals, which were announced publicly with much ado, offered a different wrapping but the same content. The USSR continued to oppose Western deployment of medium-range weapons but it was not prepared to pay a price. Even the last proposal made at the end of October, 1983, meant that the USSR would only have to scrap 103 of 378 SS-20 missiles worldwide but would be able to keep 140 launchers in Europe and a further 135 in Asia. In return she wanted the U.S. and NATO to forgo 572 Pershing II and cruise missiles. Thus, the Soviet Union spared NATO from having to decide between the deterrence and arms control objectives of its double-track decision.

The U.S. and the USSR can therefore be said to be more or less equally responsible for the failure of the first attempt to subject medium-range weapons to an arms control settlement. The most manifest expression of this was that the only compromise which was taken up in Geneva - the «walk-in-the-woods» proposal - was rejected both in Washington and Moscow.

How is the policy of the West German government to be judged? First of all, it must be emphasized that the worsening of U.S.-Soviet relations after 1980 considerably limited Bonn's scope of action for successful arms control. West German INF policy could, under the prevailing circumstances, be no more than an attempt to use its remaining influence for political *damage limitation*. And initially it was successful in this. Chancellor Schmidt was able to persuade the Soviet leadership in 1980 to enter into negotiations despite the NATO decision of 1979. *Here* at least the concept of the double-track decision, i.e., determination to deploy if necessary but also willingness to negotiate, was successful. In addition, the West European allies were able to persuade the new U.S. Administration in 1981 to abide by NATO consensus and resume negotiations. Indeed, the compromise offer made by the U.S. in 1983 was likewise the result of West European initiative.

Further, the policy pursued since the seventies which used the INF issue to ensure West German involvement in nuclear arms control, despite not being or wishing to be a negotiating partner, was successful with one notable exception. A new Alliance institution was created in the SCG which was also to be of importance later. However, the exception, the non-consultation of the allies on the «walk-in-the-woods» proposal *before* American rejection, illustrates the limits of the Alliance mechanism. The *extent* of West European influence on the U.S. negotiating position was dependent on America's readiness to consult them and on which side in the internal wrangling within the U.S. government wished to orchestrate West European support for its position. Helmut Schmidt was unfortunate in that the «walk-in-the-woods» formula was worked out at a time when the unilateralist arms control opponents like Richard Perle dominated in Washington. That was in the spring and summer of 1982. Just one year later this group already began to lose influence. The European NATO allies contributed greatly to the coming about of negotiations on intermediate-range weapons, but they were unable to alter the fact that neither the U.S. nor the USSR were prepared to make earnest attempts at compromise.

Should the West German government in 1983 have refused to consent to the deployment of Pershing II and cruise missiles as was demanded by the SPD, the Greens, the trade unions and the peace movements? An unambiguous «yes» or «no» is only possible if one believed, as did the peace movements, that NATO's double-track decision could not be justified with defensive motives, or, alternatively, if one assigned clear priority to the military logic of the NATO decision, as did those who insisted on deployment. However, if one (like the author) accepted the double-track decision in principle (but not every detail) as a reaction to the blatant Soviet disregard of West European security interests in the seventies, yet took its arms control component seriously, then the answer is bound to be more complex. On the one hand, the U.S. certainly did not make the «greatest efforts» to bring about a compromise, as called for by Helmut Schmidt in his final speech as Chancellor on October 1, 1982.[48] In addition, the reference to the changed Soviet policy in 1986/87 can only partly serve to justify deployment in 1983. When Pershing missiles came to West Germany, nobody could have known whether INF negotiations would ever be re-assumed.

On the other hand, one must ask what the consequences of rejecting deployment would have been. The West German government would have provoked a large-scale crisis in the Alliance. This would have been an acceptable sacrifice *if* the rejection could have improved the chances of arms control. There were no signs of this in 1983, however. Rather, it would have confirmed the U.S. inflexibility by enforcing the opinion already prevailing in Washington that the West Europeans were «soft on defense», gave in to every form of Soviet pressure, and wanted once again to evade responsibility for the double-track decision which was of their own making. It seems highly unlikely that refusal by Bonn to carry out the double-track decison would have increased American willingness for arms control.

Very probably the same applies to the Soviet Union. The Soviet attitude during the Geneva talks, up to the end of 1983, did not indicate that the USSR would have honored Western renunciation of deployment by limiting the SS-20. This fact remains despite all their moratorium proposals and public campaigns. Instead, the Soviets would probably have celebrated Western restraint as a major foreign policy victory, with devastating consequences for NATO. The Soviet leadership under Andropov would most likely have interpreted a Western decision not to carry out the INF deployment as a sign that it could benefit from showing intransigence in its negotiating policy.

What should be stressed is that one is hardly justified - even in terms of arms control - in criticizing the West German government in fall 1983 for insisting on implementing the double-track decision and beginning with deployment. Whether it was necessary to base in *this* form is another matter.[49] With or without deployment, things looked bleak for arms control in 1983. The first attempt to limit the medium-range forces of both sides had failed. New efforts were necessary.

---

48 See Helmut Schmidt's speech to the *Bundestag* on October 1, 1982, *Bulletin*, no.90, 1982, p.286.

49 Perhaps Pershing II should not have been deployed at all events since it was inconsistent with criteria of crisis stability.

4

Phase III: Getting Involved With Disarmament - The Path to the Double Zero Option

4.1 The Stalemate Continues: Negotiations up to Late 1985

Following the start of Western deployment of new intermediate-range missiles and the Soviet walk-out from the Geneva negotiations, progress in 1984 was zero. Each side clung firmly to its respective position and waited for the other to make the first move towards the resumption of talks. At the end of February 1984, the Soviet Foreign Minister Gromyko declared that Moscow would only return to the negotiating table upon restoration of the status quo which existed prior to Western deployment - meaning the dismantling of Pershing II and cruise missiles.[1] Unaffected by her major foreign policy defeat in not preventing the start of Western deployment, the USSR upheld this condition until fall.

Neither the U.S. nor NATO saw any reason to rethink their own positions. To their minds, it was up to the USSR to make the first move back to the negotiating table. Nevertheless, ideas on how to allow Moscow to resume negotiations without too great a loss of face were broached on various sides, in part publicly. The proposal to merge strategic arms reduction (START) and INF talks played an important role in this connection. All the West European governments were committed to the continuation of negotiations and urged the U.S. to adopt a more amenable stance towards the Soviet Union.

---

1   Cf. «Gromyko spricht wieder von Verhandlungen,» *Süddeutsche Zeitung* (SZ), February 29, 1984.

There were also renewed public debates in 1984 on the possibility of a bilateral deployment moratorium. Aside from the West German and British opposition parties, SPD and Labour, this proposal received backing above all from smaller deployment countries such as the Netherlands, Belgium and Italy. On May 4, Italy's Prime Minister Craxi declared that a resumption of the talks on medium-range weapons could be achieved if NATO would agree to freeze its missiles in Europe at the present level.[2] This initiative led to considerable annoyance in Washington and surprised reactions within NATO.

In Belgium and in the Netherlands the idea of a moratorium was also fairly well received. One has to take into account that neither country had reached a final decision on whether to consent to the deployment of 48 missiles respectively on their territories. In both countries, the ruling coalitions of Christian Democrats and Liberals were totally at odds over modernization.[3] A moratorium would have allowed them to further delay a decision. On June 15, the Hague temporarily postponed the deployment decision on condition that the USSR would forgo basing further missiles. On November 30, the Belgian government followed suit after the Christian Democrats had spoken out in favor of postponement. On March 20, 1985, after a 35-hour debate, the Belgian Chamber of Deputies approved deployment of the first 16 missiles. Over six months later, on November 1, 1985, the Dutch government came to the conclusion that the Soviets had deployed further SS-20 missiles since June 1984 and gave its final consent to basing. At the same time the Hague announced that the Netherlands was to discontinue several of its NATO nuclear missions. It was the fifth and last of the deployment countries to accept modernization on its soil.

In the meantime, movement had begun to occur in U.S.-Soviet relations. On September 24, 1984, President Reagan proposed before the United Nations in New York that the Soviets participate in «umbrella talks». START and INF negotiations were to be combined with talks on

---

2   Cf. «U.S., Bonn Bar NATO Missile Moratorium,» *Los Angeles Times*, May 8, 1984.

3   See «Ein vermummtes Ja zu den Raketen,» *Die Zeit*, May 11, 1984; «Wieder Nachrüstungsdebatte in Belgien,» *SZ*, November 28, 1984; «Belgiens Parlament billigt Stationierung,» *SZ*, March 21, 1985; «Lubbers hält am Stationierungsbeschluss fest,» *FAZ*, October 31, 1985; *ACR*, no.11, 1985, pp.403.B345-348.

missile defense and space weapons.[4] This proposal was aimed at allowing the USSR to return to the negotiating table without too much loss of face, since the talks could be presented as a new negotiating forum.

Initially, Reagan's appeal brought no response. Apparently, the Soviets wanted to await the outcome of the U.S. presidential elections. Then in November the Soviet Union softened its terms. Following an exchange of letters between President Reagan and General Secretary Chernenko, the two sides agreed that Secretary of State Shultz and Foreign Minister Gromyko should meet at the beginning of January 1985 in Geneva to discuss negotiations «on all questions related to nuclear and space weapons.»[5] The Soviet leadership dropped its insistence on preconditions and thus retreated from the dead end into which it had maneuvered itself. Chernenko declared on several occasions that the new negotiations should be related to the entire complex of interrelated issues of space weapons, the reduction of strategic offensive weapons, and of INF. No further mention was made of a moratorium or of the withdrawal of the Western INF deployments. Instead, the Kremlin leadership concentrated its efforts on the prevention of an arms race in space in response to the U.S. Strategic Defense Initiative (SDI). It indicated that it would only agree to reductions of offensive weapons if settlement could be reached on ballistic missile defense and space weapons.

In a meeting between Secretary of State Shultz and Foreign Minister Gromyko in Geneva in January 1985, it was agreed to begin combined negotiations on strategic offensive weapons, strategic defense/space weapons, and intermediate-range systems. The communiqué read: «The objective of the negotiations will be to work out effective agreements aimed at preventing an arms race in space and in terminating it on earth, at limiting and reducing nuclear arms, and at strengthening strategic stability.»[6]

Nevertheless, Gromyko made it clear from the outset that progress would only be reached on INF and START if the U.S. agreed to abandon space weapons and the development of SDI-type systems. This linkage

---

4   Cf. «President's Address at U.N. Conciliatory Toward Soviets,» *Washington Post* (WP), September 25, 1984.

5   See Lothar Ruehl, *Mittelstreckenwaffen in Europa* (Baden-Baden: Nomos, 1987), p.333.

6   Quoted from «U.S. and Soviet Set Talks on Missiles and Arms in Space,» *The New York Times* (NYT), January 9, 1985.

was reaffirmed at the start of the new talks (NST = Nuclear and Space Talks) on March 12 in Geneva.

On the resumption of talks there were approximately 54 Pershing II missiles in West Germany, 32 cruise missiles in Great Britain and 16 in Italy - a total of 102 intermediate-range missiles. Belgium's first 16 systems were shortly to be deployed. The Soviet Union, in the meantime, had 414 SS-20 missiles with 1,242 warheads in deployment. Since the start of Western modernization the number had been increased by 36 systems.[7]

Both sides began the new INF talks where they had left off in 1983. Soviet INF chief negotiator Aleksei Obukhov called on both sides to forgo the deployment of new systems and repeated the old Soviet proposal that, in return for the total renunciation of Western modernization, the Soviets would reduce their SS-20s in Europe to the number of French and British warheads combined, i.e., to 420 according to Soviet counting. In a counterproposal the American INF delegation headed by Maynard Glitman renewed its global zero option as a negotiation proposal and added an interim solution which was apparently similar to the American offer of September 1983.[8] The aim was to show flexibility to the USSR from the beginning. The American negotiators now had enough leeway to sound out various options. The reason was that, in Reagan's second term, American arms control policy was moving towards greater preparedness for flexibility and compromise. This change coincided with a gradual loss of power by the unilateralist hardliners in the Pentagon and a gain by the pragmatic conservative advocates of arms control in the State Department. At any rate, Secretary of State Shultz's influence on the U.S. arms control policy increased steadily, the exception being SDI. However, the changes in Washington did not alter the fact that in March 1985 the positions of both sides were just as incompatible as they had been in November 1983. Generally speaking, the

---

7   «Burt: Soviets deploying SS-20s at 'Steady Pace',» *The Wireless Bulletin from Washington* (WB), March 13, 1985, p.17; «Die NATO hält Zahlen zurück,» *SZ*, March 21, 1985.

8   Cf. Arms Control Association (ACA), «INF Background and Negotiating History,» Background Paper, December 1986, p.4. For the following see Michael Staack, *Kurswechsel in Washington. Entspannungsgegner und Rüstungskontrolle unter der Präsidentschaft Ronald Reagans*, Forschungsberichte Internationale Politik, (Berlin: Quorum Verlag, 1987).

INF issue took a back seat as a result of the controversies surrounding SDI. As was to be expected, the first round of negotiations produced no results.

On April 7, 1985, the new Soviet General Secretary Gorbachev announced the cessation of SS-20 deployments in Europe, initially up to November 1 of that year (after that there were no further increases in the 270 launchers west of the 80th degree of latitude). At the same time, the SS-20 missiles based in Europe were to be reduced to 243, i.e., to the level prior to the breaking off of INF negotiations.[9] The offer was obviously designed to influence the decision-making process in the Netherlands but remained unsuccessful (see above). NATO contended that the announced reductions had in fact taken place and continued to base its calculations on 270 SS-20 missiles in the European zone.

In fall 1985, the Soviets made their long-awaited «comprehensive proposal» for the entire range of weapon systems dealt with in Geneva. In return for a settlement on the ban of development, testing and deployment of space weapons, the Soviet Union was prepared to reduce strategic nuclear forces by 50%. Their definition of «strategic», however, encompassed all weapons capable of reaching the territory of either superpower. This counting rule was de facto a step back to the early phase of SALT negotiations and brought the old FBS issue back into the talks (cf. 2.1). The SS-20, on the other hand, remained outside the Soviet «comprehensive proposal». In addition, Gorbachev demanded that, in keeping with the SALT II treaty protocol, there be a ban on cruise missiles with a range of more than 600 km. Clearly these terms were unacceptable to the U.S. One might therefore suspect that Gorbachev wished to count 1,149 forward-based systems as U.S. strategic weapons in order to maintain negotiating leverage for START.

In a speech before the French National Assembly in Paris on October 3, Gorbachev de-linked INF from the space and START negotiations and announced Soviet willingness to work out a separate agreement on intermediate-range weapons. He further proposed direct negotiations between the Soviet Union, Great Britain and France on the limitation of

---

9   See Gorbachev's interview with *Pravda*, April 7, 1985, in «Gorbachev Ready for Reagan Talks; Freeze Missiles,» *NYT*, April 8, 1985. Cf. also the Western reaction, e.g., the SCG press report, April 23, 1985, *NATO Review*, no.2, 1985, p.30; «Holmes: 'No evidence' of SS-20 Dismantlement,» *WB*, October 28, 1985, pp.25-31.

their nuclear weapons.[10] The reactions in London and Paris to this proposal ranged from extreme caution to outright rejection, and both governments later returned to their traditional insistence that they would only be prepared to enter into such negotiations once both superpowers had made drastic cuts in their strategic arsenals.

That did not prevent the Soviet leadership from presenting new offers on medium-range weapons in Geneva which for the first time indicated some flexibility. The Soviet proposal for an interim solution on INF was as follows:[11]

- American and Soviet ground-launched INF (i.e., Pershing II, cruise missiles and SS-20s) should be initially frozen at the present level. Subsequently, U.S. and Soviet INF in Europe would be reduced. The U.S. would be allowed to base 100-120 ground-launched cruise missiles, but no Pershing II. The USSR offered to reduce her SS-20 missiles to the total of these warheads plus the sum of British and French warheads.
- The number of SS-20 missiles based in Asia would be frozen, likewise short-range INF.
- Intermediate-range aircraft should not be included in this interim agreement (they were counted as FBS in the Soviet START proposal).

The offer contained one new aspect. For the first time, the USSR was prepared to accept U.S. land-based INF in Western Europe - a position which it had categorically rejected in previous years. It did not change its position on the Pershing II ban, however. In a further concession it offered to include SRINF in the deployment moratorium. Otherwise the Soviet position did not differ from its stance at the end of 1983. Its insistence that French and British nuclear weapons be included in full, still constituted the main obstacle to a treaty.

On November 1, 1985 the U.S. presented a counterproposal in Geneva which differed only slightly from the offer made two years before:

- Ground-launched INF in Europe should be reduced to 140 launchers with up to 420 warheads.

---

10 For details see *ACR*, no.10, 1985, pp.403.B.336-338.

11 For details see Ruehl, *Mittelstreckenwaffen*, note 5, p.335; ACA, «INF Background,» note 8, p.4; «Nitze sees some hope on INF,» *WB*, October 23, 1985, pp.23-27.

- U.S. systems should consist of Pershing II and cruise missiles with the *composition* of the ratio being negotiable.
- The SS-20 missiles based in Asia were to be reduced proportionately by approximately 50%, e.g., to 100 missiles. The U.S. reserved the right to base the same number of INF systems on American territory.
- The U.S. continued to insist on concurrent constraints for systems between 500 and 1,000 km (SRINF).

If one compares the American and Soviet proposals, both sides can be said to have come closer on a number of points. Both agreed that INF based in Asia should be treated differently from those deployed in Europe. Aircraft were to be initially excluded, and it was generally agreed that a solution had to be found for SRINF. The issue of British and French nuclear weapons continued to be the main stumbling block; the positions were still irreconcilable. Considerable sticking points also remained on other issues (e.g., deployment of Pershing II and limitation of the SS-20 based in Asia). The stalemate was not yet overcome.

The first summit meeting between President Reagan and General Secretary Gorbachev in Geneva from November 19-21, 1985, did not bring the two sides any closer. Both leaders merely reaffirmed that they would strive for a separate interim agreement on INF, regardless of their differences on SDI and space weapons.[12] This first summit meeting between the U.S. and the Soviet Union since the signing of the SALT II treaty of 1979 was, however, a symbolic expression of the improved relations between the superpowers. The communiqué contained a rejection of the strive for superiority and of the concept that nuclear war could be won. The summit thus eliminated a number of irritations in U.S.-Soviet relations. It also indicated a relaxation of tensions between the superpowers - an important prerequisite for successful arms control.

Were an agreement to be reached on medium-range weapons, additional impulses were now necessary. It was the Soviet General Secretary Gorbachev who brought a turnaround on INF.

---

12 See the Joint Declaration on the talks between President Reagan and General Secretary Gorbachev in Geneva, November 19-21, 1985, *WB*, no.214, Nov. 22, 1985.

4.2 The Stalemate Starts to Give: Gorbachev and the Road to Reykjavik

More than six years after the passing of NATO's double-track decision in 1979, more than four years after negotiations on intermediate-range weapons had begun at the end of 1981, and after a stalemate had been reached in which the two sides had maneuvered into incompatible positions, General Secretary Gorbachev began on January 15, 1986, to disentangle the Gordian knot. His proposal to free the world of nuclear weapons by the year 2000 contained new aspects for dealing with INF in the «small print». Though it was tempting to see the proposal as some kind of propaganda stunt in reply to Ronald Reagan's SDI vision, the details of the offer could hardly be dismissed as the mere repetition of former positions. On INF, Gorbachev proposed:
- within five to eight years - the first stage of his comprehensive disarmament plan - to eliminate all ground-launched LRINF in the European zone;
- to prohibit transfer of these systems to third parties by the superpowers during this period of time;
- also in the first stage to freeze the French and British arsenals at their present levels;
- as of 1990 - within the second stage - to include the other nuclear powers in the disarmament process while continuing with the total elimination of American and Soviet INF weapons and to freeze the remaining tactical nuclear weapons;
- a global elimination of tactical nuclear weapons (ranges below 1,000 km);
- by the year 2000, to eliminate all nuclear weapons worldwide by all states.[13]

Thus the Soviet Union came close to the Western zero option, but restricted to the European zone, i.e., west of the 80th degree of latitude. She declared her willingness to scrap the remaining 112 SS-4 missiles as well as 243 SS-20 missiles with 729 warheads (according to NATO figures at that time, 270 SS-20 with 810 warheads).

---

13 See Gorbachev Statement, January 15, 1986, *ACR*, no.2, 1986, pp.611.D.53-59.

The Soviet move indicated that Gorbachev was abandoning the legacy of the security policy associated with Brezhnev. The November 1985 proposal had already dropped insistence on a Soviet monopoly in medium-range systems in Europe. Further, the USSR was now prepared to trade away all SS-20 missiles based in Europe for the removal of the Pershing II and cruise missiles. From now on, nuclear balance in Europe, if possible at zero, meant *parity between the U.S. and the Soviet Union* and not, as during Brezhnev's time in office, «zero plus» in favor of the USSR.

However, the Soviet offer still contained several cloven hoofs for the West:

- The SS-20 missiles based in Soviet Asia (a considerable 171 missile force with 513 warheads) were to be totally excluded in the first reduction period.
- Admittedly, French and British nuclear weapons were no longer included in the Soviet nuclear force comparison for Europe. However, to freeze third-party systems in a *bilateral* U.S.-Soviet treaty was by no means more acceptable to the United States than the previous insistence on *counting* these systems on the American side.
- SRINF («operative tactical missiles» in Soviet terminology) were to be dismantled in a second reduction period, i.e., only after 1990. However, Soviet Foreign Minister Shevardnadze declared on February 28, 1986, in a speech to the Party Congress of the Communist Party in Moscow, that once the U.S. INF had been reduced the Soviet missiles which had been deployed in Eastern Europe as a countermeasure would also be withdrawn. The weapons in question were approximately 48 modernized SS-12 systems (range: 400 km).[14]

Given five years of fruitless INF negotiations, Gorbachev's proposal for a European zero option signified the first substantial concession to the West. Gorbachev indicated that, unlike his predecessors, he was prepared to take West European security interests seriously. It was now up to NATO and the U.S. to make the next move. It remained to be seen how seriously the West had taken its own proposals over the years. From now on, the decisive controversy in the Alliance centered on whether a zero option was still an objective or not.

Initially, everything seemed to go well. After intensive preliminary discussions in Washington, the U.S. National Security Council met on February 3 to discuss the different options for a reply to Gorbachev. The

14 See Shevardnadze's speech at the CPSU Party Congress, Feb. 28, 1986, *ACR*, no.4, 1986, pp.403.B.370/371.

Arms Control and Disarmament Agency (ACDA) suggested that the Soviet proposal for a European zero option be accepted, provided that certain conditions were met. One term was that the SS-20 missiles based in Asia be reduced by 50%. With regard to third-party systems, the U.S. remained unwilling to make any kind of compromise. U.S. Secretary of State Shultz gave his backing to this proposal. It was Defense Secretary Weinberger who hesitated. A day later, President Reagan decided to provisionally accept the ACDA proposal. A final decision was not to be made until after consultation with the allies.[15]

The U.S. was thus prepared to abandon the deployment of Pershing II and cruise missiles in Europe. West European governments and Japan were responsible for a U.S.-Soviet agreement in principle being delayed by six months.

The *Japanese* government informed U.S. Special Ambassador Rowny that the only possible interpretation of the fact that the SS-20 missiles in Asia were given different treatment to the systems in the European zone was that U.S. allies in Asia assumed a second-rank as compared to the West Europeans. Paul Nitze was summoned to *London* to hear the reservations of the British government regarding the zero option. The Britons were concerned about Soviet conventional superiority and argued that the elimination of Pershing II would leave a gap in NATO's nuclear escalation ladder. Finally, «decoupling» fears were voiced. After Great Britain, the *French* government voiced the strongest reservations towards a European zero option. This skepticism was also felt in *NATO headquarters* in Brussels. Here, at least 140 Western INF missiles were considered necessary to ensure the implementation of flexible response. This effectively ruled out the European zero option. The Belgian government supported the American plan. Even the Dutch government expressed criticism, fearing that the zero option could jeopardize deployment of cruise missiles which they had finally pushed through after long and hard efforts.[16]

---

15   The account is based on talks with U.S. and West European government officials. Cf. also *ACR*, no.2, 1986, pp.611.B.289, 403.B.363.

16   Cf. «Verbündete tragen Nitze ihre Vorbehalte vor,» *SZ*, February 15/16, 1986; «Kurzstreckenwaffen sind in Europa die 'eigentliche Gefahr',» *FAZ*, February 25, 1986; «Nach dem Gorbachev-Vorschlag abermals europäische Furcht vor der 'Abkoppelung',» *FAZ*, March 11, 1986. For the following see

The *West German government*, on the other hand, accepted Gorbachev's proposal for a European zero option after much hesitation. However, it wanted an INF treaty to include limitations on SRINF from the beginning. In this regard, Bonn pointed to the American negotiating position on SRINF since 1981 (cf. 3.4). But, in the meantime, the U.S. government had already reached a decision which took into account the reservations voiced by London, Paris, and Tokyo. «The West Europeans have sabotaged arms control,» said an offical of the U.S. ACDA.[17]

Finally, in a letter to Gorbachev, dated February 22, Reagan took up the old proposal of a *global* zero option and incorporated it into a step-by-step plan with the option of reducing INF launchers in Europe to 140. The details of the American offer were as follows:[18]

- Up to the end of 1987, INF missiles in Europe to be reduced to 140 launchers with 420 to 450 warheads; proportional cuts in the SS-20 missiles based in Asia to 88 systems with 264 warheads. Equal global ceiling, thus retaining the U.S. right to compensate for the Soviet systems deployed in Asia by basing INF systems on U.S. territory.
- Up to the end of 1988, the remaining INF systems to be reduced by 50% and a global zero solution on long-range INF to be achieved by the end of 1989.
- For SRINF, the U.S. proposed a global ceiling either at the Soviet current level or at the level both sides had on January 1, 1982. At the same time, the U.S. reserved the right to convert Pershing II to shorter-range Pershing I missiles.
- The inclusion or limitation of British and French systems in whatever form was out of the question.
- Finally, the U.S. introduced a proposal in Geneva on treaty verification. Initially, inspectors on both sides should establish a data base on existing missiles. The missiles not affected by the reductions would only be allowed in agreed deployment areas. Finally, inspectors on both sides should supervise the destruction of weapons at inspection and storage facilities.

---

also «Bonn für Reagan's Null-Lösung falls Kurzstreckenwaffen einbegriffen werden,» *FAZ*, February 20, 1986.

17   In conversation with the author.

18   Details in Ruehl, *Mittelstreckenwaffen*, note 5, p.339; «Nitze: U.S. Proposal Would Protect British, French Forces,» *U.S. Policy, Information, and Texts* (USPIT, previously Wireless Bulletin), March 3, 1986, p.1-3.

The U.S. offer was an attempt to present old ideas in a different but not particularly original packaging. It contained very little which had not already been proposed in one form or another. Once again, the global zero option served to prevent an INF treaty. In spring 1986, the feeling in London, Paris and partly in Bonn too, was that Gorbachev was highly unlikely to take NATO at its word.

However, the Soviet General Secretary did not let up. In June he dropped the condition that U.S. forward-based systems be counted as strategic systems. He did, however, insist that they be frozen at the present level. In August and Septemer 1986, there was movement in the INF talks. During bilateral consultations which took place outside the Geneva talks, the Soviets proposed limiting the number of intermediate-range systems based in the European zone to 100 warheads for both sides. However, they still insisted that the U.S. abandon Pershing II. The number of SS-20 missiles based in Asia was to be frozen and perhaps even slightly reduced. Soviet negotiators also indicated that the problem of British and French nuclear weapons could be solved.

On September 18, the U.S. introduced a new proposal which foresaw 200 LRINF warheads worldwide and 100 warheads in Europe. The offer represented a concession to the Soviets, in that it was an acceptance of their reduction proposal for Europe (not however the renunciation of Pershing II!) For NATO it meant «the available LRINF in Europe would be stretched to their limits in terms both of military-strategic efficiency and of security policy.»[19]

The next Soviet concession followed a day later on September 19. In a letter to President Reagan, Gorbachev finally agreed to drop the condition that French and British systems be included in any form in an INF agreement. He thus abandoned a Soviet position which his predecessors Brezhnev and Andropov had used to block negotiations for years. Finally, the USSR accepted the principal right of the United States to compensate for the weapons based in Asia. The Soviet Union thus met the West halfway on two important points, before the Reykjavik summit meeting:
- equal global ceiling;
- non-inclusion of third-party systems.

---

19   Ruehl, *Mittelstreckenwaffen*, note 5, p.344, refering to the corresponding Soviet position. See also ibid., p.343; ACA, «INF Background,» note 8, p.6.

In just nine months, between January and September 1986, the U.S. and the Soviet Union had removed more obstacles on INF than in the previous five years. A decisive factor was the «new thinking» under Gorbachev. The Soviet leadership moved step-by-step closer to Western positions which for years had remained unchanged.

The *summit meeting between Ronald Reagan and Mikhail Gorbachev* in the Hofdi House in *Reykjavik* from October 10-12, 1986, brought the hoped-for breakthrough on INF. Through Saturday night to Sunday morning, October 12, teams of experts on both sides negotiated under the direction of Paul Nitze and the Soviet General Chief of Staff Marshal Akhromeyev. They initially agreed that an INF treaty should be of indefinite duration. To the Americans' suprise, Akhromeyev agreed to a U.S. proposal on verification which foresaw the exchange of data prior to, and after reductions as well as on-site inspections for the missile destruction and the monitoring of remaining systems. On Sunday morning, Gorbachev and Reagan came to the following basic agreement on INF:[20]

- *total elimination of all ground-launched LRINF missiles in the European zone;*
- *global ceiling of 100 warheads on both sides with the Americans being allowed to base only on their own territory, the USSR being allowed to deploy 33 SS-20 (= 99 warheads) in Soviet Asia;*
- *non-inclusion of French and British nuclear weapons.*

Both sides failed to conclude an agreement because the Soviet leadership re-established the linkage between an INF treaty and the settlement on the issue of space weapons and the ABM treaty. In doing so they reversed a position which they had adopted prior to Reykjavik, namely that a separate INF treaty be concluded.

Nevertheless, the Reykjavik agreement meant that the U.S. and NATO had been able to reach almost all of their negotiating objectives since the double-track decision of 1979. The tentative accord was nearly identical with the zero proposal of 1981. It included an equal global ceiling for long-range INF as well as drastic reductions of the SS-20s

---

20 On the outcome of the Reykjavik summit see *The Reykjavik Talks: Promise or Peril*, Report of the Subcommittee on Arms Control, International Security and Science to the Committee on Foreign Affairs, U.S. House of Representatives (Washington D.C: GPO, 1987); also Gert Krell et al., *Von der Rüstungskontrolle zur Abrüstung? Zum Stand der Genfer Verhandlungen nach Reykjavik* (Frankfurt am Main: PRIF report, no.1, March 1987).

based in Asia. Third-party systems were excluded as were INF fighter-aircraft and bombers - American forward based systems, for example. If one examines the starting positions of both sides in 1981, the Soviet Union had clearly made more substantial concessions. Having dropped her insistence on the inclusion of French and British nuclear weapons prior to Reykjavik, she was prepared at the summit to drastically reduce the SS-20 missiles based in Asia. However, she was able to achieve one of her long-standing goals: there would be no more U.S. ground-launched missiles deployed in Western Europe and capable of reaching the Soviet Union.

After Reykjavik a substantial problem remained, apart from the working out of verification procedures, namely how to deal with short-range INF. Gorbachev conceded that there should be limitations on SRINF in a first treaty. In addition, the two sides agreed in Reykjavik that there should be follow-up negotiations on *reductions*. Secretary of State Shultz later hinted at the possibility of agreement being reached on total elimination.[21]

What was not decided in Reykjavik was exactly what limitations should be placed on SRINF and which systems ought to be included in follow-up negotiations. The Soviet Union called for a freeze for missiles in the ranges 500-1,000 km and rejected the American proposal for a common ceiling which would have given the U.S. the right to compensate for the existing imbalance by further deployments should negotiations bring no results. As for the follow-up talks, the Soviets wanted these to concentrate on the reduction and total elimination of *all* missiles below 1,000 km range. The Americans, on the other hand, obviously intended initially to negotiate only on the limitation of missiles with ranges 500-1,000 km and gave no thought to including the remaining short-range systems.

The Reykjavik summit had brought no concrete achievements, because Reagan and Gorbachev were not able to compromise on SDI, space weapons and the interpretation of the ABM treaty. Had an agreement been reached in Reykjavik then it would have been presented as a historic turning point in U.S.-Soviet relations. After all, the leaders of

---

21 Cf. «Shultz Calls Strategic Defense A 'Lever' in Arms Control,» *USPIT*, October 16, 1986, p.8; «Press Briefing on the Reagan-Gorbachev Meetings in Reykjavik, Iceland, by Ambassador Max Kampelman,» *USPIT*, October 20, 1986, p.6.

both superpowers had never before spoken in such specific terms about the worldwide elimination of all (ballistic) nuclear weapons. The perspective of a world free of nuclear weapons sent out shockwaves which reverberated through NATO, most capitals of Western Europe, and the United States itself. After Reykjavik the main emphasis of arms control activities, therefore, shifted initially from the U.S.-Soviet bargaining table to negotiations within America and in the Alliance.

4.3 A Zero Option After All? Reactions within NATO

At the Reykjavik summit, Ronald Reagan had gone far beyond what had been previously agreed upon in Alliance fora and the U.S. National Security Council. America's allies, therefore, did not greet events in the Icelandic capital with unqualified enthusiasm. Though disappointed that unprecedented progress in arms control had not been achieved after all, there was no denying that disappointment was tinged unmistakeably with a degree of relief. The fact that there was movement in arms control once again was received positively, however, as official statements reflected; NATO's announcements that winter, all spoke in praise of the arms control efforts made in Reykjavik.[22]

On the other hand, the West Europeans were unanimous in their criticism of the lack of consultation by their American Alliance leader. If Reagan had spoken to Gorbachev about the global elimination of all nuclear weapons, or merely the elimination of all ballistic missiles - the confusion surrounding what exactly had been discussed at the summit meeting remained even later - then this concerned the core of existing NATO strategy. The point was that the Americans had failed once again to keep the pledge laid down in the 1962 Athens guidelines, to consult their allies on all questions pertaining to nuclear weapons based in Europe.

If the Europeans were relieved that the summit meeting had finally failed due to SDI, then this stemmed from their reservations vis-à-vis Reagan's position involving the dismantling of all ballistic missiles, and reservations regarding the contemplated zero option on INF. After

---

22   See for the following Krell et al., *Rüstungskontrolle*, note 20, pp.24-29.

Reykjavik, most West European governments acted as brake blocks on the American arms control train.

It seemed to be a repetition of the situation in the seventies when SALT triggered off similar fears in Western Europe (cf. 2.1). The possible *elimination of all ballistic nuclear weapons* met with *unanimous* rejection by NATO allies. Having taken the comments made by Reagan and Gorbachev to date as nothing more than soap-box speeches, they now realized with horror that both heads of government had serious intentions after all. The two West European nuclear powers, Great Britain and France, categorically ruled out the elimination of their nuclear weapons for the time being. During a visit to Washington ten days after Reykjavik, West German Chancellor Kohl emphasized that before striving for cuts in nuclear weapons above the envisaged 50%, the problem of Soviet conventional superiority in Europe must be addressed. Finally, it was argued in principle that it was wrong to eliminate all nuclear weapons as they were the most reliable means of preventing war between East and West. Consequently, the elimination of all nuclear weapons did not feature in any NATO communiqué issued in the fall and winter of 1986. The joint declaration by Ronald Reagan and Margaret Thatcher of November 15 also failed to mention it. And since both the U.S. Joint Chiefs of Staff and Congress voiced sharp criticism of this proposal, the elimination perspective disappeared in spring 1987 from the American negotiating position in Geneva.

The situation for *intermediate-range missiles* proved to be more complicated. Since 1981, NATO had expressed its approval of the zero option in all its communiqués. Now, finally, came the moment of truth. Reagan and Gorbachev had actually reached agreement on this proposal and the fear, not only in NATO headquarters in Brussels but also in London and Paris, was great. In Brussels and in the NATO staff in Mons the Western negotiating position on INF had been taken so lightly over the years that no thought had been given to what specific implications the loss of Pershing II and cruise missiles would have for NATO nuclear target planning. On the contrary, there were endeavors to work out new guidelines for the employment of nuclear weapons, which would do justice to the new military options made available by Pershing II. For the NATO military, Pershing II remained the ideal weapon for the implementation of flexible response.

At first, NATO acted as if nothing had happened. Ten days after the two superpowers had reached a tentative agreement in Reykjavik on the elimination of Pershing II, NATO's Nuclear Planning Group (NPG) adopted new guidelines for the use of tactical nuclear weapons, which included INF, during a meeting in Gleneagles, Scotland. The «Political Guidelines for the Employment of Nuclear Weapons in Defense of NATO» replaced the «Preliminary Guidelines» of 1969. The new principles put less emphasis on the extensive use of tactical nuclear weapons in military operations, stressing instead their employment, albeit effectively in military terms, as a political signal aimed at early war termination. A further shift of emphasis which was of interest above all for West Germany, was the possibility of nuclear escalation by strikes against Soviet territory and less by the employment of battlefield weapons. Pershing II was needed for this very purpose.[23] In Gleneagles it became once again clear how little coordination existed between the arms control policy pursued by the U.S. and NATO and their military planning. During the meeting of the NPG, the European zero option came under sharp criticism. Above all British Defense Minister Younger voiced objections against the agreements reached in Reykjavik, while the German representative, Undersecretary of Defense Ruehl, remained non-commital on the zero option but drew attention once again to short-range weapons. The NPG communiqué did not contain unconditional support for the zero option but argued that reductions of offensive nuclear forces must be achieved in such a way that they strengthened stability and reduced the risk of nuclear war to a minimum. The communiqué clearly revealed the reservations of the allies. They merely repeated as a matter of course the old formulation that they were prepared to reverse, stop or reduce LRINF deployment should a balanced and verifiable treaty be achieved.[24]

The critics of the Reykjavik zero option were to be found above all in Paris, London and in NATO headquarters. The *French* government made it clear that it opposed, in principle, the withdrawal of American nuclear weapons from Europe because this would jeopardize European

---

23   Cf. «NATO-Beratungen über Richtlinien zum Einsatz von Nuklearwaffen,» *FAZ*, October 18, 1986; «Mit Null-Lösung ist nicht zu spassen,» *FAZ*, October 20, 1986.

24   Cf. «Zustimmung zu Reagan überdeckt dürftig erhebliche Vorbehalte,» *FAZ*, October 22, 1986; «Forderung nach Null-Lösung nicht mehr wiederholt,» *FAZ*, October 23, 1986; «NATO Endorses U.S. Summit Stand,» *WP*, October 23, 1986.

security and NATO cohesion. It additionally ruled out the inclusion of French nuclear weapons in the disarmament process for the foreseeable future. France wanted to avoid at all costs being forced into a tight corner by the two superpowers on nuclear disarmament. This position was supported at home by the Conservative ruling parties, as well as by the Socialist opposition party. However, French reservations did not sound particularly convincing; for, Paris had appealed to her neighbors to deploy U.S. medium-range missiles on their soil despite a highly promising Soviet offer but was not prepared to accept weapons herself. The Pershings were to remain in West Germany in order to act as a kind of additional security guarantee ultimately enhancing the credibility of the French *«force de dissuasion»*. Furthermore, the French believed that INF would prevent Bonn from drifting into neutralism.

However, President Mitterand and Prime Minister Chirac had different opinions on INF. Chirac, Foreign Minister Raimond and Defense Minister Giraud rejected the zero option while Mitterand, who in his capacity as president reserved the right to exercise the prerogative in foreign and defense policy, supported the option. In January 1983, the Socialist Mitterand had publicly expressed his support for the Christian Democratic Chancellor Helmut Kohl before the German *Bundestag* and had spoken out against the SPD and in favor of the Pershing II deployment. Mitterand's concern now was to preserve his credibility which meant standing by the zero option.

The *British* government also remained skeptical, but domestic motives prevented it from voicing its own reservations as unambigously as France had done. After all, Margaret Thatcher was in the middle of an election campaign and both the Labour Party and the Liberal-Social Democratic Alliance supported nuclear disarmament, though each emphasized different aspects. In the aforementioned Reagan-Thatcher communiqué of November 15, there was no longer any mention of eliminating INF in Europe. It was merely stated that «priority should be given to an INF agreement with restraints on shorter-range systems».[25]

Finally, the Americans faced overt rejection from *NATO headquarters* in Brussels. NATO Supreme Allied Commander Rogers and his deputy Mack made it clear that they considered the zero option a mistake. Rogers said that the very idea of withdrawing Pershing II from Europe

---

25 Quoted from *ACR*, no.12, 1986, p.403.B.413.

would give him «gas pains». A zero option on LRINF should be linked to
reductions of short-range INF and conventional weapons. It was extremely unusual how sharply Rogers, himself not only NATO Supreme
Commander but also the Chief of American troops in Europe, criticized
his own government in public.[26]

In the fall and winter of 1986 there were frantic efforts within NATO
and between the Alliance partners to develop a consensus on the outcome of Reykjavik and the Geneva negotiations. Not even NATO's Defense Planning Committee could bring itself to support the zero option
unequivocally. The Americans worked diligently to persuade their West
European allies to support their negotiating position from Reykjavik. In
the meantime, the proposal had been formally presented at Geneva.
Their efforts apparently received particular support from the West
German government, which for domestic reasons alone (parliamentary
elections) could not afford to appear to support the opponents of disarmament (cf. 4.4 on debate in Bonn). It was not until a meeting of the
foreign ministers in the NATO Council that the Washington-Bonn axis
could finally assert itself. Here too, however, the U.S. Administration
had to give up its proposal for the elimination of *all* ballistic missiles for
the sake of Alliance cohesion. In return it received backing for the zero
option on INF. The countries involved in the INF deployment decision
(i.e., *excluding France*) «fully» supported the contemplated elimination of
these weapons in Europe on condition that it was followed by immediate
negotiations on SRINF.[27]

The *Geneva negotiations* between the U.S. and the Soviet Union initially remained unaffected by the conflicts within NATO. The two parties concentrated on clarifying what exactly Reagan and Gorbachev had
agreed to in Reykjavik. Aside from the fact that the Soviets insisted on
the linkage between INF and the other negotiating tables, a number of
problems remained unsolved. The main sticking point was still short-
range weapons. The U.S. insisted on global constraints on SRINF in the
ranges between the SS-23 (500 km) and the SS-12 mod «Scaleboard»
(900 km), with an upper limit at the present Soviet level. Negotiations

26 Cf. «Skeptische Militärs im Nato-Hauptquartier,» *FAZ*, October 29, 1986;
    «Pact on Mid-Range Arms Harmful to NATO, Alliance Commander Says,»
    International Herald Tribune (IHT), November 17, 1986; «Null-Lösung nicht
    isoliert betrachten,» *FAZ*, November 27, 1986.

27 See *ACR*, no.12, 1986, pp.403.B.418/419.

on the reduction of SRINF were to begin within six months of the signing of a first treaty. Should these follow-up talks not achieve any results, the Americans would have the right to match the Soviet level. The main concern was to establish *de jure* equal rights. A decision on specific systems had been reached neither in Washington nor in NATO. The Soviet proposal for a freeze, on the other hand, would have meant that the U.S. would have been denied the right to *de jure* parity.

In addition to the SRINF issue, the following points had still to be clarified at the start of the seventh round of negotiations on January 15, 1987:

- Where exactly the permitted 100 warheads for longer-range INF were to be based;
- Which procedure should be adopted for the verification of a treaty;
- Within what timetable the reductions should take place.

The turning point in negotiations came on February 28. *General Secretary Gorbachev once again severed the linkage between INF and ABM and thus opened the way for a separate INF treaty*: «The Soviet Union proposes that the problem of intermediate-range missiles in Europe be removed from the general complex of problems and that a special treaty be concluded on these missiles as soon as possible.»[28]

Why Gorbachev indulged in this to-ing and fro-ing on the negotiating linkage remains a mystery. Possibly the Soviet strategy after Reykjavik had failed. In terms of foreign policy, the creation of a package deal could only have been designed to put Reagan under increased pressure - via the West Europeans and U.S. Congress - to make concessions on SDI and the ABM treaty. Now that an INF treaty was a real possibility, the aim was that NATO should persuade the U.S. not to let the vague possibility of «star wars» stand in the way of such a historic settlement. If this was the Soviet tactic, then it failed. The American position on the ABM treaty only hardened after the summit meeting. Moreover, the Alliance had enough to do in coming to terms with the outcome of Reykjavik. The Soviet negotiating package was ideally suited to the aims of some of the zero option opponents. Finally, if the Soviet leadership wished to conclude an arms control treaty with the Reagan Administration at all, then it would have to be signed in the course of 1987 so that it could be ratified by the Senate before summer 1988 when the U.S.

---

28 Gorbachev's declaration quoted in *FAZ*, March 2, 1987.

presidential election would have reached fever pitch. Time was running out, therefore, for diplomatic maneuvering. By severing the negotiating link once again, Gorbachev unmistakeably signaled how much a treaty with Ronald Reagan meant to him.

The Soviet General Secretary then went one step further. He indicated that it would be possible to reach an agreement on short-range systems. Once a treaty had been signed on the elimination of LRINF systems in Europe, the USSR would remove the SS-12 mod missiles from East Germany and Czechoslovakia (where they had been based since 1984 to «counter» Western INF deployment) to Soviet territory. Such a move had been hinted at several times by the Soviets and in particular by the East German SED leader Erich Honecker; Gorbachev made it official. Finally, he declared that the Soviet Union was prepared to enter into immediate negotiations on the reduction and elimination of the remaining «operative tactical missiles», i.e., SRINF.

While the Americans greeted the Soviet change of position unreservedly, the reaction of the NATO allies was more subdued but nevertheless positive. After all, they had become accustomed to the idea that a zero option might come about after all.

Gorbachev's declaration was greeted positively by the *British* government. It expressed its acceptance of a zero option which had been proposed by the West almost six years previously and which excluded British and French weapons. Nevertheless, Prime Minister Thatcher repeatedly referred to the issue of short-range missiles and insisted on a solution for them in connection with a treaty. London was afraid the Soviets might make an additional offer of a zero option for SRINF. The British argued that before consenting to follow-up negotiations on the elimination of these missiles, it should be examined whether new missiles with a range below 1,000 km could be used to compensate for the loss of Pershing II, which in their opinion would weaken deterrence. Therefore, during her visit to Moscow at the end of March, Prime Minister Thatcher stood firm on the U.S. right to compensate for Soviet superiority in these weapons.

France voiced harsh criticism once more. With the exception of the Communists, the representatives of all parties agreed that Gorbachev's proposal might, in the words of the former Defense Minister Quilès, be a mere ploy. The leader of the Liberal-Conservative parliamentary group in the French National Assembly, Gaudin, even presumed to claim that the zero option would lead to a «European Munich». He seems to have mirrored the sentiments of the Conservative party leaders Raymond Barre, Valéry Giscard d'Estaing, and François Léotard. The Foreign Ministry declared that to postpone the issue of short-range missiles to later negotiations was an unsatisfactory solution. It was once again President Mitterand who finally committed his government to the zero option. He had, after all, fought his presidential campaign in 1981 under the slogan «neither Pershing II nor SS-20». On March 4, President Mitterand, Prime Minister Chirac, Foreign Minister Raimond, and Defense Minister Giraud declared: «If a negotiation on Euromissiles takes place between the two superpowers, France naturally would not be hostile to it, on the condition, of course, that the process results in balanced, simultaneous and controlled reduction.»[29] Later Mitterand declared his support for the zero option publicly.

This time the *NATO military* voiced differing opinions. Supreme Allied Commander Rogers declared once more that the loss of Pershing II would give him «gas pains» and made his consent to the zero option conditional on the elimination of conventional disparity in Europe. The new chairman of NATO's Military Committee and former Chief of Staff of the *Bundeswehr*, General Altenburg, contradicted him publicly. He warmly welcomed Gorbachev's declaration on grounds that it seemed to offer solutions for those issues which the military considered problematic. Since the proposal recognized that NATO was particularly interested in the reduction of Soviet short-range missiles, deterrence would not be endangered, he said. Altenburg specifically rejected jeopardizing an INF treaty by linking it to conventional arms control.[30]

The response of the *West German government* to Gorbachev's declaration was equally enthusiastic. The events in Bonn just six weeks later, therefore, caused all the more surprise in Washington, London, Paris, Brussels, and presumeably in Moscow. For, on April 14, during a visit by U.S. Secretary of State Shultz to Moscow, General Secretary Gorbachev removed the last remaining major obstacle to an INF treaty. He offered an «extended zero option» which was to also include short-range INF

---

29 Quoted from *ACR*, no. 3, 1987, pp.403.B.429. See also the excellent account of British and French reactions, ibid., pp.403.B.427-430, 458. On France see also «Angst vor einem 'europäischen München',» *Die Zeit*, March 13, 1987; «Mitterand für Null-Lösung,» *SZ*, March 9, 1987.

30 Cf. *ACR*, no.3, 1987, pp.403.B.430/431; «Genscher hofft auf Abrüstung nach 1987,» *SZ*, March 3, 1987.

(500-1,000 km). A performance was now staged in Bonn which was to delay the decision-making process in the Alliance and indirectly the U.S.-Soviet negotiations by six weeks.

4.4 Between Zero and Double Zero: The Debate in Bonn

What happened within the CDU/CSU during spring 1987 was not totally unexpected but had been brewing for some time. It was clear that those Christian Democrats who had always rejected Social-Liberal détente policy and who felt that the maintenance of Western deterrence capability was the major security policy concern[31] would only support the zero option as long as the Soviet Union failed to take it up. Some of them - the Bavarian Prime Minister Franz Josef Strauss, for example - had rejected the Western offer back in 1981 (cf. 3.3). For this «peace through strength» wing of the CDU/CSU, the military justification of INF («coupling», implementation of flexible response) was decisive and ruled out total renunciation of Pershing II and cruise missiles.

Once a zero option really seemed to be in the cards, this group began to articulate its criticism, initially in spring 1986 when Gorbachev proposed a European zero option (cf. 4.2) and in particular on February 19 when it was heard that the West German Chancellor had written to the U.S. President in support of the offer.

Fronts were formed at this time which remained valid for all subsequent debates on INF. The pattern of argument also remained similar. The European zero option was criticized, but the true concern was *any* renunciation of Pershing II and cruise missiles, regardless of the form of the negotiating framework. Among its critics were the right-wing of the CDU/CSU, in particular the parliamentary working group on defense, the Bavarian CSU, some of the party's foreign policy experts and, finally, the chairman of the parliamentary group, Alfred Dregger. The parliamentary spokesman on defense policy, Willy Wimmer, declared that there was no reason to make the Soviet Union into some kind of sanctuary. Alfred Dregger stressed that, if Western intermediate-range

---

31   For details see Thomas Risse-Kappen, *Die Krise der Sicherheitspolitik. Neuorientierungen und Entscheidungsprozesse im politischen System der Bundesrepublik Deutschland, 1977-84* (Mainz-München: Grünewald-Kaiser, 1988).

missiles were withdrawn, West Germany would face an even greater threat from remaining Soviet nuclear weapons in the absence of a counterbalance. In February 1986, Dregger accepted the zero option on condition that the Soviets withdraw all their short-range missiles. The conservative critics were backed by the top echelons of the West German Defense Ministry, although Minister Wörner himself did not publicly deviate from the West German government's position. The critics were also given press backing by the *Frankfurter Allgemeine Zeitung* which conducted a veritable campaign against the zero option. In an editorial entitled «The Truth About the Zero Option», which appeared February 22, Karl Feldmeyer wrote:

> «Offering a zero option ... was the final step open to NATO to improve the chances of the then Chancellor Schmidt, of getting modernization accepted ... Schmidt who was uncertain from the outset of his party's support, had originally hoped to make his position more plausible by presenting Pershing II as a weapon which would compensate for the SS-20 which then led to the conclusion that, should Moscow abandon the SS-20, NATO's buildup would no longer be necessary. However, none of this had anything to do with the real situation ... Even before SS-20 deployment, NATO ... had become aware of its own requirements of modern medium-range weapons ...The consistent Soviet arms buildup of the sixties and seventies cost the West its so-called escalation dominance ... This loss of superiority was to be compensated by cruise and Pershing II missiles from the beginning. Since they are capable of reaching Soviet territory from Western Europe, they represent an existential threat to the Soviet Union at the moment that the Soviets attack Western Europe.»[32]

This line of argument emphasizing the military-strategic justification of NATO's double-track decision was vigorously contested by the FDP, in particular by Foreign Minister Genscher. Genscher declared that the zero option had been supported by both the present and previous West German governments. He expected that all those who had called for a zero option in the past would stand by their position and not abandon it simply because Gorbachev appeared ready to accept it. The detractors in the CDU/CSU were also subjected to contradiction by other party members. The «Genscherist» and deputy chairman of the parliamentary group, Volker Rühe, declared that West Germany would never have

---

32 «Die Wahrheit über die Null-Lösung,» *FAZ*, February 22, 1986. See also «Die Union sieht in Gorbatschows Angebot 'Kampf um die Seelen',» *FAZ*, February 21, 1986.

based the Pershing if the Soviet Union had not deployed its SS-20 missiles. Modernization could not be justified by military factors alone. Rühe likewise argued, albeit wrongly (cf. 2.), that the danger of West Germany's «decoupling» from the nuclear protection of the U.S. had only been presented as justification later. Defense Minister Wörner argued along similar lines. Wolfgang Altenburg, at that time still the *Bundeswehr's* Chief of Staff, indicated that the zero option would create problems for NATO's military strategy but spoke in its favor for domestic reasons: «None of us, and I include myself as a soldier, is going to challenge a true zero option for the simple reason that no-one can deny mankind's wish for a denuclearized world.»[33]

Six months later, prior to the Reykjavik summit, the critics of a zero option were equally unable to greatly influence the position of the West German government. Whether for tactical reasons or reasons of principle, the debate was focused increasingly on the problem of short-range missiles. The public prelude to this was a *Frankfurter Allgemeine Zeitung* report from August 15, 1986, based on information which seems to have been leaked by the West German Defense Ministry. It called for a new Western negotiating approach in which SRINF *below* a 500 km range would also be included in concurrent constraints.[34]

The West had no missiles deployed with ranges between 150 and 500 km, the East had almost 600 Scud missiles of an older type. Introduced in 1965, with a range of up to 300 km, the Scuds were to be replaced by the SS-23 (which, because of their 500 km range, were included in the original Western SRINF negotiating approach, the very objective of which was to prevent Scud modernization). Alfred Dregger now argued that these weapons constituted a particular threat to West Germany: «The acceptance of this threat in a treaty which would only deal with longer-range INF would be inconsistent with the principles of equal security and the strategic unity of NATO. Thus it would call into question the political purpose of the Alliance.»[35]

---

33 General Altenburg, interview with the *Kölner Stadt-Anzeiger*, March 14, 1986. See also «Genscher pocht auf Null-Lösung,» *FR*, February 22, 1986; «Hat Bonn eine Nachbesserung durchgesetzt?,» *FAZ*, February 26, 1986.

34 «Es geht nicht nur um eine neue 'Grauzone',» *FAZ*, August 15, 1986.

35 Dregger in an interview with the *FAZ*: «Die Union will Raketen kürzerer Reichweite einbezogen wissen,» *FAZ*, September 30, 1986.

To date people were only used to hearing such sharp criticism of the U.S. and NATO from the peace movements, the Greens or the left-wing of the SPD. Dregger's comments were a foretaste of what would happen six months later in Bonn. One might suspect that short-range missiles had now been assigned the task of preventing an INF treaty as a whole. The zero option on *long-range* INF could no longer be questioned, if only for domestic reasons. After all, the impending federal elections of January 1987 had to be taken into account.

Once again it was Foreign Minister Genscher who opposed these demands. He insisted that the call for the inclusion of missiles below 500 km must not be allowed to block the first step (i.e., the treaty on the reduction of SS-20, Pershing II, and cruise missiles). Genscher warned against «discovering» new conditions.

On September 30, there was a reportedly passionate debate in the Chancellery at the end of which Genscher's line of argument gained general acceptance. According to the West German government, an initial INF treaty should first of all reduce the longer-range missiles, setting equal global and regional ceilings, and, secondly, include constraints on SRINF with ranges of 500-1,000 km. A ceiling in keeping with Soviet actual numbers was envisaged (ca. 160 missiles worldwide) which would grant the U.S. the principal right to arm up to this level. This was of course consistent with the American negotiating position. In addition, the West German government asked that in an initial treaty both sides enter a binding commitment for follow-up negotiations on the missiles with ranges of 150-500 km, again with the aim of setting an equal and global ceiling. This was the position which Bonn presented during Alliance consultations prior to the U.S.-Soviet summit meeting in Reykjavik. Obviously, no-one had given serious consideration to adopting zero as the limit. The Defense Ministry could not get its condition accepted that limitations of these weapons be negotiated in a *first* treaty. [36]

While the settlements envisaged in Reykjavik caused shocked reactions in other West European capitals, Bonn remained calm this time round. Only cautious criticism of the European zero option was expressed. After all, the West German government had already accepted the proposal in spring. The deputy leader of the CDU/CSU parliamen-

---

36 Cf. «Bonn will Zusage weiterer Verhandlungen über Raketen kürzerer Reichweite,» *FAZ*, October 1, 1986; «Bonn dringt auf Zwischenabkommen,» *FAZ*, October 3, 1986.

tary group, Rühe, succeeded in backing up the Chancellor in the *Bundestag* faction. However, the West German government remained committed to the condition that follow-up negotiations for short-range missiles be negotiated in a first INF treaty. In the governmental declaration of November 6, 1986, Chancellor Kohl defined the West German position as follows:

- Support of the zero option on long-range INF;
- Concrete commitment to further negotiations on SRINF with the objective of reducing them and agreeing on equal ceilings for both sides;
- Call for conventional arms control in the event of nuclear weapons reductions exceeding the 50% envisaged in the first phase of START;
- Observance of the ABM treaty and agreement on its interpretation by the two superpowers until a new settlement could be agreed;
- The necessity of continuous and intensive consultations in the Alliance.[37]

The West German government argued in NATO that the Alliance should give the fullest possible backing to the results achieved in Reykjavik concerning INF. In *this* phase of the Alliance decision-making process, the Bonn government, above all Foreign Minister Genscher, pursued an active arms control policy. Aside from U.S. pressure, it was due to the West Germans that the NATO Council gave its approval to the zero option in December 1986 (cf. 4.3).

It was no surprise, therefore, that General Secretary Gorbachev's severing of the linkage between INF and ABM at the end of February 1987 was greeted with approval by all parties. In his governmental declaration of March 18, Chancellor Kohl reaffirmed his government's position:

«The West German government is in agreement with the INF settlement as envisaged in Reykjavik ... One concern ... remains the serious Soviet superiority in short-range INF. The West German government, therefore, expects both superpowers to enter into a concrete and binding agreement to conduct immediate follow-up negotiations on shorter-range systems. The aim of these

---

37 Cf. Helmut Kohl's declaration before the *Bundestag*, November 6, 1986, *Bulletin*, no.135, 1986, pp.1131/1132.

negotiations has to be to reduce all the systems to a low level with equal common ceilings.»[38]

In the debate two days later, all the speakers expressed their support for a zero option. However, Alfred Dregger and the chairman of the CSU group, Theo Waigel, pointed out the risks which this would involve. Dregger also expressed serious doubts concerning the continuation of America's nuclear guarantee for Western Europe. The more U.S. systems were withdrawn from Europe, the more important the British and French nuclear weapons would become for the non-nuclear weapons states on the continent. There would have to be a discussion, he argued, on how the deterrence effect of these forces could be extended to those allies who did not have nuclear weapons.

Dregger's deputy Volker Rühe, however, disassociated himself from such considerations. The military presence of the U.S. and her nuclear protection for Western Europe were indispensible and could not be replaced by an independent European project. The fact that Dregger and Rühe publicly set completely different priorities seemed to indicate a new round of the old controversy dating back to the sixties between «Atlanticists» and «Gaullists» in the CDU/CSU. At that time it had been President Kennedy's détente policy which had aroused the mistrust of the conservatives and triggered the search for European alternatives to the U.S. guarantee. Now it was a reaction to a possible American-Soviet settlement on intermediate-range weapons.

In February and March 1987, it became increasingly clear that Bonn's call for follow-up negotiations on *all* SRINF, which enjoyed broad political backing at home (the SPD was even asking for a separate zero option), met with little acceptance in NATO. The proposal may have been compatible with the *Soviet* negotiating position but not with the American stance. The Americans demanded, and were supported in this by the British government, concurrent constraints for missiles with ranges between 500 and 1,000 km in a first INF treaty but rejected follow-up negotiations for the remaining systems. The modernization of NATO's short-range potential, above all the Lance missile, was more important to them than the reduction of Soviet superiority.

---

38 Kohl's declaration before the *Bundestag*, March 18, 1987, quoted from *SzS*, no.4, 1987, pp.2-7, 7. On what follows, see the extracts from the debate, ibid., pp.8-16.

The American demand for equal ceilings for SRINF was also motivated by considerations of weapons procurement. In the event of a zero
option on LRINF Pershing II could be converted to a modern shorter-
range Pershing IB by removing the missile's second stage. Following the
replacement of the then 108 Pershing IA missiles of the U.S. Army
(range: 720 km) by Pershing II (range: 1,800 km) as part of NATO's
modernization, this increase in range was now to be reversed. Instead of
*dis*armament, *re*armament by converting LRINF into SRINF!

In Bonn, the possible conversion of Pershing II to Pershing IB made
for heated discussions. After all, the reduced-range missiles would of
course have to be based in West Germany. This led to the re-establish-
ment of the usual fronts between the Defense Ministry and the Foreign
Office. Manfred Wörner declared that the Americans must reserve the
right to equal levels of SRINF since a negotiating success was otherwise
unthinkable. His Undersecretary Ruehl even considered it to be normal
procedure to convert weapons systems - an unusual assessment given the
political sensitivity of the issue. Foreign Minister Genscher, on the other
hand, declared:

> «There is no doubt at all that the Pershing II presently based in West Ger-
> many ... will of course be withdrawn. That was the essence of the NATO dou-
> ble-track decision and is also the opinion in the Western Alliance ... And we
> state clearly that these systems must be withdrawn from West Germany as
> stipulated in the zero option.»[39]

The West German Chancellor who wished to avoid a new debate on nuclear modernization backed up his foreign minister. He reaffirmed publicly a fact which had been made known to the U.S. President weeks earlier, namely that a conversion of Pershing II was out of question.

Nevertheless, further consideration was given by the West German
Defense Ministry to new short-range nuclear weapons for NATO. In the
first draft of a letter to be sent by Kohl to Reagan which apparently
stemmed from the Defense Ministry, it was stated that the West German
government was striving for the modernization of the 72 Pershing IA
systems whose launchers were under control of the West German Air

---

39 Hans Dietrich Genscher, interview with the radio station *Deutschlandfunk*,
    April 2, 1987, quoted from *SzS*, no.4, 1987, p.42. See also Wörner's inter-
    view with the radio station *Süddeutscher Rundfunk*, March 27, 1987, ibid.,
    p.28; Lothar Ruehl's interview with *Deutschlandfunk*, March 25, 1987, ibid.,
    pp.38/39.

Force, as well as the development of a successor to the outdated Lance systems. The weapon under consideration was the U.S. Army's Tactical Missile System (ATACMS) with a variable range (200-450 km). Possibly due to Genscher's intervention, the final version of Kohl's letter reiterated Bonn's old position that it was striving for follow-up negotiations on the systems below 500 km instead of modernizing them.[40]

Once again those in West Germany who wished to prevent a zero option did not succeed in the domestic debate. When in April 1987 Gorbachev then made an offer for an «extended zero option» to include missiles with ranges between 500 and 1,000 km, the patience of the right-wing of the CDU/CSU and the top echelons of the West German Defense Ministry was exhausted. Subsequently, the arguments against renouncing Pershing II and in favor of modernizing Pershing IA were mixed with genuine concern over the Soviet superiority of short-range weapons which would remain after a double-zero option. The ensuing confusion was considerable.

The West German government found itself in an almost hopeless situation. On the one hand, large sections of the CDU/CSU parliamentary group revolted. On the other hand, U.S. pressure to accept «double zero» was growing. Not only this, President Reagan and Secretary of State Shultz were frankly enthusiastic about the double-zero option.

After all, concurrent constraints for SRINF had been demanded since 1981 and the lowest equal ceiling was, of course, zero. However, the allies were to be consulted before the United States took a decision. During a special meeting of NATO's foreign ministers in mid-April, George Shultz informed the allies of his talks in Moscow and asked them to choose between three possible responses to Gorbachev's proposals:[41]

- *Acceptance* of the extended zero option;
- *Rejection* of any zero option and a continuation of modernization up to the planned 572 Pershing II and cruise missiles;
- *Modification* of the Soviet offer, i.e., to consent to the zero option on LRINF but to insist on a low equal ceiling for systems between 500 and 1,000 km of approximately 50 to 100 weapons while arming up to this level with new missiles.

---

40 Cf. «Kohl Wants New Short-Range Missiles,» *IHT*, April 9, 1987.

41 See «Gorbachev Missiles Plan: An Offer Hard to Refuse,» *IHT*, April 23, 1987. Also «Shultz: Zweite Null-Lösung keine Schwächung,» *FAZ*, April 24, 1987.

Speaking before the NATO Council, the U.S. Secretary of State gave a clear indication of the option he favored. A week later Shultz asked the Alliance publicly to decide between «arms buildup or disarmament». It was difficult to see, he argued, how the extended zero option would weaken Western Europe's defense. NATO should decide whether to accept Gorbachev's offer or whether to settle on «something in between», i.e., reducing Soviet SRINF and deploying new Western systems.

The new Pershing IB missiles would primarily have to be based on West German territory. Chancellor Kohl was thus placed in the unpleasant position of having to decide between acceptance of a the double zero option and gaining approval at home for further modernization as the result of a U.S.-Soviet INF disarmament treaty. The middle course, «a right to equal common ceilings», was no longer possible.

In West Germany there was a complete reversal of political fronts. On the one side stood the peace movements, the Greens, SPD, and FDP in line with Ronald Reagan and Richard Perle in favor of «double zero». Foreign Minister Genscher did not commit himself in public but pursued a press policy which made it clear that he was likewise in favor of Gorbachev's proposals. On the other side stood, as was to be expected, the Defense Ministry, the CSU and the right wing of the CDU headed by Alfred Dregger. What was unusual was that Volker Rühe, who belonged to the moderate wing of the CDU/CSU, led the opposition against Moscow's proposal. Rühe declared that one should first concentrate on achieving a zero option on long-range INF then continue step-by-step without overburdening the INF treaty. He obviously overlooked the fact that it was the Americans who had insisted on collateral restrictions on SRINF in a first treaty. Rühe further said: «It is not in German security interests to negotiate further zero options before the East's threefold superiority in the conventional area has been reduced.»[42]

Moreover, West Germany would face a special threat as a result of the double zero option, due to the remaining short-range weapons. «The shorter the ranges the deader the Germans» became a standard quota-

---

42   «Rühe warnt Genscher vor Alleingängen in der Abrüstungspolitik,» *FAZ*, April 23, 1987. See also «NATO: Atomwaffen in Westeuropa zur Abschrekkung weiterhin nötig,» *SZ*, April 15, 1987; «In Bonn wird die Zustimmung Kohls zur doppelten Null-Lösung erwartet,» *SZ*, April 25/26, 1987; «Meinungsunterschiede in der Koalition über Gorbatschows Abrüstungsvorschläge,» *SZ*, April 21, 1987.

tion of opponents of the zero option. Rühe travelled to Washington to present German reservations. After Kohl's Minister of State in the Chancellery, Wolfgang Schäuble, had also voiced cautious skepticism, there was no stopping the CDU/CSU parliamentary group which launched into vigorous opposition of Moscow's offer. The belief was obviously that the Chancellor shared the reservations of his confidants Rühe and Schäuble. Kohl, who was still enjoying his Easter vacation when opinion was formed in his parliamentary group, was no longer able to control the debate. On April 27, there was a meeting in the Chancellery between Ministers Genscher, Wörner, Zimmermann (representing the CSU) and Schäuble. After a three-hour debate it was decided to defer the decision. Genscher who had the backing of the FDP, spoke afterwards of the «government's most difficult situation» since its formation in fall 1982.[43]

The arguments put forward by arms control opponents became increasingly confused. Alfred Dregger argued that the extended zero option could only be accepted once parity had been achieved in the range below 500 km, in chemical weapons, and in conventional forces. The parliamentary disarmament policy spokesman, Todenhöfer, spoke out against *any* zero option and proposed that a minimum reserve of nuclear missiles of every range be kept. On the other hand, the CSU foreign policy spokeswoman, Michaela Geiger, called for an additional zero option on the Soviet Scud missiles. Member of the *Bundestag* Friedmann even suggested establishing a linkage between disarmament and German reunification. Only CDU Secretary-General Geissler indicated that he did not reject the extended zero option and felt strongly that the INF treaty should not be overburdened by adding further conditions.[44]

Given these conflicting arguments, one might ask what the real issue of the debate was. For all practical purposes there were only two alternatives: *either* one rejected the elimination of the Pershing II LRINF missile *or* one decided in favor of modernization for the ranges between 500 and 1,000 km. For some such as Jürgen Todenhöfer, criticism of the ex-

---

43 Cf. «Bundesregierung vertagt die Entscheidung über ihre Haltung zur doppelten Null-Lösung,» *SZ*, April 28, 1987; «Genscher spricht von der schwierigsten Situation der Regierung seit 1982,» *FAZ*, April 28, 1987.

44 Cf. «Rühe: Bundesregierung ist im westlichen Bündnis nicht isoliert,» *FAZ*, May 2, 1987; «Meinungsstreit über Null-Lösung auch in der Union,» *FAZ*, May 4, 1987; «Zusammenhang zwischen Abrüstung und deutscher Frage hergestellt,» *FAZ*, May 6, 1987.

tended zero option was nothing more than a pretext for the rejection of the zero option on *LRINF*. Some of the arguments used against «double zero», e.g., the decoupling issue, were, thus, aimed at «zero long-range». Even Defense Minister Wörner spoke out against such an argument:

> «Neither coupling nor decoupling can ever be assigned to a single weapons system. They stem primarily from political will and this is nowhere more strongly expressed than in the stationing of over 300,000 American soldiers. We will not be without means with which to strike Soviet territory from Western Europe. After all, apart from the American aircraft deployed in Great Britain, there are also submarines which are assigned to SACEUR.»[45]

Wörner thus rounded off the subject. As for the argument that the loss of Pershing II would leave a gap in the escalation spectrum of the NATO strategy, well-advanced ideas of how to compensate for this already existed. Both NATO's Nuclear Planning Group (NPG) and its High Level Group (HLG) had, since the Reykjavik summit, discussed which of the remaining systems not affected by arms control should take over the missions of Pershing II and ground-launched cruise missiles and could threaten targets in the Western Soviet Union. Four possible options emerged:

- Equipping the approximately 150 U.S. F-111 fighter-aircraft deployed in Great Britain and the 72 FB-111 bombers based in the United States with air-launched cruise missiles (ALCM), and eventually making more F-111 available;
- Sea-launched cruise missiles (SLCM) either on surface ships or on modernized Poseidon submarines;
- Assigning part of the F-15E fighter aircraft scheduled for basing in 1989 a nuclear role.[46]

If, however, renunciation of LRINF was thought an acceptable sacrifice, then the only motive for rejection of the *extended* zero option had to be the wish to upgrade short-range weapons. Obviously Pershing IB was at stake and more specifically the conversion of the 108 Pershing II missiles and the modernization of 72 Pershing IA missiles, whose launchers were

---

45 Manfred Wörner's speech before the *Atlantik-Brücke*, Berlin, April 8, 1987, *Bulletin*, no.36, 1987, pp.305-307, 307.

46 See «To Reassure its Allies, U.S. Considers Placing More Nuclear Arms in Europe,» *IHT*, May 13, 1987; «Allies Weigh New Deployments To Offset Proposed INF Cuts,» *Aviation Week and Space Technology* (AW&ST), May 18, 1987, pp.18-20.

under West German control. As of 1991, there would be no more spare parts for this system which was first deployed in 1962. Plans for a Pershing IB had already existed during the term of the Social-Liberal government. Kohl's government specified the plans. At the end of June 1987, Undersecretary of Defense Würzbach confirmed in the *Bundestag* that the West German government had taken the necessary steps to study the military requirements for a follow-on system to Pershing IA. A decision had not yet been taken, however.[47]

The logical conclusion seemed indeed that specific modernization plans stood in the way of the double zero option. The arguments put forward in public by arms control opponents were for the most part without factual foundation. It was only possible, for example, to talk of the remaining Soviet short-range missiles posing a special threat to the FRG by concentrating alone on *ballistic missiles* and then emphasizing the short-range systems. Of course, the Soviet Union would have the means to threaten all West European countries even after the elimination of land-based INF with nuclear weapons using aircraft or even ICBMs and SLBMs (cf. table 7, pp.160/161). The «singularization of threat» argument was, therefore, not only wrong but also, after all, not an objection to the zero option but a plea for further disarmament moves in the area of shorter-range missiles. A «triple» zero option starting at 150 km meaning the unilateral disarmament of the Soviet Scud missiles as called for by peace researchers and the SPD was not, however, proposed by the CDU/CSU. It was charged this would lead to the denuclearization of Europe. Yet even after a triple zero option both sides would have possessed enough nuclear weapons to make any attack in Europe - even a conventional one - a risk no-one would be willing to take.

Just how much the missile debate paralyzed the ruling coalition was evident on May 7 in the *Bundestag*. With the exception of Chancellor Kohl who did not commit himself, the CDU/CSU speakers reaffirmed their rejection of the double zero proposal. They faced a united front of supporters made up of FDP, SPD, and Greens. FDP parliamentary group leader Wolfgang Mischnick declared:

» ... (T)he USSR has offered to strive for a zero option on the intermediate-range weapons with ranges of 500-1,000 km. If the numbers are correct, that

---

47 See «Luftwaffe will neue Pershings,» *SZ*, April 13, 1987; Q&A time in the *Bundestag*, June 24, 1987, *PlPr* 11/19, pp.1172-1179.

would mean that the USSR would scrap unilaterally 160 missiles of the said ranges. My parliamentary group not only thinks that this proposal is worthy of consideration but that it is highly desirable and worth striving for.»[48]

Foreign Minister Genscher responded to this by saying his colleague Mischnick's remarks were «worth serious consideration by us all». Though Genscher did not commit himself, he did contradict the various arguments put forward by the critics in Bonn.

West Germany's West European allies found it increasingly difficult to understand the complicated position of the CDU/CSU - *yes* to the zero option on long-range INF, *no* to the zero option on SRINF, *«yes and no»* to short-range modernization.

True, there was criticism in *Washington* also, but it was directed at the loss of the Pershing II and cruise missiles and less at the zero option on SRINF. Here too, there was a reversal of fronts. The zero option was approved by a coalition of right-wing unilateralists like Richard Perle and Caspar Weinberger and the firm supporters of arms control such as Spurgeon Keeny, Walter Slocombe and Paul Warnke, who were responsible for arms control under the Carter Administration. The U.S. Atlanticists, on the other hand, were divided. Paul Nitze and James Schlesinger, the former Defense Secretary, were in favor. Henry Kissinger, Brent Scowcroft (former Security Advisor) and the chairmen of the two Armed Services Committees in Congress, Rep. Les Aspin and Sen. Sam Nunn remained skeptical. While Nunn pointed above all to the Warsaw Pact's conventional superiority in Europe, Aspin stressed that it would have been better to begin arms control with a reduction of battlefield weapons. Within the Administration, the Special Advisor on arms control, Edward Rowny, voiced criticism. He was brought back into line by Reagan, however. Reagan, Shultz, and Weinberger stood firm on their approval of the zero option. Now it was up to the Europeans.[49]

---

48 Wolfgang Mischnick's speech in the *Bundestag*, May 7, 1987, *PlPr* 11/10, p.543. See also ibid., pp.524-565.

49 See «Nunn Calls for Conventional Upgrades To Balance Possible Nuclear Cuts,» *AW&ST*, April 20, 1987, pp.30/31; «Debate on Ending Missiles in Europe Dividing Experts,» *IHT*, April 24, 1987; Paul Nitze's article in *WP*, April 24, 1987; Les Aspin, «Eliminate Battlefield Nuclear Weapons First,» *WP*, April 27, 1987; «Senate Leadership Warns President Against 'Rushing' Into Euromissile Pact,» *AW&ST*, April 27, 1987, pp.40/41; «Reagan: Poindexter An 'Honorable Man',» *WP*, April 29, 1987.

Just how difficult it would be for the West German government to voice its reservations towards the extended zero option became clear as early as during the meeting of the Western European Union on April 28 in Luxemburg. The Benelux countries, Italy, Spain, Norway, and Denmark all spoke out in favor of the Soviet offer. At the beginning of May, Chancellor Kohl received a letter from *London* in which Prime Minister Thatcher expressed her approval of the double zero proposal and urged the West German government to reach a decision quickly. When this brought no results, the British government, which was in the midst of its election campaign, publicly announced its position. On May 14, it was made known that the Thatcher government accepted «double zero» provided the following terms were met:

- *worldwide* elimination of SRINF;
- exclusion of the 72 West German Pershing IA missiles from a treaty.[50]

When the Nuclear Planning Group convened in Stavanger, Norway, in mid-May, Defense Minister Wörner was largely isolated. His reservations were supported only by NATO Supreme Allied Commander Rogers. Furthermore, a majority opinion emerged in the NPG that an additional arms agreement on the missiles below 500 km was out of the question. Such a «firewall» was not acceptable to the West German government regardless of all its internal controversies. The fact that such considerations received acceptance in Stavanger, however, showed how isolated Bonn was at this time.[51]

Domestically too, the position of the CDU/CSU became increasingly difficult. Surveys revealed that 90% of the population - including the overwhelming majority of CDU/CSU voters were in favor of the zero option. Two-thirds did not believe that the loss of Pershing II would lead to a less credible American nuclear guarantee for Europe. Representatives of both churches had committed themselves more or less clearly to the acceptance of the Soviet proposal. Former Chancellor Helmut

---

50 Cf. «Die WEU will sich Zeit nehmen,» *SZ*, April 29, 1987; «U.K. Says It Can Accept Soviet Plan,» *IHT*, May 15, 1987.

51 Cf. «London für doppelte Null-Lösung. Nachrüstung bei den Kurzstreckenraketen,» *FAZ*, May 15, 1987; «Wörner beinahe isoliert,» *FR*, May 15, 1987; «Nach dem langen Tag in Stavanger war Wörners Traum zu Ende,» *FAZ*, May 16, 1987.

Schmidt said that the critics had no cause to quote him and came out strongly in favor of «double zero».[52]

On May 15, with the official declaration from London behind him and state elections in Rhineland-Palatinate and Hamburg to come, Chancellor Kohl made a personal statement. It was in West Germany's best interest that negotiations not only deal with one section of weapons: «A settlement for weapons with ranges between 500 and 1,000 km would exclude the very weapons which pose a particular threat to our country. Therefore, the weapons of all ranges from 0-1,000 km must be dealt with.»[53] This declaration, on which Kohl had not consulted Genscher, further increased the confusion regarding Bonn's position. Was Kohl now in favor of an absolute zero option? This was promptly denied.

In the state elections the CDU suffered heavy losses to the FDP, a fact which the CDU party executive blamed on the missile debate. That did not prevent the discussion within the CDU from becoming increasingly grotesque. Dregger said in a meeting of the parliamentary group that NATO would lose its moral importance if a zero option were to come about which failed to include short-range missiles in negotiations. At his request, MP Friedmann presented a paper which linked German reunification to the disarmament issue.[54] This time, however, Chancellor Kohl was able to nip the debate on the national question in the bud.

In the end, the critics of the zero option in the CDU/CSU lost their last international ally, France. The French government had adopted a cautious stance in the whole controversy, though Foreign Minister Raimond and Defense Minister Giraud expressed their scepticism on nu-

52 Cf. Helmut Schmidt, «Null-Lösung im deutschen Interesse,» *Die Zeit*, May 8, 1987, p.3; «Im Wortlaut: Bischof Kamphaus: Null-Lösung nicht blockieren,» *FR*, May 6, 1987; «EKD: Chance zu Abrüstung nicht vertun,» *SZ*, May 19, 1987. On opinion poll data see Hans Rattinger, «The INF Agreement and Public Opinion in West Germany,» paper prepared for the conference on *Canadian and German Perspectives on East-West Arms Control*, Toronto, Can., March 10-12, 1988.

53 Declaration by the Chancellor, May 15, 1987, according to *deutsche presseagentur*.

54 See «Die Aussprache über den Wahlausgang gilt der Raketenfrage,» *FAZ*, May 19, 1987; «Halblaute Kritik an der Führung der Union nach den Wahlniederlagen in Mainz und Hamburg,» *FAZ*, May 20, 1987; «Wiedervereinigung als Sicherheitskonzept,» *FAZ*, May 20, 1987.

merous occasions. Prime Minister Chirac also voiced his criticism. On May 21, President Mitterand put an end to the speculation concerning the French position and declared his acceptance of the extended zero option.[55]

Thus the West German government was isolated both at home and abroad. The CDU/CSU began a disorderly retreat. On May 24, the CDU regional party conference in Baden-Württemberg announced its support for the double zero option. In the end, the position of Foreign Minister Genscher and the FDP gained almost 100% acceptance. On June 1, after six weeks of to-ing and fro-ing, the West German government issued a resolution whose key sentences read:

«The West German government is in favor of negotiations to bring about step-by-step reductions, which should be substantial and verifiable, of the remaining U.S. and Soviet ground-launched nuclear systems with ranges between 0 and 1,000 km. Such negotiations should be held in context with the establishment of conventional parity and the worldwide elimination of chemical weapons. A first step would be for the United States and the Soviet Union to sign an agreement that they will not possess any further short-range INF missiles (500-1,000 km) worldwide. ... The West German government continues to hold that the 72 Pershing IA missiles cannot be included in the current negotiations. On this point we are in agreement with the U.S. and its allies.»[56]

In the CDU/CSU parliamentary group, the declaration was perceived for what it was, the surrender of the critics. Heated debates ensued. In his governmental declaration of June 4, Chancellor Kohl did not venture to mention the extended zero option specifically. In retrospect, the controversy surrounding the double zero option was in part the result of coalition mismanagement by the government. It revealed the weakness of Chancellor Kohl's own particular brand of leadership; he left his own party too long in the dark over his own preference. This quickly led to the international isolation of the government and reduced its scope of action so that it had no alternative in the end but to give in. Kohl allowed his party to pose as «worldpower no.3» for too long. However, the missile debate also showed that the «peace through strength» wing of the

---

55   On the French position see *ACR*, no.5, 1987, p.403.B.471; «Chirac will Kohl den Rücken stärken,» *SZ*, May 22, 1987; «Zwischen Kohl und Mitterand Meinungsunterschiede über die zweite Null-Lösung,» *FAZ*, May 23, 1987.

56   Declaration of the West German government, June 1, 1987, quoted from *FAZ*, June 2, 1987.

CDU/CSU and the conservative strategy experts who in the seventies had supported INF modernization with the «decoupling» argument (cf. 2.), were no longer in a position to dominate the domestic debate.

After the CDU/CSU had given up its resistance and the West German government had declared its support for the double zero proposal, the way was open for a NATO decision. On June 11-12, 1987, in Reykjavik, the NATO Council expressed its support for the worldwide elimination of all U.S. and Soviet ground-lauched missiles with ranges between 500 and 5,500 km. The West German government was able to get its call for follow-up negotiations for the remaining short-range missiles included in the communiqué, albeit in vague terms, despite British and American reservations. NATO proposed, «in conjunction with the establishment of a conventional balance and the global elimination of chemical weapons, tangible and verifiable reductions of American and Soviet land-based nuclear systems of shorter range leading to equal ceilings.»[57]

This formulation was a compromise which could not disguise the fact that NATO was deeply divided over the further treatment of the short-range missiles beyond the double zero option. This was to emerge just a few months later during an NPG meeting in Monterey.

Kohl had scarcely brought himself to support the double zero proposal when the next problem arose. To the surprise of the U.S. and NATO, the USSR had made a call already on April 27 - i.e, after the Shultz's visit to Moscow - for the destruction of the 72 U.S. warheads for the Pershing IA missiles (720 km) based in West Germany under the «double key arrangements» in the framework of an INF treaty. The U.S. government promptly rejected any such notion and stressed that it was impermissable that the «established pattern of nuclear cooperation» within NATO be influenced by bilateral U.S.-Soviet agreements. (There were even some references - albeit wrongly - to «third-party systems» in connection with the Pershing IA.) This had indeed long been Alliance practice. Cooperation agreements such as existed between the U.S. and West Germany on the Pershing IA were signed with all NATO countries who had U.S. nuclear weapons on their soil or provided the launchers for such weapons. If the call had been given in to, then a precedent would have been created with unforeseeable consequences for the sensitive framework of nuclear cooperation within NATO. There was unani-

---

57   Declaration of the NATO Council meeting, June 11/12, 1987, quoted from
     ACR, no.7, 1987, p.403.B.503.

mous agreement on the fact that the established pattern of nuclear co-operation should be kept out of superpower arms control. The U.S. government, therefore, refrained from trying to influence the position of the West German government on the Pershing IA issue, as it had done over the double zero option.[58]

However, it became clear in the course of the summer, that the Soviet call was not simply a negotiating tactic but was to be taken seriously. Moscow's pressure on Bonn increased steadily, culminating in a harsh speech by Foreign Minister Shevardnadze before the Disarmament Commission of the United Nations.[59] In fact, the Soviet call for the inclusion of the Pershing IA was justified to a far greater extent than its earlier insistence on the counting of the French and British nuclear weapons. Keeping the Pershing IA out of arms control, in the same way as the French and British nuclear weapons, would have blurred West Germany's non-nuclear status. After all, the Americans had no control over the French and British warheads. The Pershing IA warheads, on the other hand, belonged to America *alone* who would thus have sole responsibility for making a possible employment decision.

There was only one plausible way out of the dilemma. West Germany had to declare its unilateral renunciation of the Pershing IA or, rather, of the missile's modernization. Soviet negotiators indicated that this would be an acceptable solution.[60] Indeed the Soviet aim could only be to prevent the planned modernization of the Pershing IA. The missiles themselves were outdated; as of 1992 the company that produced them, Martin Marietta, would not have produced any more spare parts, anyhow.

The real subject of the domestic debate surrounding the Pershing IA was its modernization. The usual fronts formed, with the Defense Ministry and the right-wing of the CDU/CSU on the one side and the FDP (supported by the opposition parties) on the other. Foreign Minister Genscher did not commit himself in public but stressed that West Germany would do everything in its power to pave the way for an INF

---

58   This judgement is founded on interviews conducted by the author with government officials. Cf. also «New Soviet Obstacle Seen on Missile Pact,» *IHT*, April 29, 1987; «USA besorgt über Bonner Raketendebatte,» *SZ*, August 19, 1987.

59   See the extract from Shevardnadze's speech, *ACR*, no.9, 1987, p.403.B.531.

60   See «Moscow Will Consider Pershing Compromise,» *IHT*, August 4, 1987.

treaty.[61] In the end, Chancellor Kohl showed decisiveness. After consultation with the U.S. government, with the Foreign Minister, and with the leader of the CDU/CSU parliamentary group, but *without* informing the Bavarian CSU, he declared on August 26, 1987:

> «If an agreement on the worldwide ban of all medium-range missiles is reached in Geneva between the U.S. and the Soviet Union, if in particular the still open verification issues are solved in a way that is satisfactory to all sides, if such an INF agreement has been ratified by the contracting parties and become effective, and if, at last, the contracting parties keep to the agreed timetable for the elimination of their weapons systems, under these conditions I am prepared to state today that, with the definitive elimination of all Soviet and U.S. medium-range missiles, the Pershing-I-A missiles will not be modernized but dismantled.»[62]

Thus the problem of Pershing IA was largely solved. The U.S. and the Soviet Union both welcomed Kohl's decision unanimously. There was, however, a hefty altercation with the *CSU* which felt it had been passed over and linked the subject to the quarrel on domestic policy strategy within the Christian Democratic Party. On September 1, the CSU issued a ten-point declaration which summarized once again the party's criticism of the double zero option and which was apparently written largely by Franz Josef Strauss himself:

> «It is unacceptable that the Alliance be divided into three zones of varying degrees of security, with absolute risk for West Germany, reduced risk for the European partners and minimal risk for the allies on the other side of the ocean. This would not be the purpose of the Alliance. It would lead inevitably to a reorientation of West German policy. ... For this reason the zero option I was problematic and the zero option II with its direct inclusion of Pershing IA is wrong, because our position will be considerably worse after it comes into effect than before modernization.»[63]

The barely disguised threat to leave NATO shows how out of touch with reality the critics of the zero option were. The text's lack of factual foundation (it completely ignored the strategic nuclear weaponry of both su-

---

61   See «Genscher: Bonn will Null-Lösung fördern,» *KStA*, August 26, 1987; «Bewegt sich FDP hin zur SPD-Position?,» ibid.

62   Quoted from *ACR*, no.9, 1987, p.403.B.536. See also «Strauss: Mit Freunden abstimmen, nicht nur mit Genscher telefonieren,» *FAZ*, September 5, 1987.

63   «Die Null-Lösung II ist falsch,» *FAZ*, September 2, 1987. See also «Kohl mehr als vier Stunden bei Strauss in München,» *FAZ*, September 4, 1987.

perpowers, for example), also showed that the critics in Bonn had lost the battle. The resignation of the CDU/CSU's parliamentary spokesman for disarmament, Jürgen Todenhöfer, was an indication of this fact. He was replaced by Karl Lamers, a loyal supporter of the Kohl/Rühe position in the *Bundestag* faction.

4.5 The Home Stretch: Negotiating the INF Treaty

While the debates within the Alliance and in Bonn continued, the U.S.-Soviet negotiations were progressing at a fair pace. Gorbachev's severing of the linkage between INF and SDI at the end of February had given new momentum. The two sides now worked on the completion of a treaty which was to be signed that same year. However, the small print of the treaty brought a number of sensitive problems. On March 4, the U.S. presented a 40-page draft treaty in Geneva which included the agreements reached in Reykjavik but in more precise terms. It would have allowed conversion of ground-launched to sea-launched cruise missiles and Pershing II to shorter-range Pershing IB. This concept was immediately rejected by the Soviets.[64]

A further issue on which attention focused was *verification*. In the U.S., the Pentagon was able to gain acceptance for a proposal which rested on extensive on-site inspections. The Joint Chiefs of Staff showed reluctance, fearing that the Soviets would in the end be granted too many opportunities to gather information on militarily sensitive U.S. facilities. The West Europeans were likewise cautious. As inspection measures were foreseen for the missile sites of the Pershings and cruise missiles, the consent of the deployment countries would have to be obtained.

In mid-March, the Americans introduced a verification proposal in Geneva, based on the Pentagon draft which contained the most comprehensive verification measures in the history of East-West arms control. The proposal included the following points:[65]

---

64 Cf. «U.S. Missile Plan is Said to Limit Soviet Warheads To 100 in Siberia,» *IHT*, March 3, 1987; «Soviet Said to Agree to Inspection of Europe Missile Sites,» *IHT*, March 6, 1987.

65 See «Details of INF Verification Proposal Released by U.S.,» March 12, 1987, *USPIT*; *ACR*, no.3, pp.403.B.436, 438, 445/446; «Intelligence Officials Say Arms Inspections Must Exempt Some U.S. Sites,» *IHT*, June 4, 1987.

144   *Chapter 4*

- comprehensive exchange of data on missiles and their production and storage facilities which was to be checked by on-site inspections;
- on-site monitoring of the destruction, dismantling, or conversion of medium-range systems, both at missile sites and at production and storage facilities;
- permanent monitoring of certain production facilities, as well as repair and storage facilities for the remaining missiles, by some 100 inspectors on each side;
- previously agreed U.S. and Soviet sites to be subject to monitoring at short notice - «on-challenge inspections».

To the suprise of all those who had believed that the Soviets would never buy such a proposal, the Soviet arms control expert Victor Karpov declared that the USSR was in favor of on-site or challenge inspections if necessary either on Soviet, British, or West German territory. The USSR would willingly send inspectors to Greenham Common (the British cruise missile base). The Soviets' own draft treaty, presented in Geneva on April 27, contained verification measures which were truly in the spirit of «glasnost». On-site inspections were to take place at the missile sites, the facilities for the destruction and testing of missiles, at other military bases, and at production and storage facilities. They should not be restricted to monitoring the gates of the facilities in question; the inspectors should be allowed to enter the production sites themselves.[66]

Although negotiations on verification issues progressed much more quickly than even optimistic observers had expected, the question of *short-range missiles* remained the main bone of contention. As already mentioned, the visit by Shultz to Moscow from April 13 to 15 brought the decisive breakthrough when Gorbachev offered the double zero option.

The double zero proposal meant that Gorbachev was prepared to forgo modernization of the Soviet short-range missiles for the time being. The Soviets had already begun to replace the outdated Scud missiles (300 km) with the SS-23 (500 km). NATO considered the SS-23 to be the main candidate for a new military option. It was feared that the accuracy of these missiles could increase in the nineties in such a way that they

---

66 See «Soviet Said,» note 64; «Kreml kommt NATO mehr entgegen,» *FR*, April 29, 1987; *ACR*, no.3, pp.403.B.446; no.5, 1987, pp.403.B.476; «Soviets Won't Boost Gulf Fleet,» *IHT*, June 8, 1987.

could threaten important military targets of NATO using *conventional* warheads. The Soviet offer, therefore, was not just a concession over and above renunciation of the SS-20, it meant the elimination of a new Soviet military option.[67] The extended zero option was an offer of preventive arms control.

Two points connected with the Soviet offer remained unclear, however:

- Were the short-range missiles to be eliminated *worldwide* or only *in Europe*? The Soviet position presented in Geneva at the end of April referred only to the SRINF based in the European zone.
- What was to be done with the 72 Pershing IA missiles whose launchers belonged to the West German *Luftwaffe*? Nothing was said on this in Moscow. However, in Geneva, the Soviets later called for the scrapping of the *warheads* which were under American control (cf. 4.4).

The Soviet General Secretary did not receive a reply from Washington until two months later, after the West German missile debate was over (cf. 4.4). On June 16, 1987, the U.S. presented NATO's position on the SRINF in Geneva:

- *global* elimination of all ground-launched medium-range missiles with ranges between 500 and 1,000 km;
- non-inclusion of nuclear forces (such as Pershing IA) which were part of NATO's «established pattern of nuclear cooperation».

At the beginning of July, press reports indicated that the Soviet leadership was prepared to accept the double zero option worldwide on condition that the U.S. forgo converting its ground-launched to sea-based cruise missiles and Pershing II to Pershing IB. Further, a satisfactory solution still had to be found for the Pershing IA.[68] The corresponding Soviet offer followed shortly afterwards. *On July 21, General Secretary Gorbachev accepted the global elimination of all ground-launched INF missiles with ranges between 500 and 5,500 km.* This was exactly what Richard Perle had proposed as the Western negotiating position in fall 1981 and for which he had failed to gain acceptance (cf. 3.3).

---

67   For details, see Thomas Risse-Kappen (ed.), *ATBMs and West European Security* (Frankfurt am Main: PRIF report no.4, October 1987).

68   See «U.S. is Said to Favor New Proposal on Arms Accord Offered by Soviet,» *IHT*, July 2, 1987. See also *ACR*, no.7, 1987, pp.403.B.502/503.

A week later, the U.S. replied to the Soviet concession by finally agreeing to forgo conversion of ground-launched cruise missiles (GLCMs) and Pershing II to other systems. In summer 1987, the following sticking points still remained:

- treatment of Pershing IA;
- details of verification;
- details of destruction of the systems to be eliminated;
- timetable for scrapping.

At the end of August, the U.S. introduced a new verification proposal in Geneva which was a considerably watered down version of their previous offer. The official reason given was that the total elimination of the INF systems required less stringent verification provisions than would be the case if both sides were to have kept 100 warheads, as was envisaged in Reykjavik. In reality, the new verification offer was the result of vigorous infighting in the U.S. Administration itself. Above all, intelligence agencies disapproved of letting Soviet inspectors get too close a look at U.S. military facilities. American arms companies also grew increasingly nervous. They were backed by Bonn and London. In the meantime, Moscow was calling for challenge inspections to be conducted at the military bases of America's allies.

It was for these reasons that the U.S. proposal contained two important changes as compared to previous offers:[69]

- Challenge inspections would take place only at a limited number of previously agreed military facilities, particularly at former deployment areas, and even here for not more than 10 years after destruction of the last weapons.
- The call for regular on-site monitoring of missile production facilities was dropped.

In mid-September the Soviet Foreign Minister Shevardnadze paid a further visit to Washington during which settlements were reached concerning the dismantlement of warheads, and the inspection of missile sites, test areas, and repair, storage, and maintenance facilities. Originally, the USSR had called for the destruction of the warheads. The two

---

69 See «U.S. Offers Measures to 'Simplify' Arms Treaty Verification,» *IHT*, August 26, 1987; «Kurz vor dem Ziel,» *FAZ*, August 29, 1987; *ACR*, no.9, 1987, p.403.B.538; «Soviet INF Plant Visits Concern Pentagon,» *AW&ST*, November 9, 1987, p.25.

sides now agreed that only the re-entry vehicles and parts of the guidance systems should be destroyed, while the nuclear material and certain
sensitive parts of the guidance systems should be returned to the respective national arsenals. The U.S. assured the Soviets that the warheads of the Pershing IA would be dealt with in the same way, once the
cooperation agreement with West Germany had expired, in keeping
with Chancellor Kohl's declaration (cf. 4.4). While the U.S. now assumed
that the Pershing IA question was settled, the Soviets brought the subject
up again in October and insisted that a formal assurance be included in
the treaty.[70]

In Geneva work continued at a furious pace to finalize the treaty. On
October 22/23, the Soviet Foreign Minister and U.S. Secretary of State
met once more. In Moscow, agreement was reached on a timetable for
the destruction of the missiles (18 months after the treaty's entry into
force for SRINF; 3 years for LRINF), and the two sides came closer on
the verification issues. Both sides gave way on Pershing IA. Though the
system is not specifically mentioned, the Elimination Protocol stipulates
that the reentry vehicles of missiles which had been released by a unilateral decision from cooperation agreements should likewise be destroyed
within fifteen days of the final date envisaged for the destruction of the
INF systems.[71] After Gorbachev had been unwilling to set a date for the
summit to sign the treaty - presumably the *Politburo* had yet to make a
decision - the two sides announced a week later that President Reagan
and the Soviet General Secretary would meet in Washington for their
third summit, from December 7-10.

In November, a final obstacle emerged. The United States called for
the right to inspect the production facility of the Soviet mobile intercontinental missile, the SS-25, whose first propulsion stage was identical to
that of the SS-20. This had been known for some time. It seems likely,
therefore, that the American call was made in connection with the
growing domestic criticism of the treaty's contents by the extreme right.
As the date for the treaty's signature drew nearer, the criticism by opponents of any form of arms control became increasingly vociferous in the
U.S. Originally, they had given their wholehearted support to the Rea-

---

70 See *ACR*, no.9, 1987, pp.403.B.545-549; «U.S., Soviet Reach Arms Pact,»
    IHT, September 19/20, 1987; «Soviet Hitch in Arms Pact Seen,» *IHT*, Octo-
    ber 10/11, 1987.

71 Cf. *ACR*, no.10, 1987, pp.403.B.556-559.

gan Administration. Now they had to stand by and see the President on
the point of concluding a treaty with the «evil empire». In the Senate,
which had to ratify the INF treaty with a two-thirds majority (i.e., at least
67 of 100 votes) the number of principal opponents of arms control was
estimated at 15-20 senators. During a television show shortly before the
summit, Vice President Bush was the only Republican presidential candidate prepared to support the treaty. Even the Minority Leader in the
Senate, Robert Dole, would not commit himself. (However, during the
summit meeting he spoke in positive terms of the treaty and later, during the ratification debate, he was crucial to ensure bi-partisan support
for the agreement.)[72]

Although it was highly unlikely that the Soviet Union would convert
the more modern SS-25 to an SS-20 and thus violate the INF treaty, the
U.S. insisted on permanent inspectors at the gates of the Soviet missile
factory in Votkinsk («parameter portal monitoring») which produced the
SS-20, the SS-25, and other missiles. In a countermove, the USSR demanded that an American factory producing cruise missiles be subject to
a similar regulation. The U.S. rejected this, not wishing to provide the
Soviets with the chance to see the production of their advanced ALCMs
and SLCMs. Finally, the Americans consented to allow Soviet inspectors
to permanently monitor the Hercules Aerospace Cooperation in Magna,
Utah, which produced the rocket motors of the Pershing II. Further, a
division of General Dynamics in San Diego belonging to the government in which the launchers for the ground-launched cruise missiles had
been produced was made available for regular challenge inspections as
foreseen by the treaty.

This final agreement was reached a fortnight before the signing of
the treaty during a final meeting of the two foreign ministers in Geneva.
Work continued almost up to the last minute, to complete the treaty and
compare the translations. Just two hours after General Secretary Gorbachev had landed in Washington, the plane carrying the treaty text,
ready for signature, arrived in the American capital. *On December 8,*

---

72 Cf. «Lawmakers Predict Battle in Congress Over Missile Treaty,» *IHT*,
November 2, 1987; «Ratification Battle Expected in U.S. Senate,» *IHT*,
November 26, 1987. On the issue of the SS-25 see «Neuer Stolperstein in
Genf?,» *FR*, November 17, 1987; «Moscow to Let U.S. Inspect Missile
Plant,» *IHT*, November 20, 1987; «Pact Would Allow Soviet Officials To In-
spect U.S. Missile Plants,» AW&ST, November 30, 1987, pp.16-19.

shortly before 2:00 p.m. local time, President Reagan and General Secretary Gorbachev signed the treaty on the global elimination of all ground-launched missiles with ranges beween 500 and 5,500 km.

Ratification of the INF treaty by the U.S. Senate proved more difficult, but also simpler in the end than expected. Problems arose out of two issues. When the treaty came under scrutiny by the Senate's Foreign Relations and Armed Services Committees, it turned out that some of its verification provisions were obviously not defined precisely enough to allow common U.S.-Soviet understanding. The issue could be quickly resolved, however, during a Shultz-Shevardnadze meeting in Geneva in early May 1988. The second problem which arose during the ratification debate had nothing to do with the INF treaty as such, but all the more with the ongoing battle between the Administration and Congress on the ABM treaty interpretation. Senator Sam Nunn, who was dedicated in the ABM debate to preserving the constitutional rights of Congress, wanted to make it absolutely clear that the INF treaty, first all of, bans futuristic technologies as well as existing weapons systems and, secondly, that the treaty's interpretation by Congress during ratification would bind any future U.S. government.[73] In the end, the issue was equally resolved by a U.S.-Soviet understanding that the treaty indeed covered exotic technologies and by a compromise worked out between the Administration and the democratic majority of Congress that future interpretations of the INF treaty by another U.S. government would not be legally binding.

Ratification of the INF treaty was also simpler than had to be expected. It quickly turned out that the conservative opponents of the agreement were unable to gather enough support for their concerns. The leading critic, Senator Jesse Helms, became more and more isolated during the ratification debate. In the end, two days before the beginning of the Reagan-Gorbachev Moscow summit on May 29, 1988, an overwhelming majority of 93 U.S. Senators approved the INF treaty. Ratification documents were exchanged during the Moscow summit.

---

73 See, e.g., «Futuristic Technology Issue May Delay Senate Action on INF,» AW&ST, April 11, 1988, p.105.

4.6 «Each Party Shall Eliminate Its Intermediate-Range and Shorter-Range Missiles (and) Not Have Such Systems Thereafter»: The INF Treaty[74]

The «Treaty between the United States of America and the Union of Soviet Socialist Republics on the Elimination of their Intermediate-range and Shorter-range Missiles» consists of:

- the *Treaty* containing 17 articles;
- the *Memorandum of Understanding Regarding the Establishment of the Data Base* on the numbers of deployed and otherwise stored systems, on the missile bases, the storage sites, as well as the testing, production, and maintenance facilities;
- the *Protocol on Procedures Governing the Elimination* of ballistic and cruise missiles subject to the treaty;
- the *Protocol Regarding Inspections*, with an annex containing the agreed verification procedures.

Article I of the treaty states in succinct terms that each side should eliminate its INF systems. The missiles, their operating bases and support facilities are defined in *Article II*. Articles II.5 and II.6 distinguish between intermediate-range (1,000-5,500 km, LRINF in NATO/U.S. language) and shorter-range missiles (500-1,000 km, SRINF in NATO usage), and between ground-launched ballistic missiles (GLBM) and cruise missiles (GLCM).

Article III lists the systems to be eliminated. On the Soviet side, the SS-20, SS-4, SS-5, SS-12, and SS-23, and on the American side, Pershing II, the BGM-109G cruise missile, and Pershing IA (i.e., the reserve systems stored in the U.S.). Article X.6 adds the Soviet cruise missile SSC-X-4 and the American Pershing IB which both had been tested but not yet deployed.

The data memorandum brought some surprises. It was common knowledge that both sides had produced substantially larger numbers of systems than they had deployed. This includes reloading stocks, missiles for testing purposes, reserves, etc. As a result, both sides must scrap a to-

74 Art. I of the INF treaty. The agreement and its protocols are published in *USPIT*, Special Edition, December 10, 1987.

tal of 3,472 cruise missiles with almost 4,000 warheads (including the 72 Pershing IA missiles belonging to the *Bundeswehr* and the 84 SSC-X-4 cruise missiles already produced by the Soviets; see table 6 for details).

Most suprising was the fact that the Soviet Union had deployed considerably more shorter-range missiles according to its own data than had been assumed by NATO in its published force comparisons. Most of the 167 SS-23 missiles, for example, had obviously been deployed shortly before the completion of the INF treaty. Equally suprising was that the USSR had already produced 84 SSC-X-4 ground-launched cruise missiles with a range of 1,800 km.[75] On the other hand, the Soviets have 40 SS-20s less in deployment according to their figures than Western estimates supposed. This discrepancy is obviously due to the fact that NATO judged more SS-20 missiles to be operative than were located at the declared missile sites. The reload and reserve numbers are not overwhelming at 245 systems. On the other hand, it emerged that both sides had considerable numbers of non-deployed shorter-range weapons, the USSR over 539 SS-12 and SS-23 in reserve, the U.S. over 170 Pershing IA stored in the United States.

Article IV of the treaty stipulates long-range INF systems and all equipment and maintenance facilities must be destroyed within three years. The elimination of the weapons should take place in two phases. After two-and-a-half years each side may *possess* launchers for only 200 warheads and is permitted to *deploy* missiles with no more than 180 warheads, and launchers for 171 warheads. Further, the ratio of ballistic missiles to cruise missiles must remain the same as it was in November 1, 1987. This regulation affects the U.S. which has to dismantle its Pershing II and GLCMs in the ratio of 1:1.8 (November 1, 1987: 247 Pershing, 442 cruise missiles), i.e., it may not possess Pershing II missiles alone in two-and-a-half years. The regulation means that the Soviet Union may only keep 60 SS-20 missiles in deployment, with a maximum of 57 launchers. The U.S. may have deployed a further 64 Pershing II missiles as well as 116 cruise missiles after 30 months.

---

75 Cf. «Moscow Numbers on Missiles Differ Widely From U.S. Data,» *IHT*, December 17, 1987.

Table 6: Missiles to be Eliminated According to the INF Treaty

	deployed	non-deployed[1]	training	total
1. LRINF (1,000-5,500 km)				
a) USSR				
SS-20 (5,000 km)	405	245	42	692
SS-4 (2,000 km)	65	105	147	317
SS-5 (2,300 km)	-	6	-	6
total	470	356	189	1,015
b) USA				
Pershing II (1,800 km)	120[2]	127	178	425
GLCM (2,500 km)	309[2]	133	3	445
total	429	260	181	870
c) total missiles	899	616	370	1,885
total warheads[3]				2,815
2. SRINF (500-1,000 km)				
a) USSR				
SS-12 (900 km)	220	506	185	911
SS-23 (500 km)	167	33	96	296
total	387	539	281	1,207
b) USA				
Pershing IA (720 km)	-	170	54	224
c) USA/FRG[4]				
Pershing IA	72	?	?	72?
d) total missiles	459	709?	335?	1,503?
3. Missiles Tested				
a) USSR				
SSC-X-4 GLCM	-	84	-	84
b) USA				
Pershing IB	-	-	-	-

total missiles to be eliminated	1,358	1,409	705	3,472
total warheads[3]				3,983

1   missiles stored in a support facility (production, storage, testing, maintenance) as defined by the treaty;
2   including 12 Pershing II and 35 GLCM reserve missiles at the missile operating bases;
3   not including training missiles or those in the testing phase (SS-20x3);
4   not part of the treaty but also to be eliminated in accordance with the declaration of Chancellor Kohl of August 26, 1987, and Article II.9 of the Protocol on Elimination.

Source: *«Memorandum of Understanding Regarding the Establishment of the Data Base» of the INF treaty.*

When the INF missiles are brought to the elimination facilities, they should arrive in complete organizational units (Art. X.3). Thirty days after the treaty's coming into force, neither side may still have missiles or launchers stored at production sites or testing facilities.

Article V lays down the procedure for the destruction of the shorter-range missiles which must be completed after 18 months. To this end the systems including their launchers, are to be taken to specially designated elimination locations. A further stipulation is that the destruction facilities for the missiles and those for the launchers must be over 1,000 km apart. The aim here is to ensure that the missiles are no longer operable once they have reached their elimination facilities.

The arrangements for the destruction itself are laid down in the *Protocol on Elimination.* Distinctions are to be made between launchers, missiles, and reentry vehicles. With regard to the *launchers*, the erector launcher mechanisms will be dismantled from the launcher chassis and cut into two pieces. The same happens to the chassis. The SS-20 will have its launcher chassis shortened by about 80 cm at the rear axle and can then by used for other purposes. The Pershing II trucks can also be returned to the U.S. arsenals once all the instruments and devices which serve to launch the missile have been removed.

As for the *missiles*, first of all the reentry vehicles will be removed, i.e., the front sections that carry the warheads dismantled. Rocket stages may either be burned or exploded. The airframe of the cruise missiles will be cut in two pieces lengthwise. Within the first six months after the treaty comes into effect, each side may, according to Article X.5, destroy up to 100 missiles by launching them. The *reentry vehicles* will be crushed, once the nuclear warheads and parts of the guidance system have been removed. These will likewise be returned to the national arsenals. The nuclear material may be re-used for either military or civilian purposes.

Article VI of the treaty contains a general ban on production and testing for all existing and future intermediate- and short-range systems. Exempted from this is the use of stages which are externally similar to those of INF systems, for ground-launched missiles not limited by the treaty (Art. VI.2). This affects the Soviet SS-25 ICBM (cf. 4.5). Surface-to-air missiles are likewise excluded from this arrangement (Art. VII.3), i.e., air-defense systems and tactical missile defenses (ATBMs). There is no ban on the launching of sea- or air-launched missiles (e.g. ALCMs and SLCMs) from fixed, land-based launchers for test purposes (Art. VII.11). Finally, both sides may continue to use boosters which would otherwise count as medium- or short-range systems, provided that their stages can be distinguished from those limited by the INF treaty. They may, however, only be used for research and development purposes in specially designated testing facilities; the maximum number of launchers allowed is 35 (Art. VII.12).

The *verification of treaty compliance* is set out both in the main treaty and in the Protocol on Verification. Aside from the generally permitted national technical means, e.g., satellite monitoring (Art. XII), the INF treaty allows *on-site inspections* for the following purposes:
- verification of the data provided by both sides;
- monitoring the destruction of systems and the dismantling of operating bases, repair and maintenance facilities;
- challenge inspections of facilities identified in the Memorandum of Understanding;
- permanent monitoring of two production facilities.

The «Memorandum of Understanding» establishes the data base on the INF systems and their maintenance and repair facilities as of November 1, 1987. Not later than 30 days after the treaty has come into effect both sides must have brought these figures up to date (Art. IX.3). In addition, they are to be brought up to date every six months. For the purpose of data verification, both sides may conduct on-site inspections at all missile bases and missile support sites with the exclusion of missile production facilities. Apart from the deployment areas, these are, according to Article II.9, launcher production facilities, testing, repair, and training sites, storage facilities, and missile elimination sites. The «Memorandum of Understanding» lists these facilities separately, namely 19 in the U.S., 12 in Western Europe, 7 in Eastern Europe, and 77 in the Soviet Union. Verification of data base, for which each side may appoint up to 200 inspectors, must be complete 90 days after the treaty has come into effect. Inspection of the missiles is to be by external observation; the inspectors further have the right to monitor the immediate vicinity of each facility in question.

The second type of on-site inspection is concerned with the monitoring of the destruction of weapons systems and the dismantlement of deployment sites and repair and maintenance facilities (Art. XI.4). The elimination of the missiles and their launchers can be monitored at the designated destruction locations, either during or after scrapping (Art. XI.7 and 8). The elimination of missile bases and repair and maintenance facilities can be monitored by inspectors within 60 days of their previously announced retirement. Again this does not apply to missile production facilities (Art. XI.4).

Over and above this, both sides have the right to conduct challenge inspections for 13 years after entry into force of the treaty, either to check data specifications or to ensure that former missile bases or testing, repair, and maintenance facilities are not being used contrary to the terms of the treaty (Art. XI.5). Within the first three years, 20 such challenge inspections may be conducted annually, 15 in the following five years, and in the final five years 10 annually. The facilities subject to these inspections are likewise listed in the «Memorandum of Understanding». Again, missile production facilities are excluded. This is where both sides draw the line on on-site inspections so as to ensure that sensitive military secrets do not become subject to «legalized spying». Strictly speaking, therefore, both the U.S. and the USSR could continue to produce INF missiles in secret. However, since the production facilities for the launchers are subject to challenge inspections, likewise deployment areas and testing equipment, they would not be able to make these missiles operational.

Two missile production factories will be subject to permanent on-site inspection, however, in accordance with Article XI.6. The facilities in question are the Votkinsk Machine Building Plant which produced the

SS-20 and still produces the SS-25 and other Soviet missiles. The U.S. insisted on parameter portal monitoring since the propulsion stage of the SS-25 is similar to that of the SS-20. In reciprocity, the Soviet Union was granted the same right of monitoring at the entrance of the missile factory Hercules Plant No.1 in the U.S. state of Utah. The motors for Pershing II were produced here.

In order to be able to distinguish between mobile ICBMs like the SS-25 and prohibited intermediate-range weapons, it was further agreed in Article XII.3 that, on the request of one side, the roofs of all fixed structures at the launchers bases concerned must be opened and the missiles be displayed to allow the missiles to be counted on their launchers via satellite.

Two commissions were assigned with cooperative monitoring of treaty observance and achieving settlements for problems regarding verification. To this purpose a Special Verification Commission was created. In addition, the Nuclear Risk Reduction Centers, which were set up in summer 1987, were tasked with the exchange of data and the announcement of dates for the elimination of systems, as foreseen in the treaty (Art. XIII).

Analogous to Article XIII of the SALT II treaty, Article XIV of the INF treaty stipulates that none of the parties may «assume any international obligations or undertakings which would conflict with its provisions». This applies to future cooperation agreements between the U.S. and NATO members (as well as between the USSR and WTO members) - «double key arrangements» - regarding missiles with ranges between 500 and 5,500 km.

The INF treaty is valid indefinitely, but contains in Article XV.2 the usual right of withdrawal on six months notice should one side decide that «extraordinary events related to the subject matter of this Treaty have jeopardized its supreme interests». This article also corresponds to the provisions in the SALT treaties.

Provided that both sides comply with the INF treaty, there will be no more U.S. or Soviet ground-launched missiles within the specified ranges by approximately mid-1991.

5

Conclusions

5.1 A First Step: An Evaluation of the INF Treaty

In the past ten years, there has been an extensive debate on the pros and cons of negotiated arms control. The concept of cooperative arms control became subject to increasing criticism from both the left and the right. Most experts came to the conclusion that negotiated arms control had no chance of success:

> «Anyone seeking weapons reductions today through negotiated arms control to the levels achieved in say 1965, might just as well propose total disarmament in these negotiations - neither proposal would have the slightest chance of success. Conclusion: any hopes that arms control policies would have a decisive political effect on the dynamics of the arms race have not been fulfilled. Arms control has not led to disarmament.»[1]

Meanwhile, the INF treaty shows that negotiated arms control under certain conditions can lead to substantial results for both sides:
- This is the first genuine disarmament treaty in the nuclear area. It would be incorrect to speak of «levelling-up» in this instance, i.e., setting high ceilings and building up to these levels. Double zero, on the contrary, will result in the scrapping of more than 3,400 missiles with almost 4,000 warheads (see table 6, pp.152/153).
- The treaty will bring about the elimination of newly-developed weapons on both sides (exceptions: SS-4, SS-5, Pershing IA) and not, as was often the case in previous arms control, the withdrawal from

---

1   Volker Böge, «Rüstungssteuerung am Ende - mit einseitig-unabhängiger Abrüstung einen neuen Anfang machen!,» in *Sicherheitspolitik kontrovers*, eds. W. Heisenberg/D.S. Lutz (Bonn: Bundeszentrale für politische Bildung, 1987), pp.737-750, 737.

service of missiles which were obsolete anyway. By now, the Pershing II is still among the most modern nuclear weapons in the American arsenals.

- In a quantitative sense, asymmetric arms reductions have proved to be possible. The USSR has to eliminate about twice as many missiles and about three times as many nuclear warheads as the West. Yet, a comparison on a purely numerical basis is misleading. If one takes into account qualitative parameters - in particular how military options are to be affected - then one can truly speak of a balanced treaty. While disarmament on the Soviet side involves greater numbers, NATO and the U.S. will forgo, once and for all, deploying ground-launched missiles in Western Europe capable of reaching hardened military targets in the Soviet Union within in a very short flight-time.

- Moreover, the treaty increases stability in Europe considerably. It eliminates highly modern counterforce weapons which could strike military targets on both sides, not only with extreme accuracy but with little or no advance warning time. This at least was the evaluation of those who considered the SS-20 to represent a strategic threat to Western Europe,[2] as well as of those who rejected the Pershing II due to its short flight time.[3] The elimination of INF thus improves crisis stability in Europe. Equally, the arms race in land-based missiles of the specified ranges has come to an end. Finally, one has to consider the political gains for East-West détente in Europe.

- The INF treaty finally represents a dramatic improvement of verification procedures for arms control and, without doubt, will prove to be a yardstick by which future treaties on strategic and conventional weapons are measured. Aside from the observation of maneuvers as part of the CDE Stockholm agreements, this is the first time that the principle of on-site inspection has been applied in militarily sensitive areas.

Euphoria aside, one must, however, remember that the dynamics of the arms race has only been halted in a marginal area. The INF treaty will not mean - as several of its advocates hope and many of its critics fear - the denuclearization of Europe. The nuclear arsenals which will be

---

2   See, for example, Lothar Ruehl, *Mittelstreckenwaffen in Europa* (Baden-Baden: Nomos, 1987), pp.115-132.

3   See Horst Afheldt, *Atomkrieg. Das Verhängnis einer Politik mit militärischen Mitteln* (München: Hanser, 1984), pp.169-196.

eliminated represent only 3-4% of the global total; in the European context they amount to little more than 20% depending on the counting method used (see table 7). For the superpowers, therefore, a very small segment of their nuclear arsenals has to be given up. This does not, however, detract from the contribution the INF treaty will make to regional stability in Europe. What is more, pointing to the relatively insignificant quantitative cuts ignores the fact that, in qualitative terms and in the context of deterrence, a critical area of military instability in Europe is being removed.

Deserving more attention than the above criticism is the objection that efforts are already underway to compensate for the drop in deterrence potential - which will allegedly arise from the elimination of the intermediate-range weapons - by new armament programs. On the Western side, there are plans to fit the American F-111 INF bombers based in Great Britain - which NATO considers are presently hardly capable of penetrating Soviet air-defenses - with air-launched cruise missiles (ALCMs). The F-111s would then be capable of striking targets in the Western Soviet Union. The «Army Tactical Missile System» (ATACMS), the follow-up to the short-range Lance missile, should also be mentioned in this context. Equipped with either conventional or nuclear warheads and with a range of about 450 km, ATACMS could reach targets in Eastern Europe. Initial operational capability is expected in the early nineties. Finally, reference should be made to a new generation of long-range standoff weapons which, launched from aircraft, are said to be able to attack military targets in WTO countries using either nuclear or conventional munition.[4]

As far as the *Soviet Union* is concerned, it has already reallocated some of its Yankee-class submarines in the Atlantic from waters close to the U.S. coast to the West European side. These SLBMs will obviously take over part of the SS-20 targets. Observers also point out that the USSR could threaten targets in Western Europe with its new intercontinental SS-24 and SS-25 missiles and thus easily compensate for the loss of the SS-20. Moreover, the USSR could develop a new generation of shorter-range missiles as well, replacing the Scud. Finally, the Soviet Union is

---

4   Cf. «Allies Weigh New Deployments to Offset Proposed INF Cuts,» *AW&ST*, May 18, 1987, pp.18-20; «Die Nato begrüsst das Mittelstrecken-Abkommen,» *FAZ*, November 5, 1987; «NATO Discusses Placing New N-Arms in Europe,» *IHT*, November 4, 1987.

said to be in the process of introducing a new generation of fighter-aircraft.

Table 7:   Remaining Nuclear Forces in and Targeted on Europe After the INF Treaty

---

	Number of Launchers
1. *Strategic Forces for European Purposes*	
USSR (assumed):	
- ICBMs SS-11/-17/-19	?
- SLBMs SS-N-5	39
USA:	
- B-52 Bomber/Minuteman III ICBM (assumed)	?
- SLBM Poseidon C-3 (assigned to NATO; 10 warheads each)	ca. 40
Great Britain:	
- SLBM Polaris A-3	64
France:	
- SLBM M-20/M-4	96
2. *INF Missiles*	
France:	
- SSBS S-3 D	18
3. *Short-Range Missiles (0-500 km)*	
USSR:	
- Scud (300 km)	ca. 580
- SS-21 (120 km)	ca. 130
- Frog (80 km)	ca. 650
USA/NATO:	
- Lance (110 km)	88
France:	
- Pluton (120 km)	32

4. *Nuclear Capable Long-Range INF Aircraft*
    (excluding naval aviation)

    USSR:
    - Badger, Blinder, Backfire   360

    USA/NATO:
    - F-111, FB-111 (in U.S.)   210

    France:
    - Mirage IV A + P   ca. 30

5. *Nuclear Capable Short-Range INF Aircraft*
    (excluding naval aviation)

    USSR:
    - Fitter, Fishbed, Flogger, Fencer   ca. 3,900

    USA/NATO:
    - F-104, F-4, F-16, MRCA Tornado   ca. 1,800

    France:
    - Mirage III E, Jaguar   75

6. *Nuclear Capable Artillery*

    USSR: ca. 7,500
    USA/NATO: ca. 4,000

Sources: *Bundesministerium der Verteidigung: Streitkräftevergleich NATO-Warschauer Pakt
[Rohfassung] (Bonn: July 1987); John M. Collins/Bernard C. Victory: U.S./Soviet
Military Balance, Congressional Research Service (Washington D.C.: September 1,
1987); IISS: The Military Balance 1987/88 (London: 1987).*

No-one would deny that the USSR, even after the elimination of the SS-20, still has sufficient nuclear weapons to be capable of striking all targets in Western Europe it considers important. (Similarly, NATO and the U.S. can still threaten Soviet targets; cf. Table 7.) One can even argue that this was the case *before* the deployment of the SS-20, thus calling into question the strategic sense of the Soviet INF buildup. It would only be possible to talk of «displacement» of the arms race from one area to another, however, if the USSR developed new weapons in order to make up for the elimination of the SS-20. This can hardly be substantiated for the SS-24 and SS-25. Moreover, if the Soviet Union designates a substantial portion of these new ICBMs for European target coverage, it must do so at the expense of strategic target coverage, especially after the conclusion of a START treaty.

On the Western side, too, one can only partly speak of a displacement effect. True, the air-launched cruise missiles would fully compensate for the loss of the GLCMs, but not for the elimination of the Pershing II with its short flight time combined with extreme accuracy. There remains a gain in crisis stability. The Army Tactical Missile System could only partly replace the Pershing IA due to its shorter range. And it remains an open question whether this system will be based in West Germany at all (see 5.5).

Despite these reservations, the INF treaty represents historic progress in the sphere of negotiated arms control. Agreements have been reached which would have been considered impossible years ago. The double zero agreement is a first step which could lead to further deep cuts in the nuclear arsenals - nothing more and nothing less.

5.2   The Artfulness of Reason: The Breakthrough in Geneva and Lessons for Arms Control

If one compares the results of the INF negotiations in Geneva to the official stances first adopted by both sides in 1981 when talks began, one does not observe a classic case of negotiated compromise in which both sides approach each other from incompatible starting positions. Rather, the INF treaty was accomplished following 100 percent acceptance by the Soviet Union of a proposal made by the West in November 1981 (see 3.3). This is at least true for the mutual zero-option on long-range INF. The situation is a little more complicated for short-range systems. Here, too, the U.S. had insisted since 1981 on concurrent constraints, and the lowest possible level on both sides is, of course, zero. If one consults the arms control criteria of NATO's double-track decision of 1979 and compares them to the initial Soviet bargaining position of 1981, one can conclude that the West has succeeded in getting its conditions accepted almost to the letter:[5]

- Any limitation of American INF was to be accompanied by a corresponding cut in respective Soviet missiles (first criterion). Yet initially the USSR had demanded that the U.S. forgo deployment, while wanting to keep up to 100 of its SS-20 missiles in Europe.
- Limitations on U.S. and Soviet LRINF were to be negotiated step-by-step bilaterally within the framework of SALT III (second criterion). The step-by-step approach did assert itself. INF aircraft, for example, were not made subject to any restrictions. The Soviet Union again dropped the demand which it had repeatedly made during the SALT negotiations, that U.S. «forward-based systems» (FBS) be included in U.S.-Soviet arms control agreements.
- The INF treaty limits only American and Soviet intermediate-range missiles (third criterion). This, too, was due to the Soviets backing off. Nuclear weapons of third countries as well as the established pattern of nuclear cooperation between the U.S. and NATO remain unaffected by the treaty.[6] Originally, however, the USSR had insisted on the inclusion of the British and French forces, and later, with respect to short-range INF that the elimination of the 72 Pershing IA warheads based in West Germany be *formally included in the treaty*. Moscow's concession not to insist on the inclusion of third party systems and the declaration made by Chancellor Kohl on August 26, 1987, together with the provision of the treaty prohibiting modernization, elim-inated the remaining obstacles without jeopardizing the Alliance's established pattern of nuclear cooperation.
- *De jure* and *de facto* parity was achieved both for the common ceilings (zero) and for the resulting rights (fourth criterion). Yet, initially, the USSR had refused to include its SS-20 force based in Soviet Asia and was unwilling to accord the U.S. the same ceiling even in Europe.
- The treaty is adequately verifiable in a way acceptable for both sides (fifth criterion). The verification procedures exceed anything that the

---

5   See the Communiqué of the Special Session of NATO's Foreign and Defense Ministers, December 12, 1979, quoted from *American Foreign Policy Basic Documents 1977-1980*, ed. Dept. of State (Washington D.C.: GPO, 1983), pp.494-496.

6   This criterion was not part of the published version, but was included in the Integrated Decision Document.

USSR was willing to accept through 1985. On-site inspections, on the other hand, have always been demanded by the West - and have finally been achieved.

How is the almost complete success of the Western negotiating position to be explained? One possible interpretation represents the official NATO view and was expressed by Chancellor Kohl on June 4, 1987, in the following way (at that time he still used the subjunctive):

«This success would be accredited to the firm and decisive stance taken by the West German government and the entire Alliance in implementing the NATO double-track decision.»[7]

This explanation stresses the fact that the Alliance, firstly, responded to the Soviet SS-20 challenge by agreeing to the double-track decision in 1979 and, secondly, proved by its own INF deployment in 1983 that it would neither be influenced by the Soviet propaganda campaign nor by the pressures of domestic opposition. Without Western INF deployment there would be no double zero agreement! At the same time, the U.S. and NATO stuck to their negotiation concept and thus signalled to the USSR that they were prepared to seriously consider arms reductions *provided* the Soviet Union took West European security interests into account. In the end, alliance cohesion, decisiveness, but also unwillingness to compromise on «second best» solutions, had paid off. «Disarmament through Western strength» would be an apt description of this evaluation of events.

One could also take the opposite view, however, and declare the zero option to be a late victory of the advocates of détente, arms control, and disarmament in Europe, namely the West European Social Democrats and the peace movements. This account would point to the fact that there was an unspoken consensus within NATO in 1979 that Soviet concessions could eventually influence the extent but not the necessity in principle of Western INF deployment. Arms control should *complement* the modernization but not substitute for it. On the other hand, the demand for some sort of zero option had been raised from the beginning by the Dutch and, in particular, by the West German Social Democrats as early as Summer 1979. Without the pressures exerted by the peace

---

7   Declaration of Chancellor Kohl to the *Bundestag*, June 4, 1987, *PlPr* 11/16, p.925.

movements in Great Britain, the Federal Republic, and the Netherlands, the zero proposal would not have become the Western negotiating position two years later. However, at that time nobody believed in the achievability of zero INF. It became apparent just how ill-prepared the West European governments were for the achievement of the zero option as late as 1986/87 in the wake of the summit meeting in Reykjavik. Rather than agreeing to eliminate the Pershing II, West European conservatives came up with further conditions one after the other. The governments in London and Bonn only agreed to the zero solution because the domestic situation in their respective countries had changed. «Secret victory of the peace movements,» one might call this explanation of the INF treaty.

Both interpretations fail to take into account the moves in the *Soviet INF policy under Gorbachev*. In recent years the USSR largely featured in the Western INF debate among politicians and experts as a political constant. There were those who described Soviet policy as inflexible and concerned with gaining military superiority in all areas by splitting and politically blackmailing the Alliance and by using arms control primarily as an instrument of political propaganda.[8] Opponents of Western INF deployment, on the other hand, ignored the Soviet arms buildup almost completely and concentrated on criticizing Western INF decisions for which the SS-20 had only been an excuse.[9] Neither side predicted the turnabout in Soviet policy and accordingly did perceive the zero option to be feasible. This author was no exception.[10] The «Gorbachev turnabout» came as a surprise to everyone involved in the debate; this even includes the small group of experts whose analyses were seriously concerned with the motives behind Soviet INF policy.[11]

---

8   This is the evaluation by Lothar Ruehl who has been West German Undersecretary of Defense. See his *Mittelstreckenwaffen*, note 2.

9   See, for example, Ulrich Albrecht, *Kündigt den Nachrüstungsbeschluss!* (Frankfurt/M.: Fischer, 1982); Anton Andreas Guha, *Die Nachrüstung. Der Holocaust Europas* (Freiburg: Dreisam, 1981); Alfred Mechtersheimer, *Rüstung und Frieden* (München: Langen-Müller & Herbig, 1982).

10 See, for example, my own research report «*Fahrplan zur Abrüstung*»? *Zur INF-Politik der Bundesrepublik Deutschland 1970/83* (Frankfurt/M.: PRIF, 1985).

11 See, e.g., Raymond Garthoff, *Détente and Confrontation* (Washington D.C.: Brookings, 1985), pp.870-886; David Holloway, «The INF policy of the So-

The «peace through strength» explanation, however, contains a hypothesis which attempts to explain Soviet concessions. The changed stance of the Soviet Union, it is argued, was principally a reaction in response to Western strength and the decisiveness with which the zero option had been proffered by the U.S. and NATO. This explanation is questionable from a methodological viewpoint because is makes cause and effect connections out of a mere chain of events. It is impossible to prove the hypothesis without detailed knowledge of the Soviet decision-making process. What is plausible, however, is that Western INF policy, including the deployment of the Pershing II and cruise missiles, must have illustrated clearly to the Soviet leadership the complete failure of the security policy pursued by Brezhnev and Gromyko. Since the mid-1970s, these policies were largely characterized by détente rhetoric accompanied by unceasing armament. As a result, the Soviets annoyed the greatest advocate of arms control among U.S. presidents since World War 2 - Jimmy Carter - and contributed to his political failure at home (intervention in Afghanistan) and - albeit indirectly - to the election of Ronald Reagan as U.S. president. Western Europe fared similarly. The Soviet Union's SS-20 deployment earned it opponents among the most important supporters of détente at that time in Great Britain (James Callaghan), France (Valéry Giscard d'Estaing) and last but not least in West Germany (Helmut Schmidt). Western INF deployment in 1983 was a signal to the Soviet leadership that, in the end, narrow-minded superpower behavior would not improve the security position of the USSR but, rather, backfire. Up to this point, therefore, it is plausible to agree with the «disarmament through strength» explanation. NATO's double-track policy, including INF deployment, can thus be regarded as a necessary prerequisite for the reorientation in Soviet policy - something which could however not have been foreseen in 1983.

But the «disarmament through strength» version cannot account completely for the *turnabout* under Gorbachev and especially not for his acceptance of the zero option. The USSR could, after all, have pursued its traditional course as it had done in 1984 and 1985 (*after* Western deployment but *before* Gorbachev). It might even have accepted some compromise solution like the «walk-in-the-woods». That the Soviet Union chose instead to re-examine its policy and finally revised it completely,

---

viet Union,» in H. H. Holm/N. Petersen (eds.), *The European Missile Crisis* (London: Frances Pinter, 1983), pp.92-114.

can only be plausibly explained by internal developments in the Soviet Union. Without Gorbachev and the «new thinking», there would have been no *double zero* agreement. «Perestroika» seemed from the start not to have been confined to Soviet domestic and economic politics but was equally related to foreign and security policy. The change in the INF policy of the USSR which overturned all the positions of the Brezhnev era (FBS, third-country forces, SS-20 based in Asia) is itself an indication of this more fundamental change. The *Politburo* of the C.P.S.U. obviously re-evaluated the military worth of the SS-20 in 1985, as a result of which Gorbachev later agreed to the zero proposal.[12] The reconsideration of Soviet INF policy might have shown that the USSR also gains from double zero. The U.S. has forsaken the right to target Soviet territory from Western Europe with highly accurate, short flight-time, land-based missiles. Moreover, the modernization of the Pershing IA has been prevented and, thereby, to a certain extent the accurate targeting of WTO troop concentrations deep inside Eastern Europe. Furthermore, the INF treaty will affect the domestic context of foreign policy in the West inasmuch as it will put an end finally to the coalition between the conservative security establishment, whose main concern is to strengthen Western deterrence capability, and dedicated supporters of NATO's «Harmel concept», who ascribe equal importance to deterrence *and* détente. This transatlantic alliance brought about the NATO double-track decision in the 1970s and the INF deployment in 1983 (see 5.3). The double zero option, on the other hand, was pushed through in Western Europe against the concerns of the traditional security establishment, who wanted to uphold Western INF at any cost out of «extended deterrence» considerations. Gorbachev's offers have largely isolated these groups at home.

---

12 For details see Matthew Evangelista, «The New Soviet Approach to Security,» *World Policy Journal*, vol.III, no.4, Fall 1986, pp.561-599; the same author, «Words and Deeds in Gorbachev's Security Policy,» to appear in *Friedensanalysen*, (Frankfurt/M.: Suhrkamp) in prep.; Stephen Larabee, «Gorbachev and the Soviet Military,» *Foreign Affairs*, vol.66, no.5, Summer 1988, pp.1002-1026; Jack Snyder, «The Gorbachev Revolution: A Waning of Soviet Expansionism,» *International Security*, vol.12, no.3, Winter 1987/88, pp.93-131; Jutta Tiedtke, «Neuorientierung oder Etikettenschwindel? Sowjetische Sicherheitspolitik unter Gorbacev,» *antimilitarismus information*, no.11, 1987, pp.III 173-180.

To conclude, the Soviet Union is not giving up its security interests in agreeing to the INF treaty. Even the scrapping of the SS-20, SS-12 and SS-23 missiles does not mean that the USSR has no other means of covering targets in Western Europe which it considers of military importance (cf. table 7). The Soviets are merely accepting a restriction of certain military options. Contrary to Brezhnev and Andropov, Gorbachev evidently rates the benefits to be gained from double zero higher than the disadvantages for deterrence of scrapping the SS-20 force.

The decisive factor in the realization of the INF treaty is, therefore, the change in Soviet politics which itself stems primarily from internal factors in the USSR. The West can be said to have contributed by making clear to the Soviet leadership the failure of the security policy of the Brezhnev era.

Why, though, did the West agree to the zero option in the first place? The military rationale for NATO's INF buildup - aside from reacting to the SS-20 threat - did not permit complete renunciation of deployment. The military purpose of the Pershing II and ground-launched cruise missiles was to ensure the implementation of NATO's flexible response strategy in a certain range spectrum and to visibly couple the U.S. to the nuclear risk in Western Europe in an era of strategic parity between the superpowers.

The fact that the zero option was nonetheless mentioned already in the Integrated Decision Document in 1979 and, moreover, adopted by the West as its official negotiating position in 1981, is due mainly to the efforts of West European advocates of détente. As mentioned above, the zero option had been «invented» by West German and Dutch Social Democrats as early as Summer 1979. Here, one can justify the hypothesis of the «late victory of the peace movements». Firstly, the West European proponents of arms control ensured that an offer to negotiate was added to INF modernization. The growing peace movements in Western Europe were then instrumental in 1981 in letting the U.S. and NATO agree to a proposal for the worldwide elimination of LRINF. The zero option was brought about by a strange coalition of West European arms control advocates, under severe domestic pressure from peace groups, and firm opponents of détente among the Reagan Administration, who, firstly, did not consider Western INF deployment to be of military significance and, secondly, felt the zero option to be an excellent propaganda tool for the voting public. (Richard Perle was a typical representative of this position.) At any rate, hardly anybody could have imagined in

1981 that the zero proposal would one day become reality. For several of its proponents, it was in 1981 an extreme demand which was not considered to be realistic but which six years later became a burden which they were obliged to accept.

The agreements reached in Reykjavik in 1986 and the INF treaty itself can also be explained on the Western side as resulting from domestic factors on both sides of the Atlantic. Even before Iran/Contragate came to light, President Reagan needed a resounding foreign policy success as the end of his second term drew near. He would otherwise have remained the only American president since Kennedy not to have brought about an arms control treaty with the Soviet Union despite his eight years in office. At the Reykjavik summit, it had already become obvious that he would probably be able to achieve such a success in an area that was not of central importance for him. The Iran affair made Reagan vulnerable at home, thus increasing the need an agreement with the Soviets. In addition, the security policy of the Reagan Administration came under growing pressure by the Democrat-controlled Congress. When in late February 1987, Gorbachev no longer insisted on the package he had presented in Reykjavik and untied INF from the START and ABM talks, the way for a treaty was made clear. The Americans began to concentrate all their efforts to that end.

The failure of conservatives in Western Europe in the aftermath of Reykjavik to dissuade their ideological partners in Washington from pursuing the double zero course can be explained both by strong U.S. pressure but also by domestic changes - this time in Western Europe. Instead of strengthening the transatlantic ties, the Pershing II and cruise missiles brought about a crisis of legitimacy with regard to nuclear weapons in the most important European deployment countries - Great Britain, West Germany, and the Netherlands. Societal demands thus helped to ensure that the conservative governments in London and Bonn finally accepted the INF treaty despite heavy infighting. Not to do so would have cost them their credibility as supporters of arms control - a risk which neither Prime Minister Thatcher nor Chancellor Kohl were prepared to take in the midst of national elections.

In conclusion, one can say that the realization of the most important arms control treaty for Europe since 1945, can be convincingly explained as resulting from the interaction of domestic changes within the Soviet Union, the U.S., and Western Europe. To put it in very concise terms, the treaty was the achievement of the following groups of actors:

- the West Europeans, West Germany and the then Chancellor Helmut Schmidt in particular, who brought up the INF issue on the U.S.-Soviet agenda and who were also crucial in bringing about the double-track decision in both of its components in 1979;
- the West European Social Democrats and the peace movements who, firstly, made sure that the U.S. and NATO would take INF arms control seriously and, secondly, exerted enough domestic pressure for NATO to accept the zero proposal as its bargaining position in 1981;
- NATO who carried out the deployment decision in 1983 and, thus, made it clear to the Soviets that their intransigence did not pay off;
- the USSR under Gorbachev who completely reversed its INF policy in 1986/87 and finally accepted the zero proposal;
- Ronald Reagan, Margret Thatcher, and Helmut Kohl, who, for a variety of domestic reasons, had to stick to NATO's 1981 bargaining position once the Soviets accepted it.

In the end, reason won the day, but for reasons which had precious little to do with arms control as such. This can be clearly seen from the fact that neither the SS-20 nor the Pershing II would have been deployed, had both sides given special attention to considerations of political and military stability in Europe.

If one is generous, INF can be said to illustrate that East and West are at least capable of making good their mistakes. First of all, they engaged in a costly arms race for about ten years only to realize in the end that neither side could improve its security situation. The Soviet Union had to recognize that the SS-20 was not only of minimal value for deterrence but had furthermore made havoc of the threat perceptions in Western Europe. If the USSR had ever intended to use its INF as an instrument of political blackmail against Western Europe, this gambit had well and truly backfired. On the other hand, Gorbachev in 1986/87 created more confusion in NATO in just six months with his acceptance of the Western proposal to eliminate the SS-20 than the deployment of this very missile ever did. It must also be said, however, that the willingness of the West to accept compromises on INF was not unreserved. True, NATO reacted to Soviet moves in INF much more than vice versa, and the double-track decision can certainly be regarded as an innovation in arms control. During the first phase of INF negotiations between 1981 and 1983, however, neither the Reagan Administration nor most West European governments (with the partial exclusion of Bonn) were really interested in achieving an agreement. They were much more concerned with showing Western strength both towards the Soviet Union and against domestic opposition. This became especially clear through the fate of the so-called «walk-in-the-woods» compromise which, unlike the zero option, would at least have permitted the West to retain some INF. The brusque rejection of this proposal by the U.S. government reveals that, at that time, it intended to go ahead with deployment come what may.

Summing up, one can say that during the first phase of the INF story, up to 1979, the USSR in particular was responsible for ensuring that an INF arms buildup on both sides got under way. At the time of the conclusion of NATO's double-track decision, on the other hand, it had not been clear which of its two components would finally be accorded priority in Western politics. From 1981-83 *both parties* were equally responsible for the failure of the first INF negotiations. Then in 1986/87 it was first and foremost the domestic constellation in the USSR which helped to bring about an arms control success.

What conclusions can be drawn from the history of INF for the preconditions of successful arms control?

1. The explicit orientation of the actors involved towards stability criteria is not a necessary requirement for the conclusion of a treaty. What is necessary, however, is that the main decision-makers on both sides accord a higher status to cooperation with the opponent - at least to some extent - than to unceasing confrontation. A complex foreign policy strategy such as the double-track decision which attempts to combine deterrence requirements with arms control objectives is not only likely to fail under unfavorable general circumstances, but can even contribute to a stalemate in arms control, as was the case during the first INF negotiations.

2. The decision to give priority to cooperation is influenced by a whole variety of factors. In Western democracies, a key factor is apparently the existence of stable public demands for détente and arms reductions.[13] A favorable constellation in the domestic environment, which

---

13 For the case of West Germany see Thomas Risse-Kappen, *Die Krise der Sicherheitspolitik. Neuorientierungen und Entscheidungsprozesse im politischen System der Bundesrepublik Deutschland, 1977-84* (Mainz-München: Grünewald-Kaiser, 1988).

in the case of the U.S. in 1986/87 (Iran/Contra affair) had very little connection with U.S.-Soviet relations as such, is probably more crucial to the prospects of successful arms control than actors who consciously pursue arms control and stability oriented policies but are incapable of asserting themselves either in the domestic (Jimmy Carter) or in the international arena (Helmut Schmidt).

3. The history of the INF treaty by and large confirms the hypothesis that arms control is a poor «ice-breaker» in international affairs. The hypothesis claims that arms control alone is not able to create an atmosphere of détente in the first place but, on the contrary, that its success largely depends on relations between the opponents which have *already* become more cooperative.[14] The failure of the first round of negotiations in 1981-83 illustrates that, in the absence of fairly relaxed East-West relations, arms control cannot succeed. It merely becomes part of the superpowers' confrontation. Nevertheless, the gradual improvement in U.S.-Soviet relations occured in parallel with the resumption of arms control talks in January 1985. In this respect, arms control served as a handy mechanism once the two sides had decided that the ice should be broken. Results were not achieved however for another one-and-a-half years (the Reykjavik summit meeting), by which time the overall political relationship between the superpowers had already drastically improved.

4. Under favorable domestic and international conditions it is relatively easy to resolve the military and, in the narrow sense, technical problems of negotiations. Under these conditions, both sides are likely to pave the way for an agreement by compromises and/or unilateral concessions. If the circumstances are unfavorable, then negotiations will appear to fail as a result of these very military problems (e.g. third-country forces in the case of INF). The real cause for failure though is the lack - domestically and internationally - of an opportune environment.

5. The INF treaty also serves to modify the view of many observers that the military significance of arms control agreements tends to be

---

14 See Joseph Kruzel, «From Rush-Bagot to START: Lessons from Arms Control,» *Orbis*, Spring 1986, pp.193-216.

marginal.[15] On the one hand, the double zero treaty does not deal with weapons systems central to the arms race between the superpowers despite the fact that highly-modern missiles will be scrapped on both sides. Moreover, INF seems to support the line of argument that important cuts in the weapons arsenals are only possible when both players have actually carried out their arms buildups. This was what happened with long-range INF, where the concept of preventive arms control failed. The zero option was only possible *after* both sides had carried out their respective deployments. On the other hand, the second zero solution on SRINF can be said to represent successful preventive arms control. The USSR had only just begun to replace the Scud missile with the SS-23, and NATO had not yet decided on the modernization of the Pershing IA.

6. The history of the INF treaty also demonstrates the limitations of the gradualist approach to arms control emphasizing unilateral initiatives. This is particularly true of the hope that preparedness to cooperate on one side might induce corresponding behavior on the other side. Before 1979, the USSR did not concede anything to those in Western Europe (i.e. the West German SPD and the Dutch Labour Party) who needed a signal of Soviet restraint in order to prevent NATO's double-track decision. It is also extremely doubtful whether Western readiness to forgo deployment in 1983 would have induced the Soviet Union to cut their SS-20 force. In 1986/87, on the other hand, it took considerable effort on the part of the Soviet General Secretary to get double zero accepted by NATO. Thus, strategies of unilateral restraint are not likely to *create* incentives for cooperation. Rather, they *invoke* already existing mutual interests.[16]

---

15 For this argument see Kruzel, «Rush-Bagot,» note 14. See also Albert Carnesale/Richard N. Haass (eds.), *Superpower Arms Control. Setting the Record Straight* (Cambridge, Mass.: Ballinger, 1987).

16 See Alexander George, «Incentives for U.S.-Soviet Security Cooperation and Mutual Adjustment,» in *U.S.-Soviet Security Cooperation*, eds. George, P.J. Farley, and A. Dallin (New York, Oxford: Oxford University Press, 1988), pp.641-654.

5.3 On the Threshold of World Politics? INF and West German - U.S. Relations

Those who observed the reactions of many West Europeans after the Reykjavik summit meeting in 1986 and followed the disputes in West Germany over the double zero option could well momentarily forget that they were not in the 1970s:

- Fears were voiced again that too close a U.S.-Soviet bilateralism would damage West European security interests. The concern was raised that the U.S. could reach an agreement without first consulting its allies. The future of «extended deterrence» was at stake again. The well-known «decoupling» fears that the U.S. wanted to quietly and unobtrusively distance itself from the nuclear risk involved in the defense of Western Europe re-emerged.
- Ronald Reagan tried to soothe his European allies with the assurance that the U.S. security guarantee for Western Europe was not being undermined - as did Jimmy Carter in the 1970s.
- Finally, the fears in Western Europe stemmed less from a thorough strategic than were the political-psychological expression of relations in an alliance of unequal partners.

In the context of the SALT process of the 1970s, many West Europeans feared that parity between the superpowers would neutralize the strategic arsenals on both sides so that the U.S. ICBMs would no longer be available for purposes of «extended deterrence». Even worse, instead of bearing in mind West European concerns, the Carter Administration seemed to be eager to negotiate away the very (cruise) missiles which could serve the security needs of Western Europe. At the same time, the Soviet SS-20 buildup increased the INF threat to NATO, thereby worsening NATO's position still further. Today, the double zero solution is interpreted by some West Germans as another American attempt to reduce the risks involved in «extended deterrence». Withdrawal of visible, land-based American INF able to threaten the Soviet homeland from Western Europe would signal to the Soviets, it was argued, that the U.S. is reducing its commitment to NATO defense. Worse still, a U.S. president whose reputation at home had severely suffered (Iran/Contragate) was rushing into a treaty with the Soviets without taking into account the concerns of its allies. Thus, while «decoupling» fears and the concern about far-reaching arms limitations seemed to dominate Western European reactions to U.S.-Soviet relations in the seventies as well as in the late eighties, during the *early* eighties the Americans heard just the opposite demands. Following the Afghanistan crisis and the subsequent worsening in the superpower relationship, West Europeans became worried about the future of arms control and détente. At that time, they urged the U.S. to resume the INF negotiations as soon as possible and to search for an arms control compromise. In 1986/87, however, once the talks produced concrete results, the West Europeans were still not satisfied. This, at least, must have been the impression in Washington.

One can attempt to explain the back and forth of West European demands and American reactions to them by means of a cyclic pattern resulting from the security dilemma in alliance relations.[17] In protecting its members from external aggression, every alliance faces two problems. The partners have to be able to rely on one another and stick together in times of crisis (concern of «abandonment»). Conversely, they have as great an interest in not being drawn into a confrontation between one member and the opponent too early (fear of «entrapment»). One could argue, therefore, that the demands of NATO members concerning U.S. arms control policy oscillate between the fear of being let down by the Americans and the concern of being drawn into a U.S.-Soviet confrontation.

The «abandonment-entrapment» cycle sounds plausible since it is related to the structural conditions within alliances and is not characterized by abstract calculations of deterrence theory («decoupling») which rest on questionable premises. But the cycle concept leaves out fundamental aspects and is therefore only a superficial account of U.S.-West European relations. It treats both the U.S. and its allies as unified actors and disregards the diversity among the West European countries as well as the domestic environment of security policy on both sides of the Atlantic. It is impossible, however, to explain the history of the INF treaty in the context of alliance relations without these factors. This will now be illustrated by examining the course of *West German-American relations*. Firstly, there was no uniform West German concern about U.S.-Soviet arms control in the seventies, not even on the government level. Leav-

---

17   See for the following Jane M. O. Sharp, «After Reykjavik: arms control and the allies,» *International Affairs*, vol.63, no.2, Spring 1987, pp.239-257; Glenn H. Snyder, «The Security Dilemma in Alliance Politics,» *World Politics*, vol.36, no.4, July 1984, pp.461-495.

ing aside all criticism of SALT, strategic arms control was supported in principle by a broad coalition which encompassed the SPD, the FDP (at that time the governing parties), but also the mainstream Christian Democrats. SALT was considered an imperative requirement to provide favorable conditions for West European *Ostpolitik*. Initially, «decoupling» fears were almost exclusively raised by minorities based in the conservative security and military establishment and among sections of the CDU/CSU who regard deterrence as the top priority in security policy. However, this group had excellent transatlantic connections, especially to the anti-SALT coalition in the U.S. Domestically, criticism of U.S. arms control policy and demands for a military compensation for the alleged loss of «extended deterrence» due to strategic parity did not gain support until the USSR began its SS-20 buildup - a move which was perceived as a new threat even by firm supporters of détente. The security elites of the CDU, the FDP, and partly of the SPD for whom deterrence and arms control are, in the sense of the *Harmel* report, complementary objectives of Western security policy (from Helmut Schmidt to Hans-Dietrich Genscher to Helmut Kohl) realized that the West must respond to this new challenge.[18] The deployment component of NATO's double-track decision can therefore be traced back to a domestic coalition of conservative arms control critics and supporters of the Harmel concept.

The *arms control* component, on the other hand, goes back in West Germany to a domestic alliance between the aforementioned group and the ardent supporters of détente and arms reductions in the SPD who did not accept the military logic of Western INF deployment but tolerated it in light of the Soviet arms buildup. In this respect, NATO's 1979 decision almost perfectly fulfilled the domestic demands voiced in the Federal Republic in the 1970s. Thus, both modernization of NATO's INF posture and arms control stemmed from West European demands, not least of all West German ones. For this reason, it is necessary to modify the argument that «decoupling» fears dominated the debate in the late seventies. Decision-makers like Helmut Schmidt wanted neither to be abandoned by the U.S. with respect to their security interests nor to be entrapped into an unrestricted INF arms race.

---

18   While almost everybody in West Germany would agree to the Harmel formula in general, only those will be called «Harmel supporter» in the following who - in terms of goals and instruments of security policy - give equal value to deterrence/defense and arms control/détente.

The domestic constellation in the Federal Republic faced changes in the American domestic setting.[19] Towards the end of the 1970s the anti-SALT coalition began increasingly to dominate the security debate. Modernization of NATO's INF posture fitted well into their list of demands, while eurostrategic arms control was only taken seriously by American advocates of détente who were already on the defensive at this point. The Carter Administration initially responded with caution to the demands in order not to jeopardize the conclusion of SALT II. Not until the debacle over the neutron bomb in 1978 did it increase efforts to speed up the INF decision-making process in NATO, wishing above all to preserve alliance cohesion. Thus, West German supporters of the double-track approach like Helmut Schmidt faced a dilemma. They had entered into an alliance with opponents of SALT in the U.S. in order to bring about INF *modernization*. In doing so, they simultaneously helped to undermine the domestic basis for arms control in the U.S. - a prerequisite for the success of the second component in NATO's decision. The consequences became apparent in the early 1980s.

It would be just as inappropriate to speak at the beginning of the 1980s of a *volte face* by the West Europeans. In view of the deterioration of U.S.-Soviet relations after Afghanistan and a U.S. government who came into power by rejecting the SALT process, it was now of utmost importance to implement the arms control part of the double-track decision. In West Germany the domestic coalition between «Harmel supporters» and those who gave top priority to arms reductions remained intact. The position of the conservative opponents of détente and arms control was considerably weakened by the emergence of the peace movements, whose influence even extended into the CDU/CSU. In the face of opposition from right-wing deployment supporters - Franz Joseph Strauss, the conservative prime minister of Bavaria, had been against the zero proposal as early as 1981 - this option was finally pushed through as the Western negotiating position. It came about, as shown above, through an unholy transatlantic alliance between West European adherents of détente like Helmut Schmidt and unilateralist opponents of arms control in the U.S. like Richard Perle, who did not

---

19   Cf. Bernd W. Kubbig, *Gleichgewicht oder Überlegenheit. Amerikanische Rüstungskontrollpolitik und das Scheitern von SALT II* (Frankfurt/M.: Campus, 1983); Ernst-Christoph Meier, *Deutsch-amerikanische Sicherheitsbeziehungen und der NATO-Doppelbeschluss*, 2 vols. (Rheinfelden: Schäuble-Verlag, 1986).

believe very much in the military sense of NATO's INF deployment. This coalition was, however, only of short duration.

Then in 1983, in West Germany the «deployment coalition» of 1979 was revived between the arms control opponents and the «Harmel supporters». This was due to the intransigence of Soviet policy, despite peace movements and the legitimacy crisis of nuclear deterrence. On account of the latter, there was little change in the INF policy practised by Bonn following the change in government from the Social-Liberal to the CDU/CSU-FDP coalition, even though the critics of détente and arms control now formed part of the government. On the American side, it was clear that deployment would have to take place in almost any circumstance in order to demonstrate strength to the Soviets.

It was Gorbachev who succeeded in splitting the «deployment coalition» in West Germany and ensured that the contradictions underlying the NATO double-track decision were cleared in favor of arms control. Here, too, it would be wrong to ascribe the West European reactions to the outcome of the Reykjavik summit solely to «decoupling» fears. Above all, it is necessary to distinguish between zero INF and the proposal made in Reykjavik to scrap *all* (ballistic) nuclear missiles. While the elimination proposal was subject to wideranging criticism, those who rejected a zero option for INF were unable to gather domestic support. They did succeed in causing a great stir on both sides of the Atlantic and in delaying NATO's decision-making process with respect to zero shortrange INF in spring 1987 for about six weeks. But on the whole the transatlantic «zero option coalition» of 1981 stood the test and increased its ranks by the U.S. State Department on the one hand, and ardent supporters of disarmament from the SPD to the Greens and the peace movements in West Germany on the other. In the end, the combined forces of Alfred Dregger (chairman of the Christian Democrats' *Bundestag* faction), Franz Joseph Strauss, the Defense Ministry, and the *Frankfurter Allgemeine Zeitung* (the leading center-right newspaper) could do little against the alliance composing Ronald Reagan and Richard Perle as well as Oskar Lafontaine (left-wing deputy chairman of the SPD) and Petra Kelly (the Greens). It is therefore an exaggeration to claim that the U.S. had to wear down much opposition in West Germany in order to push through the INF treaty. In fact, the conservative critics of arms control had already lost considerable domestic support.

One can therefore say that alliance structure determines the framework of transatlantic relations. The way in which U.S. security policies

are perceived in Western Europe, though, depends on the domestic cor-
relation of forces in each of the West European countries. In the Federal
Republic, for example, there exists today, compared to the situation in
the 1970s, a firm domestic consensus in favor of détente and arms control comprising the CDU/CSU majority to the Green party. This explains why «decoupling» fears of the traditional nature are voiced solely
by a minority. According to surveys, there is overwhelming support for
the INF treaty in the public. 65% of the West Germans do not believe
that the American nuclear guarantee for the defense of Europe will be
weakened through the elimination of the intermediate-range missiles.
Only 10% of the population shares this view of the conservative section
of the security elite.[20] Thus, «decoupling» fears seem to be a typical example of an elite trauma.

Moreover, the role of West Germany in NATO over the course of the
past fifteen years has changed to some extent, although it remains a
non-nuclear weapons state and subject to regulations of the Non-Prolif-
eration Treaty (NPT). But it is the very fact of the Federal Republic's
non-nuclear status together with its geostrategic position at the East-
West borderline which makes the country vulnerable in security matters,
leading in turn to dependence on the U.S. guarantee and on U.S.-Soviet
relations. West Germany's INF policy was the attempt of a medium-size
power to keep her dependence on the superpowers within acceptable
limits. NATO's double-track decision can be described as «U.S. nuclear
policy shaped under European influence».[21] Without the West Europeans, and the West Germans in particular, INF would not have become
an issue on the agenda of the superpowers' security relationship. For the
first time in the history of the Nuclear Planning Group, the West Europeans were directly involved in an American nuclear decision affecting
Europe. The deployment decision was the result of West European *par-*

---

20 See data in Michael Gordon, «Dateline Washington: INF: A Hollow Vic-
    tory?,» *Foreign Policy*, no.68, Fall 1987, pp.159-179; Hans Rattinger, «The
    INF Agreement and Public Opinion in West Germany,» paper prepared for
    the conference on *Canadian and German Perspectives on East-West Arms Con-
    trol*, Toronto, March 10-12, 1988.

21 Meier, *Sicherheitsbeziehungen*, note 19, vol.2, p.444. See also Helga Haften-
    dorn, «Das doppelte Missverständnis. Zur Vorgeschichte des NATO-Dop-
    pelbeschlusses von 1979,» *Vierteljahreshefte für Zeitgeschichte*, vol.33, no.2,
    April 1985, pp.244-287.

ticipation in the U.S. decision-making process which far exceeded *consultation*. Thus a precedent was set which will have an influence on future American decisions concerning its nuclear forces in Europe. West German involvement in U.S. nuclear planning has increased in the sense that it has been granted right of veto. Whether West Germany will take advantage of its room to maneuver will become apparent through the forthcoming decisions on short-range missile modernization.

Another innovation is that, for the first time, forms of cooperation within NATO have been established not only for armament decisions, but also for U.S. arms control policy with an impact on Western Europe. This development is again attributable among others to the West German government, who initiated the setting up of the «Special Consultative Group» (SCG) for arms control in NATO. The West Europeans gradually succeeded in increasing their influence on U.S. nuclear arms control policy affecting Europe. This is an important step forward compared to SALT when the allies were informed by the U.S. but were hardly consulted in advance and only in exceptional cases had the opportunity to influence the American negotiating position, even though both SALT I and II affected alliance concerns (FBS, cruise missiles).

During the INF talks, the European allies were consulted - with two important exceptions - before every change in the U.S. negotiating position. The two exceptions were the rejection of the «walk-in-the-woods» compromise in 1982 and the tentative agreements reached at the Reykjavik summit in 1986. U.S. unwillingness to inform its allies of the Nitze-Kvitsinsky formula *before* the decision to reject it had been taken in Washington represented a serious breach of its obligations. Worse still, those in the Reagan Administration who withheld information from the allies, did so in the clear knowledge that at least the West German government of the day (Helmut Schmidt was still in office) would most probably have supported the «walk-in-the-woods» compromise.

The lack of consultation in connection with the Reykjavik summit may have been significant concerning Reagan's offer to eliminate *all* ballistic nuclear missiles. (Even important parts of the American government were not informed either, e.g., the Joint Chiefs of Staff.) In the case of INF, however, non-consultation represented a less serious offense since the zero option lay entirely within the framework of what had been discussed in NATO for years. The proposal itself was a perfect example of European-American or, more precisely, U.S.-West German consultation with the coalitions mentioned above.

INF saw the West German government pursue, for the first time, an active nuclear arms control policy within the limits set by its non-nuclear status. As mentioned, this relates to the double-track decision itself as well as to the origins of the zero proposal. Following the Reykjavik summit meeting, Bonn, in particular the Foreign Ministry, worked with the State Department behind the scenes to secure NATO support for the American position. The infighting in Bonn in spring 1987 on a second zero option for SRINF was an important exception. The disruptive efforts of the conservative wing of the CDU/CSU, which were - for reasons which are difficult to comprehend - defended by the «Harmel supporters» of the party (e.g. Volker Rühe), delayed the NATO decision for roughly six weeks and drove the West German government into international isolation. The decision to give up the Pershing IA by Chancellor Kohl in late August signalled Bonn's return to an active arms control policy.

The history of INF not only shows the extent of West European influence on U.S.-Soviet relations, but also very clearly its *limitations*. Though the superpower relationship is of direct impact for West European security, the allies can do little to profoundly influence these relations. Prior to 1979, neither Helmut Schmidt nor British Prime Minister Callaghan succeeded in convincing the Soviet Union to adopt a softer stance on its INF policy. During the first INF talks the West Germans were just as powerless to move *both* superpowers towards an arms control agreement. Bonn's influence on the improved U.S.-Soviet relations after 1985 was also limited. In this case, though, the West Europeans could be said to have paved the way, since the European East-West détente had more or less survived the phase of U.S.-Soviet confrontation. While the *issue* and the *content* of the INF treaty were largely determined by West European influence, the *timing* lay by and large out of their reach.

5.4 Misjudgments on All Sides: INF and the National Security Debate in West Germany

In recent years, no other security policy topic has moved the West German public quite like the INF deployment. On the surface, the debate seemed to revolve around the Pershing II and the SS-20 missiles. However, the real issues at stake were the general orientation of West German foreign and security policy, the relationship between deterrence and détente, and the role which nuclear weapons should or should not play in NATO's defense strategy.[22] In the course of the debate, misjudgements were made on nearly all sides, with the result that in 1986/87 a number of central arguments which were made in 1981-83 changed side, thus leading to the formation of highly unusual transatlantic coalitions. Some of the assessments made are commented on in the following, but not from a sense of know-all - we are, as the saying goes, always wiser after the event. Rather, the aim is to draw consequences for the future.

It has already been mentioned that hardly anyone in West Germany seriously considered that the zero option could be achieved. The policies and interests of both superpowers were grossly misinterpreted by most security-policy groupings. This applies to the *Soviet Union* whose turnabout in security policy could hardly have been anticipated. Conservative advocates of NATO's INF deployment now face the problem of abandoning their carefully cultivated preconceptions of the opponent and of adjusting to the fact that a drastic improvement in East-West relations could be possible under Gorbachev. One of the topics underlying the stormy debate on double zero in spring 1987 was what response the change in Soviet politics required. Those who spoke of Brezhnev's security policy in most negative terms had to accept that this evaluation showed Gorbachev to much better advantage. This in turn had the unfortunate effect of making superfluous arguments justifying Western arms buildups which were needed for domestic purposes. Several conservatives, therefore, tried to play down the importance of double zero. Paradoxically, this only led the threat posed by the SS-20s - a threat which had been particularly emphasized in previous years - to fade into insignificance. Therefore, the critics of détente in the CDU/CSU faced the dilemma that it was impossible to continue portraying the SS-20 as a serious threat against Western Europe and, at the same time, to refer to the Soviet willingness to eliminate this weapon as a small concession.

Social Democrats, members of the Green Party, and the peace movements faced the opposite problem. It was easiest for those who had ignored the Soviet arms buildup entirely and were concentrating mostly on opposing Western defense policy, demanding unilateral disarma-

---

22   For a general account of the debate see Risse-Kappen, *Krise*, note 13.

ment. These groups welcomed the turnabout in Soviet politics, since it underscored the necessity of their own demands. On the other hand, those who critized the Western INF deployment as an overreaction to what was admittedly regarded as an unfair move by the Soviets believed that, by the principle of gradualism, non-deployment would lead the USSR to reduce their own arsenals. In order to prove their point, this group tended during the deployment debate of 1981-83 to hail every slight softening in the Soviet position as a substantial concession. In particular, the majority of the SPD now has to face the fact that Gorbachev was overturning positions which the Social Democrats themselves had supported in the debate as legitimate Soviet demands (for example, the inclusion of third-country forces in a U.S.-Soviet agreement). Those on the left, who today sing Gorbachev's praises, must be asked how critical they were of Brezhnev.

The problem of the SPD with Gorbachev and double zero is more complex, however. Many Social Democrats had believed that the rejection of INF deployment adopted at the Party congress in Cologne in 1983 and the reorientation of SPD's security policy during the subsequent congresses in Essen in 1984 and in Nuremberg in 1986 signalled the end of the «Schmidt era». They were tempted to dissociate themselves from the period 1979-82 when the SPD was in power and had tolerated the double-track decision. Now the history of the SPD's security policy under Schmidt has caught up with the party once again. While it is impossible to prove that Gorbachev's acceptance of the zero option came about as a result of Western INF deployment (see 5.2), it is even more difficult to argue convincingly that *non-deployment* in 1983 - which, in opposition to Schmidt, the SPD favored at that time - would have led to something similar to the double zero agreement. To put it the other way round: It is Gorbachev who forces the SPD to reassess Helmut Schmidt's security policy, a policy which they would have understandably preferred to forget once and for all.

The second fundamental misjudgment in West Germany's security debate concerns the evaluation of *American* politics. In the course of the domestic confrontation, deployment of the Pershing II and cruise missiles assumed a symbolic status for the German-American relationship which grew out of all proportion to the military significance of these weapons. Conservative advocates of INF deployment considered them a symbol of alliance cohesion and the visible strengthening of the American nuclear guarantee in an era of strategic parity. However, it is hard to say whether the Pershing II has a «coupling» or a «decoupling» effect (both arguments were made in the debate). No matter how many U.S. nuclear weapons are deployed in Western Europe, they cannot provide the certainty that an American president would use them for the defense of Western Europe, thus jeopardizing the survival of the American population. Indeed, this certainty is not necessary for deterrence purposes. It is sufficient that the *Soviet Union* cannot rule out the possibility that these weapons might be used. One can therefore list the following basic requirements for «extended deterrence»:

- American self-interest in Western Europe;
- the basing of U.S. troops in Western Europe and their integration in NATO's frontline defense; this would lead to every East-West war becoming a direct U.S.-Soviet confrontation;
- a minimum flexibility in the U.S. nuclear arsenals to prevent a situation where any use of nuclear weapons would immediately lead to all-out nuclear war (however unlikely escalation control might be to achieve). It is of little importance whether this «minimum extended deterrence» is a characteristic of U.S. strategic nuclear forces or is created through the deployment of nuclear weapons in NATO Europe.

The «decoupling» fears of the West German conservatives obviously stem from reasons which do not lie in considerations of «extended deterrence» alone. Firstly, there are deep-seated feelings of being threatened by the Soviet Union which consequently lead deterrence demands to increase. But there seems to be an equally strong feeling of mistrust towards the U.S. which was already apparent during first Chancellor Adenauer's term and which is possibly rooted in the traditional cultural anti-Americanism of the German national-conservatives. This mistrust has been strengthened by President Reagan's renunciation of the Pershing II which the right-wing of the CDU/CSU sees as a proof of his being first and foremost an American and only then their ideological partner. At any rate, this faction of the CDU/CSU displays little trust in the much-quoted ideology of transatlantic *Wertegemeinschaft* (community of shared values). Right-wing Christian Democrats even argued that the INF treaty reduces the nuclear risk for the U.S., thereby increasing the danger for the Federal Republic (see 4.4). They pointed to the remaining Soviet short-range missiles - the Scud, Frog, and SS-21 - and called this the «singularization of the threat».

The dangerous aspect of these kinds of arguments - which, of course, do not have a sound basis in reality - is that they accurately reflect emotions which were expressed by those on the opposite ends of the political spectrum in West Germany in 1981-83. What the conservative critics of the INF treaty today term «singularization of the threat» was referred to by the peace movements as «battlefield of the superpowers». The pattern of thinking was similar: Germany as the innocent victim, then of the hegemonial confrontation of the superpowers, now of the new U.S.-Soviet bilateralism. The following sentence could have been uttered during the controversy over the double zero option:

> «If there is war in Europe, the superpowers will fight out to the end the World War which was interrupted in 1945, and that would mean the end of Europe.»[23]

Here, an analogy is drawn between the freeing of Germany from Hitler in 1945 and a third world war between East and West. Alfred Mechtersheimer, former member of the Bavarian CSU and today Green Party MP in Bonn, wrote the above in 1982 and thus linked together the relativization of the national socialist crimes and the INF deployment. In fall 1987, it was CSU chairman Franz Joseph Strauss who made a similar comparison between the *Historikerdebatte* (the «battle of the historians» on how to interpret Hitler) and the criticism of the zero solution.[24]

In the aftermath of the INF treaty the peace movements and the West German left see themselves obliged to rethink their image of America and their perception of American politics. They viewed the Pershing II as a symbol of U.S. arms buildup. If there was, aside from the general agreement to oppose deployment, a minimal consensus among the peace movements, this consensus focused on making American politics responsible for the INF arms buildup. Some argued it was part of a first-strike and decapitating strategy of the U.S. against the Soviet Union aimed at engaging in and winning a protracted nuclear

---

23 Mechtersheimer, *Rüstung*, note 9, p.88.

24 At a CSU party-congress in Munich, see *Süddeutsche Zeitung*, November 23, 1987. For nationalist arguments in the peace movements see the excellent article by Dan Diner, «Die 'nationale Frage' in der Friedensbewegung,» *Die neue Friedensbewegung, Friedensanalysen 16* (Frankfurt/M.: Suhrkamp, 1982), pp.86-112.

war.[25] Others, including Mechtersheimer, did not accept the first-strike explanation but interpreted INF deployment as an attempt to confine the nuclear risk to Europe (just as the opponents of the zero option now criticize the *elimination* of the Pershings in the context of the «singularization» concept). Western INF deployment was declared by large sections of the peace movements to be a crucial component of the U.S. nuclear strategy. To quote Mechtersheimer again:

> «Thus this missile (Pershing II/T.R.-K.) together with the cruise missiles forms the most important instrument of the change in the American deterrence strategy, in which global deterrence is to be replaced by a greater number of regional deterrence systems.»[26]

There is no question that the new U.S. INF fitted with the American nuclear strategy, its counterforce orientation aimed at flexible and selective options. Yet, it was grotesque to make this the cornerstone of the U.S. deterrent, thereby ignoring the background of NATO's double-track decision (see 2.4). And now the most conservative president the United States has seen in years is willing to forgo «the most important instrument» of its nuclear strategy. The main opponents of the double zero solution were to be found in Western Europe which - as a victim of U.S.-Soviet confrontation - parts of the West German left had granted absolution from any responsibility for the nuclear arms race.

To conclude, the INF treaty will hopefully be a healthy experience for West Germans involved in the security debate. In the long run, it could result in a more rational evaluation of Soviet as well as American foreign policies. Double zero might free the conservatives from their «decoupling» paranoia, while the left must reconsider its image of America in light of the new situation.[27] The West German security debate should refocus on the part played by Western Europe and by the

---

25 This argument was even made by some peace researchers. See, for example, Dieter S. Lutz, «Dolus eventualis. Überlegungen zur Gefahr eines bedingt vorsätzlichen (Welt-)Krieges in und um Europa,» in *Kriegsursachen, Friedensanalysen 21* (Frankfurt/M.: Suhrkamp, 1987), pp.294-307.

26 Mechtersheimer, *Rüstung*, note 9, p.120.

27 For an attempt to explain the anti-Americanism among the West German left and the peace movements see Harald Müller/Thomas Risse-Kappen, «Origins of Estrangement. The Peace Movement and the Changed Image of America in West Germany,» *International Security*, vol.12, no.1, Summer 1987, pp.52-88.

Federal Republic in the arms race as well as in arms control, and should face responsibilities.

5.5 «Firewall» or «Triple Zero»? The Future of Nuclear Weapons and Arms Control in Europe

From the beginning to its very end, the INF debate was overloaded with arguments related to the general security situation of Western Europe which completely outweighed the military impact of the weapons systems in question. And this continues to be the case in the aftermath of the INF treaty. How else can one explain that the removal of less than 20% of the nuclear arsenals in Europe leads to a reassessment of the role of nuclear weapons in NATO?

Such a re-evaluation, however, has to take into account the profound changes in the international as well as in the domestic environment of Western security since the seventies and early eighties. There is, first of all, the turnabout of *Soviet security policy under Gorbachev*. The USSR might still aim at the de-nuclearization of Europe as part of its shift towards conventional emphasis in its military doctrine.[28] But, unlike Brezhnev, Gorbachev seems to be willing to pay a price for this objective, and, for the first time, the Soviet Union appears to be taking West European security interests seriously. As a consequence, NATO's nuclear policy cannot count any longer on a «benign» international environment when it comes to modernization decisions. The easy justification for Western arms buildups - the «Soviet threat» - is not available anymore. While Soviet intransigence helped NATO to carry out its INF deployments in 1983 despite mass protests, Gorbachev's flexibility is the new reality which has to be taken into account.

The second change concerns the *domestic* environment of Western security policy. The INF debate resulted in a breakdown of the consensus on the role of nuclear weapons in NATO's defense posture in Great Britain, West Germany, and the Netherlands. While the INF treaty had a reassuring effect on the public and took out much of the heat from the domestic nuclear debates, further modernization decisions on NATO's arsenals have to take the following conditions into account:

---

28 See Michael MccGwire, *Military Objectives in Soviet Foreign Policy* (Washington D.C.: Brookings, 1987).

- Nuclear weapons are only acceptable in the framework of *general deterrence*. Any significant military role in the defense of Western Europe will therefore continue to meet with harsh opposition by large segments of the public as well as of the national security elites in the countries mentioned. The interpretation of NATO's flexible response doctrine which dominated in the seventies and put the emphasis on nuclear flexibility, selectivity, and a «continuous spectrum of escalation» cannot provide a basis anymore to restore the domestic nuclear consensus. Instead, some kind of *minimum nuclear deterrence for Europe*, which needs to be precisely defined, will carry the day.
- The West European public as well as the overwhelming majorities of the security elites in West Germany and the Benelux countries take the Harmel approach seriously. Any future modernization of NATO's nuclear weapons has therefore to take place within a framework of an elaborated arms control concept. «Firewalls» to prevent further nuclear arms control negotiations in Europe will almost certainly fail.
- There is still no consensus in Western Europe on the long-term role of nuclear weapons. The left (with the exception of France) favors the denuclearization of Europe, at least in the long run and provided that conventional stabilization is achieved. Most of the conservatives, on the other hand, continue to support the deployment of nuclear forces in Western Europe as a means of general deterrence regardless of the conventional situation. They believe in nuclear deterrence as the best means to prevent *any* war. Future zero options are unacceptable for them.

While the long-term role of nuclear weapons in Europe remains controversial, there nevertheless is enough room for a new nuclear consensus in Western Europe, at least for the time being. It can be labelled «neither firewall nor triple-zero». To understand this and given the fact that the Federal Republic will play a crucial role in this context, one has to come back to the nuclear debate in West Germany in the aftermath of the INF treaty.

In spring 1988, a new West German anti-nuclear consensus seemed, at first glance, to have emerged. When U.S., British, and French officials pressed for the modernization of NATO's outmoded short-range missiles, they met with almost unanimous opposition from all West German political groups. It marked the first time that Alfred Dregger, the conservative chairman of the CDU/CSU *Bundestag* faction, agreed with the left-wing deputy chairman of the SPD, Oskar Lafontaine, and with Petra Kelly of the Greens, on a security policy issue.

«The shorter the ranges, the deader the Germans» was a dictum quickly adopted by all political groups, having been introduced into the debate in early 1987 by Volker Rühe, the moderate deputy chairman of the CDU/CSU *Bundestag* faction. (The statement is, of course, wrong in assuming that only Germans, on both sides of the Iron Curtain, will be threatened by nuclear missiles after the INF treaty is implemented [see Table 7, pp.160/161].) But, along with the above-mentioned notion - «singularization of the threat» - it expresses clearly a general sense of West Germany's vulnerability to nuclear weapons and of the nation's specific defense dilemma.

However, the surprisingly unanimous West German consensus against new short-range missiles stemmed from very different, even contradictory motives. The *conservatives*, to begin with, did not change their minds about nuclear weapons and became nuclear pacifists during the debate. Rather, their opposition to modernization of short-range weapons stemmed from their «decoupling» fears; they did not want to pay what they saw as the price of «double zero». The replacement of the Pershing II missiles with modernized battlefield weapons fitted into their worst assumptions about U.S. policies and motives: the United States first removes the intermediate-range forces from Western Europe and then deploys new battlefield weapons in order to decouple itself from the nuclear risk in Central Europe. And West Germany, the victim of the superpowers, would have to pay the price again.

The Social Democrats - to say nothing of the Greens and the peace movements, who oppose nuclear weapons anyway - for the most part support triple zero. While there is no intra-party consensus on the future role of nuclear weapons in Europe, even Social Democrats who favor some «minimum extended deterrence» see little deterrent value in battlefield and short-range missiles.

Chancellor Kohl and the mainstream Christian Democrats shared the conservatives' critical attitude but their motives were not the same. Along with Foreign Minister Genscher and the FDP, they preferred an arms control solution to the problem of both NATO and Soviet short-range missiles. Their dilemma is that they did not want «triple zero» either, which in their view could ultimately lead to the total denuclearization of Europe. (In this sense, they shared the French and the British opposition to further «zero solutions».) Kohl's and Genscher's ideal solution

was a modified double-track approach. They preferred continuing follow-up talks on the short-range missiles not covered by the INF treaty in
parallel with the ongoing negotiations on conventional and chemical
weapons. They wanted these negotiations to establish a common ceiling
«at the lowest possible level» (excluding zero). *Only in this context* were the
mainstream Christian Democrats and the FDP prepared to tolerate a
modest modernization of the remaining short-range systems.

This is indeed the direction in which the emerging nuclear consensus
in NATO will probably lead. It will be worked out in the years to come
and should be acceptable to most West European governments and the
U.S. While the *Gesamtkonzept* («comprehensive concept») will not entirely
satisfy the demands of the left-wing of the security debate, it could at
least be tolerated by it. A new nuclear consensus in NATO could contain
the following elements:
- continuing arms control negotiations on the remaining nuclear
  weapons in Europe, especially those short-range systems with ranges
  below 500 km, *in parallel* with the conventional stabilization talks;
  rather than aiming at new zero options, these talks would be designed
  to establish common ceilings at very low levels of armaments;
- drastic, even unilateral reductions of NATO's nuclear battlefield arsenals, nuclear artillery in particular; there is now unanimous consensus
  in West Germany on this;
- a *minimum nuclear force* composed of U.S., British, and French systems
  and containing some missiles capable of holding a small set of Soviet
  targets at risk (probably air-launched cruise missiles) and small numbers of a successor model to the *Lance* with increased range (about
  400-450 km). This force should be subject to arms control from the
  very beginning, either by unilateral restraint or by negotiated ceilings.

The main problem for the future of nuclear arms control in Europe,
however, will be the inclusion of British and French forces into the process. Once a START I agreement has been worked out and the process
of conventional arms control is underway, there is no further rational
argument left to exclude third-country systems from arms control any
longer. On the other hand, participation of Great Britain and France in
nuclear arms control could be acceptable for these countries, once it has
been made clear that this does not mean that they have to give up their
independent nuclear forces altogether.

While there is some reason to believe that the nuclear issue in Europe could be settled in a satisfying way for everybody involved, the major problem in the future will of course be *conventional arms control*, which will present a much more complex task than ending the INF arms race.[29] On the other hand, there is some chance that, in future negotiations on conventional disarmament from the Atlantic to the Urals, there will not be a repeat of the MBFR talks in Vienna. Both sides have pressing economic motives for wishing to limit conventional arms, as they constitute the most expensive item on the defense budgets. No government in Western Europe is prepared to increase defense spending at the cost of social expenditures. Paris, London, and Bonn may talk of increasing their conventional arsenals, but despite this their present and foreseeable budget levels are unlikely to allow them to even maintain the status quo.

The Soviet Union faces a similar situation. Gorbachev's economic reforms would only seem feasible if there are considerable cuts in military spending. Here, too, conventional weapons account for the highest percentage of total arms expenditure. There are signs, though, that the USSR under Gorbachev might be prepared to question its offensive military strategy in the conventional field.[30] After all, the success or failure of conventional arms control in Europe will be determined by the Soviet preparedness to alter its military strategy. Should cuts in conventional arms be achieved, this would put an entirely new face on East-West relations in Europe, the political consequences of which are rarely understood.

It cannot yet be said whether the double zero solution will ring in the start of a fundamental change in East-West military relations in Europe. In any case, further efforts are required of both sides if the chances which INF has created are to be fully exploited.

---

29 For details see Hans-Joachim Schmidt, *Konventionelle Stabilisierung? Zu den Problemen konventioneller Rüstungskontrolle in Europa* (Frankfurt/M.: PRIF-Report), forthcoming.

30 See, in particular, Jack Snyder, «Limiting Offensive Conventional Forces: Soviet Proposals and Western Options,» *International Security*, vol.12, no.4, Spring 1988, pp.48-77.

Index

Aaron, David, 33
ABM Treaty, 114, 115, 121, 128
ACDA. *See* Arms Control and
  Disarmament Agency
Afghanistan, 60, 98, 175
Aircraft, 15, 88(table), 89(table)
  Backfire bomber, 16, 17, 22
  F-111, 9, 15, 32, 159
  and Geneva talks, 87, 89, 96, 108
Akhromeyev, Sergai (Marshal), 114
ALCMs. *See* Cruise missiles, air-
  launched
Altenburg, Wolfgang, 34, 123, 126
Andropov, Yuri, 94, 99, 101
Apel, Hans, 44(n), 45, 46, 58, 65
Arms control, 6, 157
  and alliance management, 82, 84
  and asymmetric reductions, 158
  as confrontation, 172
  conventional, 190, 191
  criteria for, 50, 162–164
  and détente, 172. *See also* Détente
  and deterrence, 21, 22, 23, 61, 171
  future, 190–191
  gradualist approach to, 173
  and INF, 16, 46(n), 49, 59, 84,
    171–173. *See also* INF Treaty
  and levelling-up, 157
  vs. military-political objectives,
    57–59, 118
  and peace through strength, 164,
    166
  preconditions for success of, 171–
    173
  preventive, 145, 173

and Reagan Administration, 60,
  84, 98
See also Double-track decision;
  Strategic Arms Limitation Talks;
  Strategic Arms Reduction Talks
Arms Control and Disarmament
  Agency (ACDA), 82, 110
Aspin, Les, 136
ATACMS. *See* United States, Army's
  Tactical Missile System
Athens guidelines, 14, 116

Bahr, Egon, 26, 79
Ballistic missiles, 160(table), 178,
  180
  intercontinental (ICBMs), 135
  submarine-launched (SLBMs), 32,
    39, 135, 159
Barre, Raymond, 123
Belgium, 50, 53, 68, 103, 111
Benelux countries, 137, 188
Borm, William, 41
Brezhnev, Leonid, 15, 19, 39, 43,
  51–52, 85–86, 99, 166, 182
Brown, Harold, 32, 33, 34
Brzezinski, Zbigniew, 37
Burt, Richard, 67, 68, 68(n), 82, 94,
  94–95(n41)
Bush, George, 148

Calculated inferiority, 51, 57
Callaghan, James, 49, 49(n61), 166,
  181
Carter, Jimmy, 12, 16, 166, 172, 174
  and Afghanistan, 60, 98